VARIETY OF ATTEMPT

*British and American Fiction in the
Early Nineteenth Century*

NEAL FRANK DOUBLEDAY

UNIVERSITY OF NEBRASKA PRESS
LINCOLN & LONDON

Copyright © 1976 by the University of Nebraska Press
All Rights Reserved
Manufactured in the United States of America

Library of Congress Cataloging in Publication Data

Doubleday, Neal Frank.
  Variety of attempt.

  Includes bibliographical references and index.
  1. English fiction—19th century—History and
criticism. 2. American fiction—19th century—History
and criticism. I. Title.
PR861.D6   823'.7'09   75–38057
ISBN 0–8032–0876–6

FOR FRANCES

Contents

Variety of Attempt

1

Variety of Attempt

"Art lives upon discussion," Henry James writes in "The Art of Fiction," "upon experiment, upon variety of attempt." Of course in any period writers use what writers before them have done; and variety of attempt is carried on within, and here and there emerges from, the whole set of conventions that the writers of the period have inherited or developed. But the early nineteenth century is, it seems to me, especially a time in which fiction writers were thinking of new possibilities and using their resources for new purposes. If we have not fully realized that point—as probably James did not—it may be because neither the writers, most of them, nor their critics were much in the habit of technical discussion, although letters and prefatory material are evidence that the writers defined their own aims. As in other periods, the art of fiction in the early nineteenth century lived upon variety of attempt.

The common quality of the examples of early nineteenth-century writing here considered is that in all of them the writers were, on the evidence of what they did, thinking hard about the uses and the means of fiction, whether or not the thinking itself is ever made explicit. A short book can do no more than discuss selected examples of variety of attempt in a rich period; but the examples are, I believe, interesting and significant—some of them well known, some of them less well known nowadays than they deserve to be, all of them in some particular way illustrative. The effort is to seize upon work in which the writer departs from what his predecessors had done and his contemporaries were doing. The attempts are new in subject, interest, or technique. Sometimes a new subject or interest seems to have required a new technique, and in nearly all of our examples there is at least some technical accommodation to new aims. We have, therefore, examples of the extension of the uses of the means of fiction, and sometimes of the means themselves.

Some of the work here examined is minor work, and some is, although of great excellence, often so considered. Yet a minor work may contribute quite as much to the development of a literary kind as a major work does. Indeed the minor status of some works and even of some writers may be the result of historical accident or, more often, of the development of unintelligible academic conventions in which we seem to produce endless studies of a relatively few writers and few studies of some very interesting ones.

Our discussion will often entail consideration of the interplay between convention and the new attempt, and the interplay will be of various kinds. Jane Austen's *Northanger Abbey* has its inception in a realization of absurdities in a convention and works out therefrom. Or, to take a very different example, James Fenimore Cooper's *The Pioneers* uses material new to fiction with a conventional plot. The interplay may be more subtle than it is in either of these two examples, but in some fashion there will be interplay. And, in curious ways, the new attempt of one writer may affect or stimulate the new attempt of another.

Sir Walter Scott is of course the towering figure in the period of our concern; the Waverley novels were, Mary Russell Mitford remarks, "the most approved topic of discussion among civilized people," and all of the writers we consider have some sort of connection with Scott's work. We need not be very much concerned with the imitation of Scott; his important influence was in opening up fiction to varieties of attempt beyond his own. At the end of the eighteenth century Jane Austen in *Northanger Abbey* was making her kind of fun of sterile fictional conventions, yet by 1818 when that novel was finally published, Scott was well along with the Waverley novels and his liberating influence already felt.

As Scott concludes a discussion of the novels of Charlotte Smith, he remarks the surprising number of women novelists in his time. Perhaps, he thinks, a complex modern society is "more happily painted by the finer pencil of a woman," or perhaps a delicate age that dislikes the coarseness of the middle eighteenth century "has rendered competition more easy to female writers."[1] But he does not remark what one would think might have been as obvious to him as to us: fiction writing was the only intellectual activity in which women competed on equal terms with men.

For some of the writers Scott mentions—for Susan Ferrier, for instance—novel writing was primarily an interesting outlet for their energy and intelligence, although Miss Ferrier found it also profitable. Some of them—like the Mrs. Smith who is the subject of Scott's discussion, and like Miss Mitford—wrote in a desperate need for the money they could earn with their pens. In the United States, too, women writers of fiction abounded; in the 1830s Eliza Leslie and Catharine Maria Sedgwick had attained the sort of reputation Nathaniel Hawthorne was still struggling for. The five works by women writers discussed in this book markedly extend, each in its own way, the uses of the means of fiction.

The American writers here considered, no less than the British, carry on a variety of attempt, but they share a special problem. In their every attempt we are aware of the problem of the function and possibilities of fiction in a new nation without a literary tradition of its own—the more because a vigorous critical discussion both urged the problem on them and tried to help them solve it. Since the novels of Scott that were concerned with the recent past in Scotland seemed to critics and writers alike to show the readiest way to extend the means of fiction to American experience and American needs, Scott's example informs the early critical discussion and his influence persists from 1815 well into the century. Yet the emulation of Scott was but a starting point in working out American problems, and in a measure perhaps unparalleled at any other time and place, the new attempts were stimulated by critical discussion—a discussion of surprisingly persistent effect. Though the work by Hawthorne considered here was written at mid-century or later, it was much affected by the literary thinking of the 1820s, and is best understood in relation to that thinking.

We may not be much used to the discussion of specimens of British and of American fiction in the same book, but it is well to think about American fiction in the early nineteenth century, when it was finding its direction, in some connection with the only tradition it had to work out from and to modify. The intention of writers of early American fiction may be clearer to us if we see how elements British in origin combine in their work with American purposes. And there are other connections. Cooper, for instance, had a London publisher for *The Pioneers*, and thought of both British and American readers. Washington Irving was both a British and an American writer; examples of his work in both roles are here considered. Miss Mitford, who edited three collections of American writing, was in her own work influenced by Irving's.[2]

"The highest instruction we can derive from the tedious tale of a dull fellow," Henry Fielding remarks in *A Voyage to Lisbon*, "scarce ever pays for our attention." Of course it is true; no critic would dispute it. The trouble is that in academic criticism we take it too much for granted, and then proceed as if we were after all discussing dull fellows who wrote, not first of all to interest and to entertain, but so that their work might be interpreted. I hope that the discussion of our examples of variety of attempt may be sufficiently interpretive, but that the interpretation will not neglect or obscure what each writer has done to interest or to entertain his readers in his way, since in every instance his way is somehow a new way.

One of the pleasant connections between the work of great writers in nineteenth-century literary history is Sir Walter Scott's review of Jane Austen's *Emma* in the *Quarterly Review* in 1816,[3] the first adequate recognition of Miss Austen's gifts. Scott begins his review with an amusing account of the run of fiction in the recent past, of the novel of "romantic cast," the work of many now-forgotten novelists. Miss Austen must have been delighted by Scott's account of the stock heroine:

> She was regularly exposed to being forcibly carried off like a Sabine virgin by some frantic admirer. And even if she escaped the terrors of masked ruffians, an insidious ravisher, a cloak wrapped forcibly around her head, and a coach with blinds up driving she could not conjecture whither, she had still her share of wandering, of poverty, of obloquy, of sec-

lusion, and of imprisonment, and was frequently extended upon a bed of sickness, and reduced to her last shilling before the author condescended to shield her from persecution.

This heroine, and the hero, and the author, and the reader while he is engrossed in the novel, all live in what Scott calls "the land of fiction." The reader has long been used to it, and he does not expect its events to be like those he knows in everyday life, nor its persons to be like himself or anyone of his acquaintance; the admirable inhabitants of the land of fiction have minds and hearts purified by an extravagant sensibility the reader may delight to contemplate but would hardly wish to share. Each of the British writers we shall be discussing takes his own road out of this land of fiction.

We follow first the road Maria Edgeworth takes in *Castle Rackrent*, not only because the tale departs so strikingly from the ordinary techniques and interests of fiction in the time, but because it represents Miss Edgeworth's influence as it was most important. Scott in his Postscript to *Waverley* says of the characters in his novel: "It has been my object to describe these persons, not by a caricatured and exaggerated use of the national dialect, but by their habits, manners, and feelings; so as in some distant degree to emulate the admirable Irish portraits drawn by Miss Edgeworth."[4] And her influence seems to have been effective on John Galt and Susan Ferrier before it was effective on Scott.

We may not be able fully to understand Miss Edgeworth's reputation in her own time, not quite be able to see why she is so much a transitional figure. We do read *Castle Rackrent*, but we neglect much of her work; we see it at best against that of only a few of her immediate predecessors—against the novels of Fanny Burney, say, and a few specimens of the Gothic novel. If we come upon contemporary reviews of her novels, the praise given them seems extravagant and unwarranted.[5] But we cannot read the reviewers in their contexts; we do not have their experience with the novels of the time. Doubtless many intelligent readers would have agreed with Francis Jeffery when he wrote, looking back at the novels of the time of his youth, that "certainly a greater mass of trash and rubbish never disgraced the press of any country, than the ordinary Novels that filled and supported our circulating libraries, down nearly to the time of Miss Edgeworth's first appearance."[6] The beginning of the nineteenth century marked a new awareness of what fiction might do.

Notes

1. *The Lives of the Novelists*, Everyman ed., p. 334.

2. Miss Mitford, however, did not consider Irving an American writer and excluded his work from her anthology *Stories of American Life by American Writers* (1830), explaining that "his writings are essentially European." American critics tended to resent his use of English settings. The "Author's Introduction" to *A Tour on the Prairies* (1835) shows how much a problem his national status was to Irving himself.

3. Reprinted in *Jane Austen: The Critical Heritage*, ed. B. C. Southam (London: Routledge & Kegan Paul, 1968), pp. 58–69.

4. Scott acknowledges his emulation of his "accomplished friend' at greater length in the "General Preface to the Scott Novels" (1829).

5. For instance, an American critic, Willard Phillips, in a review of *Harrington* and *Ormond*, praises Maria Edgeworth for her concern with "men and women, animated by the passions with which real life is glowing, and busy with the pursuits in which we ourselves are interested" (*North American Review* 6 [1818]: 153).

6. Quoted in Ian Jack, *English Literature, 1815–1832* (Oxford: Clarendon Press, 1963), p. 225. Even J. M. S. Tompkins's admirable survey, *The Popular Novel in England, 1770–1800* (1932; rpt., Lincoln: University of Nebraska Press, 1961), leaves the reader bemused, so many and so undistinguished are the novels, so often indistinguishable from one another.

2

Honest Thady's Tale

Castle Rackrent was published in 1800, *Belinda* in 1801. There can be no more surprising juxtaposition in the work of any fiction writer than that of these two books by Maria Edgeworth. *Castle Rackrent* was a success in its time and has been read and admired ever since. *Belinda* was well received in its time—even Jane Austen seems to have admired it;[1] but no reader today, I should think, can believe in the figures in it, nor care about what happens to them. The only ready explanation we have for the superiority of *Castle Rackrent* over a novel so close to it in time is that Miss Edgeworth's father, Richard Lovell Edgeworth, had nothing to do with *Castle Rackrent*.

But a comparison of *Castle Rackrent* with *The Absentee* (1812) may seem more useful, for *The Absentee* has part of its action in Ireland, and it has a worthy and intelligible social purpose, energetically carried along. In the nineteenth century it had such distinguished praise as may now surprise us,[2] but it is a readable novel and certainly better than *Belinda*. Yet it has some of those characteristics that make the typical novel of the late eighteenth and early nineteenth centuries seem to us creaking and maladroit. A number of its figures, even some fairly important ones, are mere puppets. The central plot interest seems intended to be the revelation that Grace Nugent is not, after all, of illegitimate birth; and one can hardly suppose that the frayed old plot element of the hero or heroine of mysterious birth was ever less interesting. Yet for that matter, nowhere else in her work does Miss Edgeworth escape from the conventions of the novel up to her time, nor from the baleful influence of her father, so fully as she does in *Castle Rackrent*.

Nevertheless, we say too easily that, although Miss Edgeworth's overt didacticism was acceptable to her first readers, it is the quality that nearly spoils most of her novels for us—as if we did not know any great and successful didactic novels. The trouble is, rather, that her moral thinking is untouched by religious feeling or indeed by any ideal.[3] It is as doctrinaire and as imaginatively sterile as the teaching of Richard Lovell Edgeworth himself. As early as 1821 Richard Whately pointed out in the *Quarterly Review* that Miss Edgeworth's stories usually started in her mind with her sort of moral, and that she "framed a fable to illustrate it," a fable that proceeds by "a sort of independent machinery of accidents" in which good or ill conduct is requited.[4] Because the narrative point of view in *Castle Rackrent* precludes the didactic approach common in Miss Edgeworth's fiction, it is not only her best work, but it is most untypical— surprising to find among the rest of her stories and in the fiction of her time.

The puzzle about *Castle Rackrent*, then, is its emergence early in Miss Edgeworth's career. We can see that it does have one quality in common with the rest of her novels: Miss Edgeworth was able to make her characters—or some of them—speak effectively. Lady Delacour in *Belinda* has such fluency and such hectic vivacity that we may even mistake what she says for wit; her maid, Merriot, is often amusing. The speech of Lady Clonbrony in *The Absentee* represents her admirably. In *Ormond* the Irishmen speak convincingly. And throughout *Castle Rackrent* we hear the effective voice of Thady Quirk—honest Thady—for as narrator he seems to write as he would talk. But beyond that— and of course a concern for Irish ills—there is not much in common between Miss Edgeworth's other work and *Castle Rackrent*.

Castle Rackrent is a nineteenth-century work by virtue of its publication date. It was written late in the eighteenth century, the last section of it (which Miss Edgeworth tells us was written two years after the first part) perhaps as late as 1799. It is particularly tied to its time of composition, for Miss Edgeworth wrote after the Independency, after the establishment in 1782 of an Irish Parliament with power to legislate,[5] and before she felt the disappointment of the new hope that had come with it. The book looks back on a period which she hopes had come to an end; the original title page itself makes that clear: "Castle Rackrent/ An Hibernian Tale/ taken from facts,/ and from/ the manners of the Irish squires,/ before the year 1782." As well as a memoir novel and a regional novel, it is therefore a historical novel, although, as George Watson, its latest editor, points out, it is about a way of life, and not centered on a historical event, as *Waverley*, for instance, is centered on the Forty-Five.[6] Yet *Castle Rackrent* has something of that feeling for period that was to distinguish Scott's fiction.[7]

Although *Castle Rackrent* is in important ways a new thing in fiction, in an ironically allusive way it is connected with a flourishing fictional convention, as perhaps Miss Edgeworth meant to indicate by its title. Michael Sadleir points out that in 1800 nearly four-fifths of the new issues in the catalog of the Minerva Library were Gothic novels—Castles, Abbeys, Mysteries, and the like.[8] Some of the first readers of *Castle Rackrent* may well have procured it under a misapprehension—yet not a complete misapprehension, for it is in its way as "horrid" a novel as any recommended by Isabella Thorpe in *Northanger Abbey*. The edifice itself seems malignant, and its inhabitants doomed. There may be even some reminiscence of the Gothic mysterious portrait in the picture of Sir Patrick Rackrent that Thady loves to look upon.

In her use of Thady as narrator, Miss Edgeworth manages an understated account of events that, told in another fashion, would seem as unbelievably appalling as any in a Gothic novel. Thady's story is of desperate lives, miserable marriages, and horrifying deaths. Sir Patrick Rackrent falls in a fit while his guests are drinking his health and dies as they continue their drinking bout—and thereafter his dead body is seized for debt. Sir Murtagh, exasperated by a dispute with his wife about money, dies when he breaks a blood vessel in a burst of passion. Sir Kit confines his wife in her bedroom for seven years, indeed until his death in a grotesquely motivated duel releases her. Sir Condy manages to attend his own wake, and comes to his death in trying to empty Sir Patrick's drinking horn at one draught.

But the ills and evil of Rackrent Castle stem from no Montoni, no Gothic villain. The Rackrents inherit the social and economic pattern of their lives, and so mismanage their inheritance that they worsen the pattern and destroy themselves. Each of them seems intended to represent some characteristic ill of the Irish gentry: Sir Patrick is ruined by drink, Sir Murtagh by avarice and a passion for litigation, Sir Kit by profligacy and gambling, the feckless Sir Condy by a political venture to which his friends persuade him and by a wife as feckless as he. On the edges of Thady's narrative we are aware of the misery of the tenants, the corruption of the agents, and the callous self-seeking of the Rackrents's friends. Yet the effective social criticism of the story inheres in its narrative point of view, for Thady tells of the events in the lives of the Rackrents as if he thought them memorable, unfortunate, and sometimes, sad, but not monstrous, not appalling. As so often to other men, long-established evil has come to seem to him merely in the nature of things.

But for critics with nineteenth-century habits of mind, the moral implications seem to have been difficult to state, although the critics themselves may have realized them well enough. Scott, within a discussion of Daniel Defoe's narrators, asks,

> And what would be the most interesting and affecting, as well as the most comic, passages of *Castle Rackrent*, if narrated by one who had a less regard for "the family" than the immortal Thady, who, while he sees that none of the dynasty which he celebrates were perfectly right, has never been able to puzzle out wherein they were certainly wrong [?][9]

But clearly Thady does not ever try to fix the rightness or wrongness of his masters' conduct; Scott, almost always a most satisfactory critic, is surely at fault here. Emily Lawless, the intelligent author of the English Men of Letters volume on Miss Edgeworth, has another kind of difficulty. Of *Castle Rackrent* and Miss Edgeworth she says:

> In it alone we find her regarding life,—not from any utilitarian, ethical, or dogmatic standpoint,—but simply and solely objectively, as it strikes, and as it ought to strike, an artist. . . . Take it from whatever point of view we like—moral, philosophical, social, political—it seems to stand outside of the entire code, human or divine.[10]

In this passage there may be some confusion of author with narrator. But the difficulty in both the quoted passages is, I suspect, that the writers are not used to taking into account in their criticism how much the reader's activity may contribute to the experience of a narrative. In *Castle Rackrent* Miss Edgeworth has given the reader much to do.

The preface to *Castle Rackrent* purports to be by the editor of Thady's narrative; it is of course part of the fiction. But it is carefully calculated to prepare for a complex effect, for when the reader gets to Thady's narrative he will find himself more perceptive than the editor has been. The purported editor is made to say that our desire for truth leads us to memoirs and private anecdotes, and that they are in an important way superior to formal biographies. "It may be maintained," he goes on, "that the merits of a biographer are inversely as the extent of his intellectual powers and literary talents," and that the naive and unskilled writer is the more apt to tell the truth; "the talents of a biographer are often fatal to his reader."

> For these reasons the public often judiciously countenances those, who without sagacity to discriminate character, without elegance of style to relieve the tediousness of narrative, without enlargement of mind to draw any conclusions from the facts they relate, simply pour forth anecdotes and retail conversations, with all the minute prolixity of a gossip in a country town.[P. 3]

The passage is far from ingenuous. Thady does not, to be sure, draw the conclusions from his story that the reader does, but he is a shrewd observer of character within the limits of his experience—as Miss Edgeworth believed the "lower Irish" commonly were.[11] And Thady's narrative style has its own elegance and great economy. Yet the editor's apprehension seems a possible appprehension of the surface of the tale. *Castle Rackrent* is a remarkable technical achievement.

The student of literature will naturally suppose some influence upon *Castle Rackrent* from Daniel Defoe and some from Henry Fielding's *Jonathan Wild the Great*, but if there was any, Miss Edgeworth seems to have been quite unconscious of it. In the often-quoted letter to a Mrs. Stark she says:

The only character drawn from the life in "Castle Rackrent" is Thady himself, the teller of the story. He was an old steward (not very old, though, at that time; I added to his age, to allow him time for the generations of the family). I heard him when I first came to Ireland, and his dialect struck me, and his character; and I became so acquainted with it, that I could think and speak in it without effort; so that when, for mere amusement, without any idea of publishing, I began to write a family history as Thady would tell it, he seemed to stand beside me and dictate; and I wrote as fast as my pen could go, the characters all imaginary. [P. xi]

In taking her narrator from this real person—he was her father's steward, John Langan—Miss Edgeworth manages an imaginative separation between author and narrator, and at the same time a complex interplay between the narrative and the reader's response to it.

The old literary term "transparency" is an attractive one, and perhaps we might follow Brander Matthews in applying it to *Castle Rackrent*.[12] But here the term seems to need some hedging round. It is not quite that we "see through" what Thady writes to another reality. All that we know of the events that went on at Castle Rackrent and of the conduct of its four masters is what Thady tells us. And Thady is after all a sensitive and perceptive observer; we do not at all doubt his accounts of events or of the relationships of persons. But we do constantly make moral estimates of the events and relationships, starting from moral premises quite different from Thady's; we "see through" his judgments to our own.

Thady is a hereditary upper servant; he has lived under the Rackrents, he says, "these two hundred years and upwards, me and mine" (p. 57); his habits of mind are ancestral. It does not and cannot behoove him to make moral judgments about the family he serves. He speaks often—the expressions come in like a refrain—of "the honor of the family" and of his "regard for the family." For him the family demands a respect that in no way depends upon the conduct of any representative of it, and the nearest he can come to any moral estimate of the conduct of any of his masters is occasional extenuation of some act that he suspects may need it from his readers' point of view. It is the special sign of the complete decay of an aristocracy that Thady's loyalty cannot come down to his son Jason, who has become a lawyer, and who battens on the improvidence of those who, in the old social pattern, would have been his masters.

Although Thady does not analyze his own attitudes, we are sometimes aware that his natural sympathies are a little at odds with his loyalties. He was much taken aback when Sir Kit brought home his new wife, who was foreign to all that Thady had ever known or imagined, and who laughed at what he had always held in regard. But when he recounts how Sir Kit locked her up, Thady says that he "could not but pity her, though she was a Jewish, and considering too it was no fault of her's to be taken with my master so young as she was at the Bath, and so fine a gentleman as Sir Kit was when he courted her" (p. 32). Even so, Thady thinks it is she and not Sir Kit who was responsible for the misfortunes of the marriage: "Her diamond cross was, they say, at the bottom of it all," Thady says: "and it was a shame for her, being his wife, not to show more duty, and to have given it up when he condescended to ask so often for such a bit of a trifle in his distresses, especially when he all along made it no secret that he married for money" (p. 36). When Thady tells how the "Jewish" became Sir Kit's widow and left Ireland, he comments that "she had taken an unaccountable prejudice against the country" (pp. 35–36).

We may accept Miss Edgeworth's statement that she could write and think in John Langan's dialect and character without effort, understanding of course that she uses the dialect and the character for her own purposes. The Anglo-Irish dialect is remarkably restrained, as Scott suggests in his Postscript to *Waverley* when he points out how different Miss Edgeworth's Irish characters are from "the 'Teagues' and the 'dear joys,' who so long, with the most perfect family resemblance to each other, occupied the drama and the novel." Some of the dialect consists of variants of English words, like "fader," "childer," "shister," "cratur." Thady uses a few words that have no parallels in English, like "gosson," "shebean-house," "whillalu." There are relatively few instances of what we think of as characteristically Irish locutions: "all entirely," "at all at all," "he never went the circuit but twice," "kilt and smashed" (severely injured), "lying for death," "out of the face" (openly). For the most part Thady writes standard, literate English, and even the recorded dialogue is far less dialectal than, say, the speech of Scotsmen in the Waverley novels.

Miss Edgeworth's great triumph is in seeming to catch so perfectly the cadences of Irish speech. Doubtless some of that effect is to be accounted for by her imitation of the speech of John Langan. But Thady's remarkable syntax—those long and carefully planned sentences that may be so inclusive—is as much a product of Miss Edgeworth's skill as, say, Huck Finn's syntax is the product of Mark Twain's. We find Huck perfectly convincing, although we know well enough that no young boy ever fashioned such sentences as his. We hear Thady's voice in what he writes, and he seems to us loquacious like an Irishman; but it is Miss Edgeworth who extends the cadences and manages at the same time a highly economical narrative, even a packed one.

Thady's sentences are sometimes little masterpieces, with a curious sort of completeness in themselves. This example comes when Sir Condy thinks of marrying Isabella Moneygawl, a disappointment to Thady, who had hoped he would marry Judy, Thady's grandniece:

> To be sure it was not his place to behave ungenerous to Miss Isabella, who had disobliged all her relations for his sake, as he remarked; and then she was locked up in her chamber and forbid to think of him any more, which raised his spirit, because his family was, as he observed, as good as theirs at any rate, and the Rackrents a suitable match for the Moneygawls any day in the year; all which was true enough; but it grieved me to see that upon the strength of all this Sir Condy was growing more in the mind to carry off Miss Isabella to Scotland, in spite of her relations, as she desired. [P. 44]

And when Sir Condy has won his seat in Parliament—in the upshot a great misfortune—Thady is left alone in Castle Rackrent. Its dilapidation and desolation foreshadow the end of things:

> There was then a great silence in Castle Rackrent, and I went moping from room to room, hearing the doors clap

for want of right locks, and the wind through the broken
windows that the glazier never would come to mend, and
the rain coming through the roof and best ceilings all over
the house, for want of the slater whose bill was not paid;
besides our having no slates or shingles for that part of the
old building which was shingled, and burnt when the chimney took fire, and had been open to the weather ever since.
[P. 61]

But even these sentences do not fully illustrate the kind of narrative economy that Miss Edgeworth manages to conceal under
what she makes the editor affirm is Thady's "minute prolixity."
   A striking example of that economy is Thady's account of the
ills that fall upon the estate when Sir Kit is its absentee landlord.
The passage represents the social problem with which *The Absentee* is concerned:

The agent was one of your middle men, who grind the face
of the poor, and can never bear a man with a hat upon his
head—he ferretted the tenants out of their lives—not a
week without a call for money—drafts upon drafts from Sir
Kit—but I laid it all to the fault of the agent; for, says I, what
can Sir Kit do with so much cash, and he a single man? but
still it went.—Rents must be all paid up to the day, and
afore—no allowance for improving tenants—no consideration for those who had built upon their farms—No sooner
was a lease out, but the land was advertised to the highest
bidder—all the old tenants turned out, when they had spent
their substance in the hope and trust of a renewal from the
landlord.—All was now set at the highest penny to a parcel
of poor wretches who meant to run away, and did so, after
taking two crops out of the ground. Then fining down the
year's rent came into fashion—any thing for the ready
penny, and with all this, and presents to the agent and the
driver, there was no such thing as standing it—I said nothing, for I had a regard for the family, but I walked about,
thinking if his honour Sir Kit, (long may he live to reign
over us!) knew all this, it would go hard with him, but he'd
see us righted. [Pp. 20–21][13]

In less than a page, this passage, it seems to me, does as much as *The Absentee* to make clear the evil of the absentee landlord, more effectively, even with more immediacy. And it is a good example of the special quality of Thady's narrative: the misery on the Rackrent estate is unambiguous; the ironic tension is between the reader's moral judgment of Sir Kit and Thady's inability to think any ill of him.

The writer who can firmly imagine a narrator who seems to have a quite independent existence and then write from that narrator's mind and heart in a style that seems to belong only to him has accomplished what must be one of the most difficult achievements in fiction, even when that narrator is merely telling his own story. When the narrator is primarily an observer and recorder, and is telling not so much his own story as the story of others, as Thady tells the story of the Rackrent family, a great success is a rare thing. George Watson affirms that *Castle Rackrent* has "a technique impossible to parallel in English before 1800" (p. xvi). In Miss Edgeworth's own time there are some partial parallels: we shall consider later the narrators of Scott's "Wandering Willie's Tale" and of John Galt's *Annals of the Parish*.

Miss Edgeworth, although she understood that *Castle Rackrent* was both a popular and an artistic success, never wrote anything else at all like it.[14] I think that we must take her letter to Mrs. Stark seriously and conclude that she needed John Langan and the cadences of his voice behind her narrator. Hers was not the kind of imagination, apparently, that could construct a narrator from a few intimations, as Scott must have constructed Wandering Willie. And she seems never to have been fortunate enough to find another person useful to her as her father's steward had been. She could hardly have used Thady more than once, as Washington Irving used his "nervous gentleman" narrator in two books; she had made Thady exhaust his experience in *Castle Rackrent*. But even if this speculation is accepted, the early emergence of a work greatly superior to all the rest of Maria Edgeworth's fiction is a problem in the ways of the imagination we probably cannot solve.

NOTES

1. The evidence for Jane Austen's admiration is only that she cites *Belinda* along with Fanny Burney's *Cecilia* and *Camilla* as examples of fine novels in her defense of novel-reading in the fifth chapter of *Northanger Abbey*. But that is an equivocal document.

2. The reviewers agreed particularly in their praise of Larry Brady's letter at the end of the novel. Francis Jeffery wrote in the *Edinburgh Review*: "If Miss Edgeworth had never written any other thing, this one letter must have placed her at the very top of our scale as an observer of character, and a mistress of the simple pathetic." Later in the century the novel had high praise from Ruskin and Macaulay. See O. Elizabeth McWhorter Harden, *Maria Edgeworth's Art of Prose Fiction* (The Hague: Mouton, 1971), p. 179 and p. 174 n.

3. *Belinda*, indeed, seems to me a morally unhealthy novel. Its moral malaise can be only partly explained by Richard Lovell Edgeworth's interference with its design.

4. See *Jane Austen: The Critical Heritage*, pp. 90–91; 93–95.

5. Miss Edgeworth herself settled in 1782 (when she was fifteen) at her father's estate in Edgeworthstown in County Longford; she was born in Oxfordshire and had been in Ireland before only as an infant.

6. Introduction to *Castle Rackrent*, ed. George Watson (London: Oxford University Press, 1969), pp. ix–x and xvii. This excellent edition is in the Oxford English Novels series. Parenthetical page references in the text of this chapter are to Mr. Watson's edition.

7. Miss Edgeworth's Glossary is one evidence of that feeling for period. The Glossary is really a set of notes very much like the notes Scott was later to append to his novels.

8. See Michael Sadleir's valuable introduction to the Oxford World's Classics edition of *Northanger Abbey*, p. xiv. A character in Thomas Henry Lister's *Granby* (1826) is made to say: "You cannot think how I was disappointed in Northanger Abbey, and Castle Rack-rent, for the titles did really promise something" (quoted in Ian Jack, *English Literature, 1815–1832*, p. 248).

9. *The Lives of the Novelists*, Everyman ed., p. 376.

10. *Maria Edgeworth* (New York: Macmillan, 1905), p. 87.

11. In her continuation of her father's *Memoirs* (1820), Miss Edgeworth writes: "The lower Irish are such acute observers, that there is no deceiving them as to the state of the real feelings of their superiors. They know the signs of what passes within, more perfectly than any physiognomist, who ever studied the human face, or the human head" (quoted in Watson's Introduction, p. xxiv).

12. Introduction to the Everyman edition of *Castle Rackrent* and *The Absentee*, p. xv.

13. Miss Edgeworth explains in a footnote that a "middle man" is an agent who leases an estate and rents the land out to undertenants at exorbitant rents. In her Glossary she explains that "fining down the year's rent" means the accepting of a smaller rent if part of it is paid at once so that the landlord has cash in hand; and that the "driver" is a man employed "to drive the cattle belonging to tenants to the pound."

14. *Ennui* has a narrator; he tells his own story. But *Ennui* has all the weaknesses of Miss Edgeworth's fiction in general.

3

Henry & Catherine

Although Jane Austen was working on *Northanger Abbey* at about the same time, and probably in the same years, that Maria Edgeworth was working on *Castle Rackrent*, it was not published until much later. The two women were in some external ways alike: both were spinsters, both lived closely with their families (very different families), neither wrote from financial need. But they viewed experience in most unlike ways. Sir Walter Scott acknowledged what he gained from Miss Edgeworth's work; in Miss Austen's he found a kind of achievement denied to him.[1]

Northanger Abbey stands somewhat apart from Miss Austen's other novels. It does not have the "confined locality" that Mary Russell Mitford admired in them; if any one of her novels is a "little bit (two inches wide) of Ivory" worked on with "so fine a Brush," this one certainly is not.[2] Jane Austen's critics have difficulty with the book. Its history is puzzling.

We need to recall something of that history. Written for the most part in 1798–99, the book in 1803 was sold outright to a publisher, Richard Crosby, who chose not to bring it out. In 1816 the manuscript and copyright were bought back, and in 1816 Miss Austen intended publication of the book and wrote for it an "Advertisement," in which she pointed out that since it was written, "places, manners, books, and opinions have undergone considerable changes." But the book was not published, and in 1817 Miss Austen wrote to a niece that it had been "put on the Shelve for the present," and that she did not know that it would ever come out. One of the ironies of literary history is that *Northanger Abbey* was published with *Persuasion* in 1818 after Miss Austen's death.[3]

It is most unlikely that *Northanger Abbey* was withdrawn because Jane Austen thought the satirical treatment of the Radcliffean novel dated. Had that been the objection, it would have been as apparent in 1816 when publication was planned as in 1817 when publication was put aside. But it hardly can have been the objection: in 1814 Miss Austen herself enjoyed reading Eaton Stannard Barrett's burlesque novel *The Heroine* (1813), a very successful book;[4] and as Michael Sadleir in his introduction to *Northanger Abbey* has shown, 1817 was a far more appropriate time for the publication of a Radcliffean satire than 1803, when publishers' lists were crowded with new Radcliffean romances. In 1817 the better of them were still current but their great vogue had run itself out—just the time parody might be acceptable to publishers and best succeed with readers. And the Gothic convention to which Mrs. Radcliffe had contributed so much was to be variously used for years thereafter. We need to seek further for a convincing reason that *Northanger Abbey* was put on the shelf.

Persuasion was written in 1815–16 and was ready for publication in 1817. Jane Austen had a new novel to offer the public; her other novels had won recognition and the praise of the discerning. Her doubt about *Northanger Abbey*, it seems to me, would have been not of its quality nor of her success in carrying out her intention, but rather whether or not such an intention was an appropriate one now that she had gained acceptance for four novels and was about to ask it for a fifth. She knew well enough that in *Northanger Abbey* she had made fun not only of the devices and expedients of Mrs. Radcliffe and of other novelists, but of the genre in which she herself had been writing. The defense of novels and of novel reading in the fifth chapter of *Northanger Abbey*—whether a part of the original manuscript or, as seems probable, added in a revision—betrays a consciousness of the problem. We may feel that it does not belong in the book; but we can see why Miss Austen thought it well to put it there, and why, when she reconsidered the book in 1817, she must have decided that it did not solve her problem.

Of course critics have seen the resemblance between the juvenilia and *Northanger Abbey*;[5] if one takes into sufficient account the development of Jane Austen's mind by, say, her twenty-third year, he must see a marked resemblance. For throughout *Northanger Abbey* Miss Austen alludes to what Scott calls "the land of fiction"; indeed she keeps that land present in our minds, while assuring us we are not in it. But her wry amusement at the predicament of the novelist goes beyond ridicule of the land of fiction. An apprehension of an inherent absurdity in the novel as a genre is apparent in Miss Austen's earliest writing and persists to the amusing "Plan of a Novel" which she wrote about 1815.[6] In some of her references to the conventions of novels in volume 1 of *Northanger Abbey*, she doubtless has in mind particular novels or novelists, but others apply to the English novel as she knew it; some indeed remind the reader today of novels unwritten in her lifetime, sometimes of novels by writers then unborn.

In many of these references (beginning with the first sentence), Jane Austen delights in pointing out how different her Catherine Morland is from the stock heroine (sometimes how like).[7] But in others she enjoys letting us see what she might do in a burlesque novel, were she writing one. Once, for example, she tells us that Catherine had reached the age of seventeen without exciting the admiration of any young man, but that it may be accounted for:

> There was not one lord in the neighbourhood; no—not even a baronet. There was not one family among their acquaintance who had reared and supported a boy accidentally found at their door—not one young man whose origin was unknown. Her father had no ward, and the squire of the parish no children. [P. 16]

Or, to take but one more example, when John Thorpe fails to appear to dance with Catherine and she feels all the discredit of lacking a partner, Miss Austen remarks:

> To be disgraced in the eye of the world, to wear the appearance of infamy while her heart is all purity, her actions all innocence, and the misconduct of another the true source of her debasement, is one of those circumstances which peculiarly belong to the heroine's life, and her fortitude under it what particularly dignifies her character. Catherine

had fortitude too; she suffered, but no murmur passed her lips. [P. 53]

Such passages are inclusive enough; they go beyond the novel of sentiment by Miss Austen's immediate predecessors, and get to those exigencies of plot with which, in one way or another, every novelist must struggle.[8]

Against this continuing comment on the absurdity of novels, Jane Austen establishes her Catherine. Now Catherine is hardly an anti-heroine, for we as readers are quite as much concerned with her hopes and fears as we are with those of any other heroine. Miss Austen takes a seventeen-year-old girl of good family, good disposition, and abounding health, and puts her under the tutelage of Isabella Thorpe, "four years older than Miss Morland, and at least four years better informed" (p. 33), of a "decided pretension" and a "resolute stilishness" (p. 55). Catherine is much impressed by Isabella—as what seventeen-year-old would not have been? But Catherine's troubles do not come from Isabella's influence; in the first volume her rather minor troubles arise from the stupidity of John Thorpe; in the second volume her major trouble arises from the conjunction of the stupidity of John Thorpe and the stupid cupidity of General Tilney. Nor is she ever corrupted by Isabella, ever led by her influence to play any role unnatural to her—a point Miss Austen carefully emphasizes. When, for instance, Catherine believes that she has offended Henry Tilney, "feelings rather natural than heroic" guide her, and without thinking her dignity injured, she is eager to explain the cause of her supposed offense (p. 93). Miss Austen may from time to time describe Catherine's feelings in a mock heroic vein, as she does in the passage quoted above, or as she does in the paragraph that ends the eleventh chapter: "And now I may dismiss my heroine to the sleepless couch, which is the true heroine's portion; to a pillow strewed with thorns and wet with tears. And lucky may she think herself if she get another good night's rest in the course of the next three months" (p. 90). But in the first volume Catherine's own feelings are always rather natural than heroic; paradoxically it might be urged that she indulges in fewer heroics than would be quite natural in a girl of her age.

The remarkable thing about Jane Austen's insistence upon the elements of absurdity in the very nature of the novel is that it accompanies some successful storytelling without lessening its effectiveness. We are interested in the charming and openhearted Catherine and in her adventures. The storytelling is so successful, indeed, that it has beguiled critics into considering *Northanger Abbey* in a manner too nearly like that in which they consider novels of very different intentions. They may not mistake Catherine; Miss Austen tells us specifically and often how she differs from the stock heroine. We are not so often instructed about how to take Henry Tilney. But at least once she makes us see clearly that he stands for a type of masculine vanity, and that we are to share in her wry amusement at it.

When Catherine finally takes the walk with Eleanor and Henry Tilney that the Thorpes have managed to delay, she is introduced to the doctrines of the picturesque, which she finds sufficiently bewildering, and is "heartily ashamed of her ignorance." It is, Miss Austen comments, "a misplaced shame. . . . A woman especially, if she have the misfortune of knowing anything, should conceal it as well as she can":

> The advantages of natural folly in a beautiful girl have been already set forth by the capital pen of a sister author;[9]—and to her treatment of the subject I will only add in justice to men, that though to the larger and more trifling part of the sex, imbecility in females is a great enhancement of their personal charms, there is a portion of them too reasonable and too well informed themselves to desire any thing more in woman than ignorance. [P. 111]

Henry Tilney desires nothing more; and if Catherine does not know her own advantages, as Miss Austen says she does not, she yet effectively employs them, and confesses and laments her ignorance. Henry at once gives her "a lecture on the picturesque": "of fore-grounds, distances, and second distances—side-screens and perspectives—lights and shades." Catherine is "so hopeful a scholar" that, when they gain the top of a hill, she voluntarily rejects "the whole city of Bath, as unworthy to make part of a landscape."[10]

Comedy sharpens toward satire in three directions here: a

ridicule of William Gilpin and the cult of the picturesque;[11] an amused realization of masculine vanity ensnared by itself; and, more subtly, an awareness of Catherine's innocent, perhaps unconscious, but surely instinctive, feminine tact. Lest we should miss that tact, Miss Austen remarks, late in the book: "I must confess that . . . a persuasion of her partiality for him had been the only cause of giving her a serious thought." It is, she adds, "A new circumstance in romance . . . dreadfully derogatory of an heroine's dignity," but not, she implies, a new circumstance in common life (p. 243).

For the most part, however, we are to understand Henry Tilney without overt authorial direction. His status as a clergyman scarcely enters into our consideration.[12] He is not, I think, developed in any particular reference to novelistic convention, but probably in reference to Jane Austen's observation, since intelligent women were as well aware of masculine condescension in her time as in any other—Miss Mitford was, as we shall see. For Catherine when she has fallen in love with Henry, there is of course no blemish in him: "His manner might sometimes surprize, but his meaning must always be just:—and what she did not understand, she was almost as ready to admire, as what she did" (p. 114).[13] But Jane Austen does not expect her readers to have the same estimate of him that Catherine has.

A century ago Mrs. Oliphant, who may be Jane Austen's best critic, pointed out that her "fine vein of feminine cynicism" is very different from the ruder masculine quality of the same name, and that it is "the natural result of the constant, though probably quite unconscious, observation in which a young woman, with no active pursuit to occupy her, spends, without knowing it, so much of her time and youth." When it manifests itself in Miss Austen's work, Mrs. Oliphant says, "she stands by and looks on, and gives a soft half-smile, and tells the story with an exquisite sense of its ridiculous side, and fine stinging yet soft-voiced contempt for the actors in it."[14] With some of her characters, the Reverend Mr. Collins, say, or General Tilney, Miss Austen allows the smile to be apparent and her voice to have some emphasis. But when the smile is not apparent, when—to use Mrs. Oliphant's extension of her metaphor—Miss Austen smiles with her eyes only, as she does, I dare suggest,

with Mr. Knightley in *Emma*, and as she does, I would insist, with
Edmund Bertram in *Mansfield Park*, one needs to regard her
carefully. With Henry Tilney, as we have seen, Miss Austen at
least once lets the smile become apparent, but often she smiles at
his conduct with her eyes only.

Some of Jane Austen's critics, it seems to me, have trouble
recognizing vanity in her characters unless it is expressed in
overt self-praise. It need not be. In *Mansfield Park* she says of
Maria and Julia Bertram: "Their vanity was in such good order,
that they seemed to be quite free of it" (p. 35). Henry Tilney's
vanity is not entirely concealed, but he is far too urbane to praise
himself. He is also intelligent and witty—self-consciously witty;
but intelligence, wit, and vanity are no impossible combination.
He is everywhere sententious—more sententious than can be
accounted for by the style of eighteenth-century conversation.
He delights to instruct Catherine, and his instruction runs even
to pedantry about her diction (pp. 107, 174, and 196). Eleanor,
who has long put up with him, can speak with a gentle satire
about that pedantry—"Come, Miss Morland, let us leave him to
meditate over our faults in the utmost propriety of diction" (p.
108)—but she is willing to interpret his poses lest Catherine mis-
understand them. Since we do not see him apart from
Catherine, we hardly see him when he is not posing in some sort;
often, of course, his poses are admirable enough.

Henry Tilney's poses are admirable enough in those passages
in which Jane Austen puts into his mouth ideas we must suppose
are also ideas of her own—in his remonstrance to Catherine
when he has become aware of the nature of the suspicions of his
father she has entertained (pp. 197–98), or in his explanation to
her of what she ought to feel (were she a proper heroine) when
she has learned of Isabella Thorpe's duplicity (p. 207). Since
these passages mark out stages in Catherine's education, Henry
Tilney, the character who will most impress her, must be made
to speak them; Miss Austen cannot depend upon authorial
comment in either instance. Yet in dealing with these passages,
her critics, it seems to me, are hampered by their own methods.
To think of Henry Tilney as Jane Austen's spokesman, or to say
that he "is never far from the author," or even to take him as a
kind of partly fallible *raisonneur*,[15] is not to measure the comic

distance at which author and character stand. Henry's comic flaw is not, of course, a very reprehensible one. Henry Fielding in his preface to *Joseph Andrews* defines it: "Affectation does not imply an absolute Negation of those Qualities that are affected: . . . when it comes from Vanity only, it partakes of the Nature of Ostentation." Henry Tilney does possess most or all of the qualities he affects: he is comic only in his persistent and self-conscious display of them.

But our consideration of Henry and Catherine needs to take into account a shift of interest in the second volume; we need to see that *Northanger Abbey*, like some other novels of its period, is really written in volumes, each with an interest of its own. The second volume not only has its action in a new place; the direction and the technique of its satire changes. Indeed, Catherine's character in the second volume is not quite consistent with that of the Catherine we have come to know in the first. Although we can readily believe that the Catherine of the first volume would enjoy connecting her reading of Mrs. Radcliffe with her visit to the Abbey in imaginative play, it must seem to us unlikely that she would let that play lead her into folly. In the first volume, naive as she is, fooled as she may be by Isabella, her conduct always evinces an essential rightness, and she never fancies herself in any heroic role. One must suppose that Jane Austen could see the inconsistency quite as well as we, and that, since it furthered her design, she did not much care.[16]

Miss Austen's design is to write the kind of parody of Mrs. Radcliffe that will fit into the fabric of her novel. She had found that parody directed specifically toward incidents of *The Romance of the Forest* would go better into the context of her story than would specific parody of the more famous *Mysteries of Udolpho*.[17] And she is keen enough to fix upon an element in Mrs. Radcliffe's procedure that, as Scott points out, is characteristic of it but in the end disappointing to her readers: "Her heroines often sustain the agony of fear, and her readers that of suspense, from incidents which, when explained, appear of an ordinary and trivial nature."[18] The parody is generally prepared for by the conversations about Mrs. Radcliffe's novels in the first volume—which have only a tenuous connection with the central interest there. In the second volume, the parody is specifically prepared for by Henry Tilney's playful prediction of the adventures Catherine may expect in the Abbey (pp. 157–60). His prediction is not burlesque of Mrs. Radcliffe; but, since it takes the form of summary narrative, it so crowds in Radcliffean elements that it has the effect of travesty—a different thing from the later parody in Catherine's adventures.

But that parody is not to exist by itself and it needs more occasion than Henry's suggestion or Catherine's delight in being in what had been a real abbey. Catherine's bewilderment at General Tilney's conduct and at Eleanor's embarrassments is skillfully used. The reader may be ahead of Catherine in his understanding of General Tilney, but he is not allowed to be very far ahead, so that Catherine's suspicions, although mistaken, seem to have some sort of basis. Even when Henry reproves Catherine after her delusion becomes known to him, he does not at all affirm that his father is beyond suspicion, rather that her suspicions have taken a form impossible in her time and place.[19]

The literary problem is not only the providing of a context for the parody in the action of the novel. It is also the writing of a kind of parody not jarringly inconsistent with the tone and temper of the novel. Miss Austen solves the problem so supremely well that the reader—while he is reading—is likely to be quite unconscious of any problem. Yet it surely was a difficult one. The parody passages must be recognizable parody; but they must not be impossible as accounts of Catherine's interpretations of her experience, and they must use commonplace properties. Take this sample:

> The dimness of the light her candle emitted made her turn to it with alarm; but there was no danger of its sudden extinction, it had yet some hours to burn; and that she might not have any greater difficulty in distinguishing the writing than what its ancient date might occasion, she hastily snuffed it. Alas! it was snuffed and extinguished in one. . . . Catherine, for a few moments, was motionless with horror. It was done completely; not a remnant of light in the wick could give hope to the rekindling breath. Darkness impenetrable and immoveable filled the room. A violent gust of wind, rising with sudden fury, added fresh horror to the

moment. Catherine trembled from head to foot. In the pause which succeeded, a sound like receding footsteps and the closing of a distant door struck on her affrighted ear. [Pp. 169–70][20]

The passage is recognizable parody, a kind of extended allusion; yet it is nowhere the parody of exaggeration. Clearly Miss Austen's danger—a danger I think she just manages to avoid—is that she may write markedly better in Mrs. Radcliffe's vein than Mrs. Radcliffe does herself, and thus lose the parody. And even though the danger is avoided, one thinks what a fine Radcliffean novel Miss Austen might have written had she cared to do so.[21]

Some of Jane Austen's critics write as if they had themselves discovered that General Tilney's conduct is in its way as outrageous as anything Mrs. Radcliffe imagined, even though they may quote Miss Austen when she tells us in the next-to-last chapter that Catherine feels "in suspecting General Tilney of either murdering or shutting up his wife, she had scarcely sinned against his character, or magnified his cruelty" (p. 247). But the parallel between Catherine's delusion and the reality of her experience is suggested earlier in the novel, in the passage in which Eleanor comes to Catherine's room to inform her of the General's determination to send her packing. There Miss Austen reverts to parody and makes a most subtle use of it:

At that moment Catherine thought she heard her step in the gallery, and listened for its continuance; but all was silent. Scarcely, however, had she convicted her fancy of error, when the noise of something moving close to her door made her start; it seemed as if some one was touching the very doorway—and in another moment a slight motion of the lock proved that some hand must be on it. She trembled a little at the idea of any one's approaching so cautiously; but resolving not to be again overcome by trivial appearances of alarm, or misled by a raised imagination, she stepped quietly forward, and opened the door. [Pp. 222–23]

The Radcliffean emanation of doubt and dread foreshadows Catherine's forlorn journey homeward, and her probable wretchedness thereafter.

Catherine's forlorn journey precedes and prepares for that

beautiful reversal, a reversal quite in the Aristotelian sense, in which the General's egregious conduct has an effect entirely the opposite of its intention. The upshot is one we can scarcely imagine provided for in any other way, for we can think of nothing else that would jolt Henry Tilney out of his complacency and his subservience to his father—a subservience that is often suggested, and that the account of the arrangements for the dinner at Woodston (pp. 209–11) is designed to enforce.

Authorial comment is relatively infrequent in the second volume of *Northanger Abbey* until the concluding chapters. It is of course withheld while Catherine builds up her own fiction with the Abbey as its setting, lest the effect of that fiction be mitigated. But there is a striking instance at the end of the skillful and affecting narration of Catherine's journey to Fullerton. The triumphant return of a heroine, Miss Austen remarks, "is an event on which the pen of the contriver may well delight to dwell . . . ":

> —But my affair is widely different; I bring back my heroine to her home in solitude and disgrace; and no sweet elation of spirits can lead me into minuteness. A heroine in a hack post-chaise, is such a blow upon sentiment, as no attempt at grandeur or pathos can withstand. Swiftly therefore shall her post-boy drive through the village, amid the gaze of Sunday groups, and speedy shall be her descent from it. [P. 232]

Here, as so often in volume 1, we seem to stand with the author surveying the action. Yet the change in point of view heightens our realization of Catherine's unhappiness—not only by its contrast with the happiness of other fictional journeys and arrivals, but by a sharing of Jane Austen's authorial concern with her Catherine. And we are reminded that this novel, like all novels, is contrived; as Miss Austen moves into its two crowded concluding chapters, authorial comment becomes a means for the amusing representation of the contriver's difficulties.

These concluding chapters show us clearly that the target of the satire in *Northanger Abbey* is ultimately the novel as a genre. They are beautifully gratuitous. There are no apparently preternatural elements to be explained away in the Radcliffean

fashion. No intractable complexity of plot forces desperate resolution. There are relatively few loose threads to gather up, and
most of those have been deliberately left so that they might be
drawn up at last. These two chapters mock a good many novels,
in some sort almost all novels—except some recent ones in which
plot and conclusion have been given up.

For surely in all our experience with novels, it is the concluding chapter or chapters that seem to us weakest, that require
from us the greatest allowances for the novelist's expedients. At
the end of a novel, both reader and writer are caught between
conflicting demands. We have a natural desire for conclusion,
for that rounding off that life denies us, for Aristotle's beginning, middle, and end. That is why we devise games like baseball
that do round off to a result, and why novelists have tried to
make their novels seem conclusive. But we know that human
experience is inconclusive, that, save death, there is no finality in
it. Miss Austen sees the novelist's predicament as comic, as she
had seen it since her fifteenth year or earlier.

In her novels other than *Northanger Abbey*, although Jane Austen conforms to convention and her readers' expectation, she
writes her concluding chapters with an air of amused embarrassment, and sometimes mocks both her readers and herself. In
Mansfield Park, for instance, she will not fix the time it takes
Edmund Bertram to cease to care about Miss Crawford and to
become anxious to marry Fanny Price; she will only "entreat
everybody to believe that exactly at the time when it was quite
natural that it should be so, and not a week earlier" the transition
occurs (p. 470). Or in *Emma*, the consent to Emma's marriage by
her valetudinarian father—who must of course be represented
as loath to consent—is brought about by his alarm at some
poultry-house robberies in the neighborhood and his desire for
Mr. Knightley's protection (pp. 483–84)—a kind of parallel to
the "probable circumstance" that provides for General Tilney's
consent to the marriage in *Northanger Abbey*. But in *Northanger
Abbey* there is no air of embarrassment in the closing chapters;
Miss Austen is enjoying herself immensely.

The next-to-last chapter begins at a normal pace, but with the
arrival of Henry Tilney at Fullerton, explanations come
breathlessly until Henry and Catherine are sure in their love but

prevented from marriage by the Morlands' unwillingness to consent to a marriage unless General Tilney also consents—not a difficulty that will much dismay experienced novel readers:

> The anxiety, which in this state of their attachment must be the portion of Henry and Catherine, and of all who loved either, as to its final event, can hardly extend, I fear, to the bosom of my readers, who will see in the tell-tale compression of the pages before them, that we are all hastening together to perfect felicity. The means by which their early marriage was effected can be the only doubt; what probable circumstance could work upon a temper like the General's? [P. 250]

A little novelistic ingenuity can supply that probable circumstance: it is the marriage of Eleanor Tilney to a gentleman who has recently acceded to the peerage. It is a most efficient probable circumstance—a triple-play probable circumstance. It provides Eleanor with a husband, rewarding her for her subdued role in the novel and gratifying the readers. It throws the General into "a fit of good-humour" in which he consents to Henry's marriage. And—fortunate stroke—it tidies up the plot. Of the gentleman who marries Eleanor, besides assuring us of his supreme eligibility, Jane Austen can affirm

> (aware that the rules of composition forbid the introduction of a character not connected with my fable)—that this was the very gentleman whose negligent servant left behind him that collection of washing-bills, resulting from a long visit at Northanger, by which my heroine was involved in one of her most alarming adventures. [P. 251]

The novel ends in an almost malicious (malicious, if we suppose that Miss Austen could foresee some of her critics) statement of alternate morals: "I leave it to be settled by whomsoever it may concern, whether the tendency of this work be altogether to recommend parental tyranny, or reward filial disobedience."

The literary moral of our consideration of *Northanger Abbey*, so far as it applies to the book itself, hardly needs stating. Obviously, if a critic approaches the book with a reverence for the

novel as a genre, he is in degree hampered in its discussion, for
he cannot easily accommodate his thinking to the work of a
writer who is amused not only by what she is doing, but by the
whole set of expedients to which any novelist must resort. It
seems to me, however, that this moral has also some application
to the criticism of Jane Austen's other novels.

Devoted students of Jane Austen may be distressed by Henry
James's unwillingness to recognize her as a conscious artist; and
as B. C. Southam remarks, it is ironic that the Jamesian critical
approach dominates the recent study of her work.[22] But I think
James was expressing, by a characteristic indirection, his realization that Jane Austen did not take the novel *qua* novel quite
seriously—not seriously in his sense, as he did. And we need that
realization, even though we reject James's depreciation of her
skill in "composition, distribution, arrangement." Doubtless she
considered literature an important activity, but we can hardly
think that the writer of *Northanger Abbey* ever considered the
novelist's activity with the reverential seriousness that most of
her best recent critics do. She would have kept that sort of reverence for what religious persons of her time called "serious
things."

NOTES

1. Scott wrote in his journal in 1826: "The Big Bow-wow strain I can
do myself like any now going, but the exquisite touch which renders
ordinary commonplace things and characters interesting from the truth
of the description and the sentiment is denied to me. What a pity such a
gifted creature died so early!" (quoted in *Jane Austen: The Critical Heritage*, p. 106).

2. Jane Austen's metaphor has been often inappropriately used. It
comes from a letter to her nephew, James Edward Austen-Leigh, author of the *Memoir*, and contrasts his presumably robust early literary
efforts with hers. See *Memoir of Jane Austen*, ed. R. W. Chapman (Oxford: Clarendon Press, 1926), p. 164. Miss Austen often works with a
pretty wide brush, and certainly so on the figures of General Tilney and
John Thorpe in *Northanger Abbey*.

3. See R. W. Chapman, *Jane Austen, Facts and Problems* (Oxford:
Clarendon Press, 1948), pp. 73–76; and his introductory note to *North-
anger Abbey* and *Persuasion*, pp. xi–xiii, in the Oxford edition of *The
Novels of Jane Austen*. The book we know as *Northanger Abbey* was first

called *Susan* and then *Catherine*; the title *Northanger Abbey* was probably chosen by Henry Austen. The title of this chapter is intended to recall the titles of the first four pieces in *Volume the First* of Miss Austen's juvenilia: "Frederick & Elfrida," "Jack & Alice," etc.

4. Of *The Heroine* Jane Austen wrote to her sister that she "was very much amused by it. . . . It is a delightful burlesque, particularly in the Radcliffean style." See *Jane Austen's Letters to Her Sister Cassandra and Others*, ed. R. W. Chapman (Oxford: Clarendon Press, 1932), pp. 376–77. Michael Sadleir in his introduction to the Oxford World's Classics edition of *Northanger Abbey* cites three other burlesques in the same period: Sarah Green, *Romance Readers and Romance Writers* (1810); *Love and Horror* (1815); and *Mystery of the Abbey* (1819).

5. A good discussion is Alan D. McKillop, "Critical Realism in *Northanger Abbey*," reprinted in *Jane Austen: A Collection of Critical Essays*, ed. Ian Watt (Englewood Cliffs, N. J.: Prentice-Hall, 1963), pp. 52–61.

6. *Minor Works*, pp. 428–30. All page references in text and notes to fiction by Jane Austen are to volumes in the Oxford edition of *The Novels of Jane Austen*, ed. R. W. Chapman, 3rd ed. (London: Oxford University Press, 1965).

7. For examples of passages in which Catherine is contrasted with the stock heroine, see pp. 19, 19–20, 23–24, 53, 60. For examples in which Catherine has some likeness to the stock heroine see pp. 15–16, 35–36.

8. For further examples of passages of a burlesque tendency that seem to be directed toward the novel as a genre, see pp. 34, 97, 119. The tendency of the last chapter will be discussed later.

9. Identified by R. W. Chapman as Fanny Burney (in *Camilla*).

10. Catherine herself delights to remain a pupil. At the Abbey she has "scarcely any curiosity about the grounds." "If Henry had been with them indeed!" she thinks, "but now she should not know what was picturesque when she saw it" (p. 177).

11. Jane Austen had probably read Sir Uvedale Price as well as Gilpin. Her brother Henry Austen says in his "Biographical Notice of the Author" that "at a very early age she was enamoured of Gilpin on the Picturesque; and she seldom changed her opinion either on books or men". (*Northanger Abbey* and *Persuasion*, p. 7). But the conversation among Edward, Elinor, and Marianne in *Sense and Sensibility* (pp. 96–98) hardly seems the work of a writer who takes the doctrine of the picturesque very seriously; even Marianne is made to say that "admiration of landscape scenery has become a mere jargon." For the influence of the doctrine of the picturesque on the account of Elizabeth's visit to Pemberley in *Pride and Prejudice* (pp. 245, 253–54), see W. L. Renwick, *English Literature, 1789–1815* (Oxford: Clarendon Press, 1963), pp. 98–99.

12. If there is such a thing as satire by silence, Jane Austen employs it on Henry Tilney's character as clergyman. There is nothing in his conversation or in his interests, I believe, that suggests his profession, although nothing in either may be necessarily inconsistent with it by the standards of late eighteenth- and early nineteenth-century Anglicanism. He tells Catherine, "Northanger is not more than half my home; I have an establishment at my own house in Woodston, which is nearly twenty miles from my father's, and some of my time is necessarily spent there" (p. 157). But in the eleven-week span of the novel he visits Woodston, reluctantly and briefly, three times; we may hope his curate is hard-working. (When early in the novel he is absent from Bath for a week, he may be in Woodston; we are not told so.) See R. W. Chapman's *Chronology* (including the amusing discussion of Henry's possible absence from his parish on Easter Day), in *Northanger Abbey* and *Persuasion*, pp. 275–79.

13. Before Catherine has fallen in love, however, she is able to wonder about Henry: when, just after she has met him, he talks with condescending politeness to Mrs. Allen, Catherine fears that he indulges himself "a little too much with the foibles of others" (p. 29). After she has fallen in love, she seems not to resent even the gratuitous rudeness of the mock moralizing with which he responds to her innocent remark that she has just "learnt to love a hyacinth" (p. 174).

14. See [Margaret Oliphant], "Miss Austen and Miss Mitford," *Blackwood's Edinburgh Magazine* 107 (1870): 294–95. The portions of this article dealing with Miss Austen's fiction are conveniently reprinted in *Jane Austen: The Critical Heritage*, pp. 215–25.

15. See Marvin Mudrick, *Jane Austen: Irony as Defense and Discovery* (Princeton: Princeton University Press, 1952), pp. 43, 48–51; A. Walton Litz, *Jane Austen: A Study of Her Artistic Development* (New York: Oxford University Press, 1965), p. 67 (also pp. 58 and 69); and Alistair M. Duckworth, *The Improvement of the Estate: A Study of Jane Austen's Novels* (Baltimore: Johns Hopkins University Press, 1971), pp. 95–98. See also John Davie's introduction to *Northanger Abbey* and *Persuasion* (London: Oxford University Press, 1971), p. xiii. Lloyd W. Brown in every reference to Henry Tilney in *Bits of Ivory* (Baton Rouge: Louisiana State University Press, 1973) takes him at the estimate Jane Austen makes him have of himself.

16. Such inconsistency troubles Jane Austen's critics, who are likely to repeat in some fashion the reservation with which Mary Lascelles begins and ends her consideration of *Northanger Abbey*: "Thus, the burlesque element . . . has a pretty intricacy and variety. Its strands are ingeniously interwoven with one another—but not so well woven into

the rest of the fabric." See *Jane Austen and Her Art* (London: Oxford University Press, 1939), pp. 59, 64.

17. *Northanger Abbey* and *Persuasion*, Appendixes, pp. 284–90.

18. *The Lives of the Novelists*, p. 235.

19. There is a fine touch in the account of Catherine's reflective recantation of Mrs. Radcliffe's influence: "Charming as were all Mrs. Radcliffe's works, and charming even as were the works of all her imitators, it was not in them perhaps that human nature, at least in the midland counties of England, was to be looked for." Parts of the Continent "might be as fruitful in horrors as they were there represented. Catherine dared not doubt beyond her own country, and even of that, if hard pressed, would have yielded the northern and western extremities" (p. 200).

20. The omitted sentence is this: "A lamp could not have expired with more awful effect." It is intended to recall the last sentence of Henry Tilney's account of Catherine's probable adventures during her visit to the Abbey (p. 160), but it is perhaps a false note in the parody.

21. Although the passages that parody Mrs. Radcliffe interest us most, not all the satire of the Gothic novel is directed specifically toward her work. For instance, when Catherine sees General Tilney in church completely collected even as he faces the monument to his wife, she thinks, not particularly of, say, Signor Montoni, but of dozens of beings hardened in guilt (p. 190); and when she sees the portrait of the mother of Henry and Eleanor, she is surprised not to find any striking resemblance to either, all her reading having taught her to expect one (p. 191).

22. See B. C. Southam's introduction to *Jane Austen: The Critical Heritage*, pp. 31–32.

4

Washington Irving
and the Mysterious Portrait

The Gothic convention has had a surprising persistence. Even in our own time a new school of women Gothic writers flourish and abound; and since *The Castle of Otranto* fiction in English has hardly been without some manifestation of the Gothic. It is like a tenacious vine which, run-out or discouraged in one place in the garden, soon flourishes in another. In 1824, when Washington Irving's *Tales of a Traveller* was published, the great vogue of the "horrid" novels recommended to Catherine Morland was some years over; but the Gothic remained an element in novels and the substance of tales—and was to be the substance of many more.

We need always to distinguish the mode of the manifestation of the Gothic convention. The Gothic presented itself to Irving in a way somewhat different from the way it had to Jane Austen when she wrote *Northanger Abbey*. *Blackwood's Edinburgh Magazine*, with its "many fine examples"—according to Poe—of *"tales of effect,"* began publication in 1817. The Gothic temper, properties, and devices were taken over into the tale, which might depend a great deal upon the readers' previous experience with the Gothic; the best Gothic tales became increasingly allusive. But Irving was early with a rather complex kind of allusiveness.

Some of Irving's work has not been justly estimated. In his lifetime his status as both a British and an American writer confused the estimate, for American critics depreciated or ignored work that did not have an American scene. But the estimate is further confused. The best work of writers—particularly of writers of short fiction—often keeps their weak work alive in the interest of readers; and often enough admiration for that best work leads scholars and critics to overestimate other pieces of little value. But somehow things have not come out quite that way with the work of Washington Irving. We take his master-pieces, "Rip Van Winkle" and "The Legend of Sleepy Hollow," for granted; and then we let those two masterpieces so over-shadow his other tales that we underestimate even the best among them. Something similar happened in Irving's day, and his *Tales of a Traveller* (1824) suffered unduly by comparison with *The Sketch Book* (1819–20) and *Bracebridge Hall* (1822).[1] Of course it is inferior to them; his critics, realizing that, could find little or nothing of merit in it, and literary history has shown relatively little interest in the book.[2] Yet Irving carried out some interesting literary experiments in *Tales of a Traveller*. We are here concerned with one of them.

When *Tales of a Traveller* was newly out, Irving wrote to his friend Henry Brevoort about it. Despite "some handling from the press," he said, "I am convinced that a great part of it was written in a freer and happier vein than almost any of my former writings. There was more of an artist like touch about it—though this is not a thing to be appreciated by the many." He had chosen, he went on to say, a line of writing peculiar to himself.[3] Now what makes Irving's writing in the first part of his career peculiar to himself is continual experimentation with genres and with conventions within genres, so that in the best of his tales we are always aware of clear likenesses to well-established forms, and of interesting—sometimes intricate and surprising—deviations from them. Irving's awareness of literary forms and conventions and his ingenuity with them help to ac-count, not only for his masterpieces, but for the excellent parts of *Knickerbocker's History of New York* and the curious interweav-ing of literary kinds in *Bracebridge Hall*. Irving was often urged to write a novel, and did consider doing so; but he seems to have been astute enough to realize that the weight of novelistic con-vention would inhibit him in what he could do best.

The continuing frame of "Strange Stories by a Nervous Gen-tleman," the first part of *Tales of a Traveller*, holds together seven stories. The three "Strange Stories" we here consider—"The Adventure of My Uncle," "The Adventure of My Aunt,"

and "The Adventure of the Mysterious Picture"—have in common the use of the Gothic property of the mysterious portrait;
and they belong to the vein in Irving that has been called "the
sportive Gothic," the vein of "The Spectre Bridegroom" in *The
Sketch Book* and of "The Stout Gentleman" in *Bracebridge Hall*. At
the end of the frame for "The Stout Gentleman," Irving slyly
remarks: "I think it has in it all the elements of that mysterious
and romantic narrative, so greedily sought after at the present
day." What Irving had delighted to do was to write a Gothic tale
of sorts without a conventional Gothic setting or any of the conventional properties, depending upon his readers' familiarity
with them for a kind of comic irony. Our three tales stem from
"The Stout Gentleman"; it is characteristic of Irving that in a
new book he continues some strain from a previous one. But our
three tales are perhaps somewhat less subtle in technique than
"The Stout Gentleman," and they make a more obvious use of
the readers' experience with Gothic tales.

Even so, the allusiveness with which we are concerned is of
rather a special sort, intended not so much to recall particular
literary experiences as to recall a set of associations with Gothic
story. It belongs, of course, to a late stage in the development of
the Gothic. If we date the Gothic from 1764—from the publication of Walpole's *The Castle of Otranto, a Gothic Story*— it had had
by the publication of Irving's *Tales of a Traveller* in 1824 a history
of sixty years. Its conventions had been used over and over again
and were very much frayed—as any writer who set about using
them well knew and, if he had any literary tact, took into account
in his use of them.

No Gothic property was more worn than the mysterious portrait. Walpole and Ann Radcliffe had used it; Charles Robert
Maturin was late in making what we may call a straight use of it
in his *Melmoth the Wanderer* (1820)—but *Melmoth* was something
of an anachronism. One can hardly guess how many stories had
made use of it, or how many times Irving had encountered it (or
how many more times Hawthorne had). It is a mistake to think
of the standard Gothic writers as the chief Gothic influences
upon early nineteenth-century writers, for they had certainly
read more Gothic stories out of the great number of the unre-
membered than they had in the work of Walpole, Mrs. Radcliffe,

William Godwin, Brockden Brown, Monk Lewis, and Maturin—and so had their readers.

At the time of *Tales of a Traveller*, the mysterious portrait might still be successfully used as a conventional Gothic property. In "The Tapestried Chamber," a tale Sir Walter Scott wrote for an annual (*The Keepsake* for 1828) and probably did not take very seriously, it is so used.[4] But about ten years earlier, in chapter 34 of *The Bride of Lammermoor* (1819), Scott had used the mysterious portrait in a much more subtle fashion and with considerable restraint. This mysterious portrait, the reader will remember, turns out to be not so very mysterious. But in the initially unexplained appearance of the portrait of Sir Malise Ravenswood in the hall of what has been his home, where it seems "to frown wrath and vengeance upon the party assembled below," there is an awe that depends upon the associations the reader can bring to the scene. The skillful writer could turn the very familiarity of the Gothic, indeed its conventionality, to his account. Poe, for example, is careful to refer to Mrs. Radcliffe in the first sentence of his mysterious portrait story, "The Oval Portrait."

The skillful writer, moreover, could use the Gothic whimsically, and take such a property as the mysterious portrait less than seriously without losing entirely its accumulation of awe. Hawthorne's use of a mysterious portrait in *The House of the Seven Gables* achieves that effect. And a somewhat like effect was what Irving was trying for in the "Strange Stories by a Nervous Gentleman"—trying for and, evidently, not quite attaining. The effect would depend not only upon his skill but upon his ability to predict what place the mysterious portrait held in the imaginative experience of his readers.

Irving's own imagination had played about old portraits before the *Tales of a Traveller*. The allegory of "The Art of Book-Making" in *The Sketch Book* turns upon the animation of the portraits of old writers in the reading room of the British Museum. In the Christmas sketches in *The Sketch Book* the full-length portrait of a crusader in armor standing by his white horse is thrice mentioned—a portrait which "was thought by the servants to have something supernatural about it; for they remarked that, in whatever part of the hall you went, the eyes of the warrior were still fixed on you"; and which, according to report, used to become animated on Midsummer eve, when the warrior rode off to visit his tomb in the church. In "Popular Superstitions" in *Bracebridge Hall*, Irving makes Geoffrey Crayon say that he had himself been startled, when suddenly catching sight of the portrait, into the notion that it was a figure advancing toward him; in "Christmas Eve" Crayon remarks on the row of black-looking portraits in his chamber, and recurs to them in *Bracebridge Hall*: in "St. Mark's Eve" one of them, with "a most pale and plaintive countenance," seems to fix her eyes mournfully upon him. In *The Sketch Book* ("The Christmas Dinner") and in *Bracebridge Hall* ("Family Relics"), Crayon reflects upon the way in which ancestral portraits are a kind of family narrative, and give their owners a certain continuity with their ancestral pasts. In "Dolph Heyliger" a ghost is identified through an old portrait—a narrative device that looks forward to "The Adventure of My Uncle."

These passages, although some of them have Gothic suggestions, may not be so much Gothic in intention as indications of the effect of Gothic story on Irving's sensibility. And of course old portraits do have inherent qualities that tease the mind and the imagination, quite apart from Gothic associations. But at any rate Irving had turned old portraits to some little literary account before he set about writing the "Strange Stories by a Nervous Gentleman" and the calculated exploiting of the mysterious portrait as a Gothic property.

The "Strange Stories" have a most intricate frame. The "Nervous Gentleman" is the same who tells the story of "The Stout Gentleman" in *Bracebridge Hall*. In the "Strange Stories" he is represented as retelling six stories he had heard at a hunting dinner prolonged by bad weather, and as relating one adventure of his own on that occasion. He purports to retell the six stories exactly as they came to him, and establishes characters for the original narrators that color their stories; he also repeats some of the comments of the original auditors. All of the stories are in some sense Gothic; out of the seven, five have to do with portraits: the three we consider, and the last two, which are told in explanation of the origin of the portrait in "The Adventure of the Mysterious Picture," the nervous gentleman's story of his own adventure.

"The Adventure of My Uncle," the first of the "Strange
Stories," has for its original narrator an old gentleman with one
side of his head "dilapidated" and a drooping eyelid. His uncle
was, he says, "rather a dry, shrewd kind of body," and he tells his
uncle's story dryly. The tale is what Scott calls "a story of supernatural terror," and its circumstances and events are conventional enough. Indeed, they are surprisingly parallel to those of
Scott's own "The Tapestried Chamber." Since Irving means to
use that conventionality, he is careful to have the narrator point
it out: the chamber in which his uncle's adventure takes place
has "a wild crazy look, enough to strike any one who had read
romances with apprehension and foreboding"; even the clock in
the turret of the chateau which so dismally strikes midnight is,
he says,"such an old clock as ghosts are fond of."

But the tale gains a curious kind of credibility just because it
comes to us through the narrator's account of his uncle's story:
the uncle seems hardly to be a subject for delusions, the narrator
hardly of easy credulity. And the tale has, too, a connection with
history we know about; Aristotle long ago pointed out that a
marvellous action may gain imaginative credence if it be connected with what we recognize as fact.

In this tale, as in Scott's "The Tapestried Chamber," the mysterious portrait is not in itself an object of terror. When the
morning after the uncle's midnight adventure, his host, a marquis, shows him some old portraits, one of them is the means by
which he identifies the figure that had visited him in his bed
chamber. The figure was that of a woman, "tall, and stately, and
of a commanding air," whose beauty "was saddened by care and
anxiety"; she had paid no attention to him, but had warmed
herself by his fire, and made her departure with arms upraised
in apparent supplication.

The uncle is informed by his host that the subject of the portrait is "the beautiful Duchess de Longueville, who figured during the minority of Louis the Fourteenth." The Duchess was
certainly such a woman as might have a distinguished apparition: she was a moving spirit in the first Fronde, largely responsible for the second Fronde, the mistress of La Rochefoucauld, a
woman of great charm and firm purpose, who was finally disappointed in all her worldly hopes and found solace at Port-Royal.
The marquis recalls something of her history and, indeed, be-

gins an account of her visit to the chateau that is the scene of the
story. He seems about to tell of an event that might account for
her appearance in the uncle's chamber, but for the honor of the
family breaks off. But when the uncle tells the story of his noc-
turnal visitation, the marquis seems to reject it.

Entries in Irving's journal at intervals over almost three
months indicate that he began writing "The Adventure of My
Uncle" without intending to identify the apparition as that of the
Duchess de Longueville. Apparently the change in plan somehow stems from the advice of Irving's friend Frank Mills "to
touch up the Frenchman tale," for in the next three entries
concerning the tale we learn of the addition of "historical anecdotes," of "inserting particulars of Duchess of Longueville," and
of "alterations of tale of my uncle."[5] Surely the change in plan
strengthened the tale. The identification of the apparition with
the Duchess allows readers who know something of the career of
that remarkable woman an experience of recognition; and even
for readers who do not, it gives the tale an imaginative solidity
that it would otherwise have lacked.

The second story in "Strange Stories" is "The Adventure of
My Aunt." The titles of the first two stories and their juxtaposition suggest that they are to stand in a complementary relationship with each other; indeed, one of the auditors, a country
clergyman, is made to regret that the uncle and the aunt had not
been married to each other, since they would have been so well
matched. The original narrator this time is "the knowing gentleman, with the flexible nose." His story is a simple one: "a
loose, idle fellow," formerly a servant in the house, hides in the
aunt's chamber behind the portrait of her late husband; he has
"borrowed an eye from the portrait by way of a reconnoitering
hole." The aunt, hearing suspicious sounds, is able to observe
the portrait in her mirror and to perceive that one of the eyes
moves. "So strange a circumstance," the narrator says, "gave her
a sudden shock. . . . The light of the taper gleamed on the eye,
and was reflected from it. She was sure it moved. Nay more, it
seemed to give her a wink, as she had sometimes known her
husband to do when living!" But after a momentary chill, the
resolute aunt calls her servants, and the intruder is ducked in the
horsepond and soundly beaten with a club.

Now glaring eyes are stock features of mysterious portraits. One remembers perhaps the portrait of the Wanderer in *Melmoth:* "*the eyes* . . . were such as one feels they wish they had never seen, and feels they can never forget." Unless the reader has some like images in his memory to bring to the story, images that function as ironic allusions, the story will not work as Irving intended it to, and probably will have little interest—though of course the reader may enjoy the lively representation of the buxom widow or be entertained by the rather persistent sexual innuendo. But the intended effect depends upon a context the reader must supply, for it is never stated, never in any ordinary way alluded to. The twist Irving seems to be trying for is a story in the convention of the "explained supernatural" that never really suggests the supernatural—for that, too, the reader must supply the context. At the end of the story the inquisitive gentleman remarks, "I don't see, after all, that there was any ghost in this last story"; but there is one, the ghost of whatever mysterious portrait stories the reader has known.

"The Adventure of the Mysterious Picture" is the nervous gentleman's own story of his adventure after four of the stories he is retelling have been told and bedtime has come. His host tries an experiment: he tells his guests that one of them will be given a haunted chamber, but no one will know who has occupied that chamber "until circumstances reveal it." The nervous gentleman finds in his room a striking picture of a man in agony, "the agony of intense bodily pain," but, too, with a scowling menace on the brow, "and a few sprinklings of blood" to add to the picture's ghastliness. The nervous gentleman tries to convince himself that his "inscrutable antipathy" toward the picture is to be accounted for by the effects of his "host's good cheer, and in some measure by the odd stories about paintings which had been told at supper." But one of those storms that frequently sound in Gothic story howls about the house, and the nervous gentleman grows increasingly nervous—although he is always aware of his own "infected imagination."

Indeed, the focus of the story is upon the narrator's analytical account of his own emotions—and that is the twist Irving has tried for in this mysterious portrait story. William L. Hedges has pointed out that in this regard the story is like some of Poe's.[6]

But the nervous gentleman himself is quite unlike any figure of Poe's, and his neuroses are much like those of the rest of us; as the narrator of "The Stout Gentleman" in *Bracebridge Hall* and the reteller of the "Strange Stories," he has been established as a comic but likable figure. In this story his concern is divided between his antipathy for the picture and his fear of ridicule in the morning: "The idea," he says, "of being hag-ridden by my own fancy all night, and then bantered on my haggard looks the next day, was intolerable; but the very idea was sufficient to produce the effect, and to render me still more nervous."

The nervous gentleman tries to solve his problem in a sensible way—a more sensible way than we expect from a Gothic narrator. He leaves his chamber and spends the rest of the night on a sofa in the drawing room. He might have escaped detection as the occupant of the haunted chamber had he not left his watch for a servant to discover under one of the sofa pillows. But his host comes to his rescue: he affirms that there is indeed a mysterious effect from the picture. The next two stories account for it.

These two stories are "The Adventure of the Mysterious Stranger" and "The Story of the Young Italian." In the first of them, the host recounts his acquaintance with a young Italian, a painter; the second story is a manuscript left by the young Italian himself and read by the host. "The Story of the Young Italian" is a Gothic story, with the unhealthiness of sentiment one is familiar with in many Gothic stories—it would seem quite at home as one of the succession of tales in *Melmoth the Wanderer*— and the young Italian's painting of the death agony of the man he has killed, a painting intended to exorcise his persistent mental image of the reality, is somewhat like the wax *memento mori* that Emily in *The Mysteries of Udolpho* supposes a mysterious portrait. Since Irving in the "Strange Stories," and indeed in the *Tales of a Traveller* as a whole, was busy about displaying his versatility, it is perhaps not surprising that he should try one tale in the straight Gothic, nor that it should remind us of Maturin.[7]

But Irving's contemporaries did not much like *Tales of a Traveller*, and liked the "Strange Stories by a Nervous Gentleman" no more than they did the other parts of the book. Nor have the "Strange Stories" been much read since Irving's time.[8]

Although "The Bold Dragoon" and "The Adventure of the German Student" do sometimes appear in anthologies, the three mysterious portrait stories have usually been neglected. From the beginning, Irving's intention has apparently bothered his critics. For instance, the reviewer in *Blackwood's* wrote of the "Strange Stories" in 1824: "the tone in which Mr. Irving does them up, is quite wrong. A ghost story *ought* to be a ghost story. Something like seriousness is absolutely necessary . . . and the sort of half-witty vein, the little dancing quirks, &c. &c. with which these are set forth entirely destroy the whole matter."[9] Subsequent criticism has indicated a discontent of somewhat the same sort.

Stanley T. Williams's judgment seems particularly instructive. In his *Life of Washington Irving* he writes: "We can never read these stories as we pore over the serious narratives of Charles Brockden Brown, with possibly a smile at their absurdity but with respect for Brown's sincere rendering of the Gothic tradition; nor are they effective as satire. . . . The tales are too brief, too wanting in substance to provoke either an honest shudder or an honest smile."[10] Now that passage may indicate a failure in the writer or in the critic. It seems to say that a writer of Irving's stature might well concern himself with "a sincere rendering of the Gothic tradition" more than twenty years after Brown's novels—yet the one story among the "Strange Stories" that is straight Gothic has certainly not been liked more than the others. On the other hand, as it seems to me, Irving's intention is hardly to be described as satiric.

It may be that Irving's intention was oversubtle and that the oversubtlety accounts for the comparative failure of these stories with his readers. Apparently he wanted to achieve both a shudder and a smile, or perhaps better to say, a shudder with a smile. There is an inherent absurdity in Gothic stories. What if a writer, Irving seems to have asked himself, instead of letting his readers "smile at their absurdity" however they may, recognize it and control it for his own purposes? If a writer could manage to evoke in his readers the simultaneous presence of two opposed reactions, amusement and a touch of terror, the effect would be a distinctive one. Irving apparently thought he could manage it by the flexible style in which he had so much confidence, and by an intricate manipulation of his narrators. He would, moreover, give each of the three mysterious portrait stories its own twist and show that there was yet some interest in the old Gothic property. He encountered problems; and our awareness of them is, of course, the sign that they were not completely solved.

Remarks in the frame of the "Strange Stories" may indicate Irving's awareness of one problem. When in "The Adventure of My Uncle," for instance, the nervous gentleman has finished his reproduction of his acquaintance's story, he remarks: "I was inclined to think the old gentleman had really an afterpart of his story in reserve; but he sipped his wine and said nothing more, and there was an odd expression about his dilapidated countenance which left me in doubt whether he were in drollery or earnest." The remark seems a tactical mistake on Irving's part, as do other comparable remarks. They are intended, I take it, merely to point up the quality of the experience of the story Irving thought his readers most likely to miss. But they suggest too readily such responses to the stories as that represented for us by the judgment of Stanley T. Williams. The quoted remark too nearly says to some readers: take this as "drollery" or take it as a tale of terror in "earnest." "The Adventure of My Uncle" would surely fail taken as either; but—given a chance—it may succeed for the reader who will take it as a tale of terror and be amused at doing so, amused partly at himself.

Yet it may be that Irving's only serious mistake in the mysterious portrait stories was a mistake in timing—that he asked from his readers a response that they were not yet ready to make. He had of course succeeded with his earlier sportive Gothic tales— some of them more complex than the mysterious portrait stories. But none of them uses a standard Gothic property irreverently or asks for a response that so much depends upon associations from a set of previous literary experiences. The *Blackwood's* reviewer of *Tales of a Traveller* may have been protecting the fiction of the magazine for which he wrote, but he was probably right in his estimate of the taste of readers and their loyalty to their habits of response.

It would have been some years after the publication of *Tales of a Traveller* that Poe made the study of the *Blackwood's* Gothic tales he recalls in his 1842 review of *Twice-Told Tales*. Hawthorne himself, early in his career had made his own study of *Blackwood's*.[11] When he came to use the Gothic convention allusively and playfully, he may have succeeded better than Irving did (although he owed something to Irving's example). But Irving tried his mysterious protrait stories ten years—at least—too early, before the convention seemed as thoroughly worn to his readers as it seemed to him.

About the enjoyment of Irving's mysterious portrait stories, of course criticism can do little; a reader may see well enough what Irving was doing and still not care for it. Yet, as it seems to me, we ought to be better readers for them than Irving's contemporaries were. Quite apparently he overestimated the literary sophistication of his public. The perspective of literary history may supply us with something like the literary sophistication that Irving expected and did not find in his first readers.

NOTES

1. The *North American Review*, for example, reviewed *The Sketch Book* and *Bracebridge Hall* carefully, but it did not bother to review *Tales of a Traveller* at all.

2. There is a good discussion of *Tales of a Traveller* in William L. Hedges, *Washington Irving: An American Study, 1802–1832* (Baltimore: Johns Hopkins University Press, 1965), pp. 191–235.

3. Quoted in *Washington Irving: Representative Selections*, ed. Henry A. Pochmann (New York: American Book Company, 1934), p. lxxv.

4. "The Tapestried Chamber or The Lady in the Sacque" is included in *Short Stories by Sir Walter Scott*, ed. Lord David Cecil (Oxford World's Classics, 1934), pp. 310–31. Like "The Adventure of My Uncle," Scott's tale has a traveler who comes to an old castle, inquires who the owner is, finds that the owner is an old friend, is invited to stay the night, and is given a bed chamber ordinarily disused and with a more antique air than that of the rest of the establishment. Both travelers are visited during the night by the figure of a woman (but in Scott's tale the figure is that of a hag and menaces the traveler). In both tales the figure is identified the next morning when the host shows his guest a portrait of a woman connected with the family's history and in particular with an episode in the chamber itself. "The Tapestried Chamber" offers us a convenient example of a straight Gothic tale with a story line nearly identical to that of "The Adventure of My Uncle."

There is another consideration, however—unimportant perhaps, but of some interest. Scott says in his introduction that his source is a fireside tale told him by Anna Seward. But since it seems unlikely that Scott would have published his tale in the form we have it had he realized its great likeness to Irving's, it seems a fair guess that a memory of Miss Seward's tale and a memory of Irving's coalesced in Scott's mind. Scott once uses the word "chateau" in reference to the edifice he describes as "a castle, as old as the wars of York and Lancaster," and which he locates in the western counties of England; "chateau" seems more likely to be an unconscious reminiscence of Irving's tale than an inappropriate piece of elegant variation.

5. See *Journals of Washington Irving (1823–1824)*, ed. Stanley T. Williams (Cambridge: Harvard University Press, 1931), pp. 135, 165, 169, 180, 184.

6. Hedges, *Washington Irving*, p. 205.

7. Irving may have intended or considered another mysterious portrait story. In a journal entry for 19 July, 1824, he records in outline a story told him by William Robert Spencer of a maid of honor at the court of Darmstadt who had an unaccountable antipathy for a portrait of a landgrave, and who was one day found dead before it, having apparently climbed upon a stool to examine it closely, lost her balance, and pulled the picture with its massive frame down upon her. Irving could not have used that source in *Tales of a Traveller*, for he was getting proof of the book before 19 July. See *Journals of Washington Irving (1823–1824)*, p. 230.

8. The most sincere tribute to the "Strange Stories" must be the young Charles Dickens's use of them in *Pickwick Papers*. The frame and the tone of the one-eyed bagman's account of his uncle's story of Tom Smart are clearly influenced by the "Strange Stories": there seems even some borrowing from the story line of "The Bold Dragoon." See *Pickwick Papers*, chapter 14. The bagman's second tale (chapter 49) has some, but less, relationship to the "Strange Stories."

9. Quoted in Hedges, *Washington Irving*, p. 197 n.

10. Stanley T. Williams, *Life of Washington Irving* (New York: Oxford University Press, 1935), 1: 274–75.

11. Hawthorne made twenty-six withdrawals of volumes of *Blackwood's* from the Salem Athenaeum, most of them of the "earlier numbers" and most of them in 1827. See Marion L. Kesselring, "Hawthorne's Reading, 1828–1850," *Bulletin of the New York Public Library* 53 (1949): 175.

5

Wandering Willie's Tale

Washington Irving's *Abbotsford,* his account of a visit to Sir Walter Scott, is our best record of the typical substance of Scott's oral storytelling. Although Irving does not attempt to reproduce Scott's manner of telling the anecdotes he records, he assures us that Scott "gave the dialogue with appropriate dialect or peculiarities": Scott's conversation, Irving says, "reminded me constantly of his novels." Apparently Scott could project his gift for the spoken vernacular to the printed page. Now writers on Scott commonly say that he was at his best when he wrote in the vernacular; Lord David Cecil says that, since "Wandering Willie's Tale" is wholly in the vernacular, "it is the only one of his works which is a sustained masterpiece of writing."[1] And of course we do find a great pleasure in Scott's vernacular writing. I find myself delighting in the freshness or the force of expressions which, I suspect, to the habituated ear would be quite commonplace. Yet it may not be the vernacular in itself that charms us; as a character in Margery Sharp's *The Innocents* suggests, "Burns and Scott between them have invested the whole Scots tongue with some insinuating glamour." At any rate the vernacular alone will hardly account for the stylistic excellence of the tale. It is Willie who speaks the vernacular, and we cannot separate his lively imagination from the expression that makes it known to us.

Scott has other achievements in the use of a narrator that mark high points in his work. For instance, in Julia Mannering's letters to Matilda (written in highly literate English), Julia combines a young girl's romantic vein with a fine intelligence and a gift for self-satire; and the combination seems to us, even though

we know that Scott gave all Julia's qualities to her, hers alone. An
equally remarkable achivement is the first few chapters of *Rob
Roy,* in which the narrative point of view of the old Frank Osbaldistone telling the story of the young Frank Osbaldistone seems
to exist by itself, without Scott's direction. In *Redguantlet* (1824),
Scott experiments with various kinds of narration, but "Wandering Willie's Tale" is the high point of the novel and Scott's masterpiece in the kind.

"Wandering Willie's Tale" is also an example of another of
Scott's strengths. "It is a kind of misnomer," Sir Leslie Stephen
remarks, "which classifies all Scott's books as novels. They are
embodied legends and traditions, descriptions of men, and
races, and epochs of history."[2] Stephen is recognizing that historical sense for which, despite some historical mistakes, Scott's
work is distinguished. "He, first of men," C. S. Lewis says,
"taught us the feeling for period. . . . If we are now so conscious
of period, that we feel more difference between decades than
our ancestors felt between centuries, we owe this, for good and
ill, to Scott."[3] And nowhere in Scott's work, I think, is this
feeling for period as vividly conveyed to us as it is in "Wandering
Willie's Tale."

Tales of the preternatural have a persistent appeal, yet there
are but a double handful of them that we cherish. Our special
interest in them must depend upon some innate sense that there
is more in experience than we can touch or see. But our interest
is in the way in which the natural world is invaded or impinged
upon, and the run of tales of the preternatural fail in the primary matter—in their representation of the world of things and
flesh and blood. The successful tales do adequately represent or
recall the ordinary world in which extraordinary things occur or
seem to occur.

The ordinary world may be the world of the writer's own time.
A few writers have managed that well: Daniel Defoe, for instance, or Henry James, or, in a tale we shall be considering,
William Austin. But the tale of the preternatural succeeds more
often when the time of its action is in some period that is in the
past for both writer and readers. And it looks as if such a tale is
best told through a narrator. Nathaniel Hawthorne remarks that

if a writer "cannot believe his own ghost story, he had better leave the task to someone else."[4] If he is able to manage it, the writer can well leave the task to someone else—to a narrator whose belief will infect the reader. But he will need that far reach of skill that is the writing from the mind and heart of a character to whom he has given imaginative life.

Wandering Willie seems to us perfectly distinct from Scott. Indeed, Willie exists to tell this tale; readers of *Redgauntlet* will remember how Scott tries and fails to connect him significantly with the action of the novel. He has, we are told, something of a prototype in a Welsh minstrel once well known in the south of Scotland. And Scott says in his note to the tale: "I have heard in my youth some such wild tale as that placed in the mouth of the blind fiddler, of which, I think, the hero was Sir Robert Grierson of Lagg, the famous persecutor." Sir Robert Grierson is clearly the prototype of Sir Robert Redgauntlet; and there is indeed a legend of one his lessees obtaining a receipt from him after his death.[5] But to our imaginations, the tale is entirely Wandering Willie's tale; we think of the skill it displays as Willie's skill—the more because Willie's narrative in its tight pattern is not much like Scott's ordinary narrative.

Willie's skill is everywhere present, even in what we may call the exposition of the tale, its first five paragraphs. As we read them for the first time, they may seen discursive and Willie garrulous—a blind fiddler recalling what he knows of his gude-sire, Steenie Steenson, and of Steenie's landlord, Sir Robert Redgauntlet. But nothing is wasted; hardly a word but has what Poe calls a "tendency, direct or indirect . . . to the one pre-established design." Yet, as Robert Louis Stevenson points out in "A Gossip on Romance," it is just in the preparation for what is to come that Scott's narrative is typically deficient.

Within these five paragraphs of exposition the special quality of Willie as narrator emerges. That quality seems to depend upon the tension the reader feels between Willie's belief in his gudesire's story in all its essentials and Willie's sceptical habit of mind, a habit of mind that makes his account often ironic or derisive. The reader—at least while he is reading the tale—can hardly think such a man deceived, nor refuse credence to a storyteller whose understanding of the persons in his tale seems so without illusion, and whose account is so trenchant. The reader almost accepts the tale for what Willie says it is—a warning against taking up with strangers on lonely roads.

From our history books we know something of Scotland during the reigns of the restored Stuart kings and of William and Mary; and in Willie's tale we recognize something of what we know, and learn more. Willie's gudesire lived in that world, and about such men as he, who had to get along in it as best they might, history tells us little. Steenie, Willie says, "wasna the sort that they made Whigs o'," and was a Tory "just out of a kind of needcessity." Since he lived on the Redgauntlet ground, he followed Sir Robert (who delighted in his skill on the pipes) and "saw muckle mischief, and maybe did some, that he couldna avoid." Sir Robert, hated and feared by Whigs and Covenanters, was not "a bad maister to his ain folk"; and his "lackies and troopers," Willie says sardonically, "wad hae drunken themsells blind to his health at ony time." When at last William and Mary came to the throne, Sir Robert could hunt down Covenanters no longer, although he suffered little for his former misdeeds. "There were ower mony great folks dipped in the same doings," Willie thinks, "to mak a spick and span new warld." But Sir Robert, reduced to the role of landed proprietor, was much concerned with his rents.

When Willie gets to the action of his tale, he moves it along briskly. In a tale of the preternatural, the use of a narrator not himself part of the action almost precludes the fixing of the interest on the narrator's psyche, precludes the kind of decadence in which the tale is not so much an account of events as it is an account of a neurotic state induced by them. Willie does of course emerge vividly as a person, but his interest is all in the persons and actions he tells about with so much zest. No story better satisfies what Stevenson calls our "demand for fit and striking incident." A discussion of the tale, therefore, requires a review of its action. Our interest is first of all in what happens; and when we remember the story, what we remember is a series of incidents "striking to the mind's eye." The incident with which Willie begins the action of his tale is striking enough.

Willie tells how at Martinmas time Steenie takes the money for his overdue rent, most of which he has borrowed, to Redgauntlet Castle. He is ushered into Sir Robert's presence by Dougal MacCallum, the old butler, and he finds Sir Robert alone except for his pet jackanapes, named Major Weir "after the warlock that was burnt."[6] Sir Robert, though fretful at Steenie's lateness with his rent and grimacing in pain with the gout, is glad to see him; Steenie, with as much confident politeness as he can manage, puts the money on the table "wi' a dash, like a man that does something clever." But before he can give Steenie his receipt, Sir Robert suffers a seizure and dies, roaring out something about hell and its flames. Steenie in terror departs from the castle, his best hope only that Dougal has seen his bag of silver and heard Sir Robert speak of the receipt. Steenie never has the benefit of Dougal's testimony; on the night before Sir Robert's funeral, Dougal, hearing the silver whistle with which his master had been wont to summon him, answers the call and is found dead beside Sir Robert's coffin. Hutcheon, an old servant whom Dougal had asked to accompany him, reports that they had seen "the foul fiend, in his ain shape, sitting on the Laird's coffin."

For the account of Steenie's interview with Sir John Redgauntlet, Sir Robert's son and heir, Scott has Willie change the pace and method of his narration. Indeed, Scott has Darsie Latimer, the recorder of Willie's tale, interrupt his record parenthetically this one time in order to mark out the change.[7] And Willie says, "I have heard their communing so often tauld ower, that I almost think I was there mysell, though I couldna be born at the time," and proceeds with a dramatic representation of the dialogue between Steenie and Sir John, who "had been bred an advocate," and who is "fair-spoken" but implacable. Steenie has no receipt, there are malicious reports concerning Sir Robert's death and Steenie seems to be taking advantage of them, the money is missing and the servants upon examination seem guiltless—Sir John demands to know where Steenie thinks the money is. Steenie, driven to exasperation, answers, "In hell, if you *will* have my thoughts of it, in hell! with you father," and runs down the stairs and out of the castle.

It may be that Steenie visits hell and sees Sir Robert there. To tell of the matter, Willie resumes his first manner of narration. Steenie, who has had nothing to eat or drink all day, stops at a

change-house for a mutchkin of brandy—something like a pint.
He drinks it in two gulps and makes two toasts: the first to the
memory of Sir Robert, "and might he never lie quiet in his grave
till he had righted his poor bond-tenant"; the second to Man's
Enemy, "if he would but get him back the pock of siller, or tell
him what came o't."

It is perhaps Man's Enemy who overtakes Steenie as he rides
through a wood of black firs, and who takes him to what seems
to be Redgauntlet Castle in a wrong place. Steenie knocks, and is
ushered in by the figure of Dougal MacCallum—"just after his
wont"—who warns him to take nothing from anyone but the
receipt that is his own. Steenie finds himself among a reveling
and profane company of figures of men who had been notorious
persecutors of Covenanters in their lifetimes—among them
Claverhouse—waited on by the figures of the worst of their serv-
ing men and troopers.[8] In the midst of them is a figure that
seems to be Sir Robert. The figure asks Steenie, "Weel, piper,
hae ye settled wi' my son for the year's rent?" and promises
Steenie his receipt in return for a tune on the pipes. But Steenie
refuses the pipes and refuses to eat or drink. Nevertheless, Sir
Robert, appealed to "for conscience-sake," gives Steenie his receipt, and tells him that Sir John may look for the rent money in
the Cat's Cradle. But he adds a condition: Steenie must return in
a twelvemonth. Steenie answers, "I refer mysell to God's pleasure, and not to yours," and loses consciousness. To this point,
Steenie, although he has been voluble enough, has been unable
to invoke the name of God; his tongue is, Willie says, "loosed of a
suddenty"—apparently by the intervention of God's grace.

When Steenie comes to himself in the kirkyard of Redgauntlet
parish in the early morning, he finds that he holds in his hand
Sir Robert's receipt, dated—he later finds— "From my appointed place this twenty-fifth of November," the day before.
He takes it to Sir John and tells his story. Sir John finds the
money in the Cat's Cradle (which Hutcheon had been able to
identify as a ruinous turret of the castle) and shoots the jackanapes, which he also finds there. The receipt he burns, but
credits Steenie with his rent. Steenie, understandably worried
about the return in a twelvemonth the figure of Sir Robert had
required, consults the parish minister, and is somewhat reas-

sured, but as a precaution gives up the pipes and brandy until the year has passed. He does not tell his story until, after the deaths of both the minister and Sir John, he is obliged to when the minister's widow tells a garbled version of it: "He might else have been charged for a warlock."

"Wandering Willie's Tale," Lord David Cecil says, is a fine example of "Scottish popular diablerie," and indeed it does have a firm basis in popular beliefs. According to some of them, Steenie may have put himself in the way of his adventure. Willie tells us that Steenie maybe did some mischief "that he couldna avoid." He is so little a religious man that, in a quarrel with his chief creditor, he says things about that creditor's doctrine that make "folks' flesh grue." He has had some acquaintance with a warlock, who has taught him the tune "Weel hoddled, Luckie";[9] Steenie had never played it very willingly, and is wise enough to refuse to play it for Sir Robert in their last strange meeting (and besides the chanter of the pipes seems to be white-hot). Above all, Steenie drinks that toast to Man's Enemy. The mysterious stranger encountered in the wood affirms that he is "the only hand" for helping his friends; perhaps Steenie has come all too close to making himself one of the devil's friends.

The tale represents other popular beliefs. The stranger tells Steenie that Sir Robert is disturbed in his grave by Steenie's curses and the wailing of Steenie's family; Scott in his note to the tale tells a story illustrative of the general belief that "excessive lamentation" disturbs the repose of the dead. Dougal or his appearance warns Steenie not to eat or drink in the strange place to which he has come; eating or drinking in any nonhuman world is very dangerous, as we know from the ballad of Thomas Rhymer. The question of the identity of the figure which seems to be Sir Robert—"Sir Robert, or his ghaist, or the deevil in his likeness"—is the question of spectral identity that puzzled Hamlet and puzzled judges in Scottish witchcraft trials—and in Massachusetts trials as well.

But there are important preternatural elements in "Wandering Willie's Tale" that, although they arise from popular belief, are transmuted in Scott's use of them. The mysterious stranger is not the black man of popular diablerie; certainly there is no figure like him in Scott's own *Letters on Demonology and Witch-*

craft.[10] He is more urbane than we should expect the devil in popular diablerie to be; and though he seems amused at Steenie's plight, he seems neither malicious nor deceitful. If he is the devil, he is the devil in rather a decent mood.

Apparently he assists Steenie from two motives: Sir Robert is disturbed—and the devil, we know, takes care of his own. But the stranger seems to have some real interest in righting Steenie. When Steenie suggests that the stranger might lend him the money for his rent, the stranger answers: "I could lend you the money on bond, but you would maybe scruple my terms." Now the devil in devil lore in general, as well as in seventeenth-century belief, seems always to have been anxious for a commitment; we read often in the records of witchcraft trials of signing the devil's book. But this stranger seems anxious to take Steenie to Sir Robert and to allow him at least a sporting chance. What connection he may have with the place to which he takes Steenie we do not know. He brings Steenie to the door; when Steenie is inside he looks for the stranger, but, Willie says cryptically, "he was gane for the time"—we do not know if he ever is, or can be there.

Nor does the concept of the afterlife in the tale seem to belong to popular diablerie. But it is not so different from Dante's in the *Inferno*, where hell is the eternal prolongation for the sinner of his sin. The retribution that has fallen upon Sir Robert is to be eternally Sir Robert, to live in Redgauntlet Castle, to be surrounded by figures like himself. It is the concept of an observant man who has seen in this world that sins become their own punishments. Willie's account of the afterlife of Sir Robert and his associates is not only striking to the mind's eye but the stimulus for moral reflection. And neither Willie nor the reader forgets that Steenie himself had been one of Sir Robert Redgauntlet's retainers.

In its careful shaping, "Wandering Willie's Tale" is not a folk or popular tale. Scott adroitly uses the convention of the "explained supernatural," the more adroitly because incompletely. Although some of the apparently marvellous events in the tale turn out not to be marvellous after all, Steenie's strange meeting with the figure of Sir Robert remains unexplained: "Steenie would have thought the whole was a dream," Willie says, "but he had the receipt in his hand, fairly written and signed by the auld Laird; only the last letters of his name were a little disorderly, written like one seized with sudden pain." Sir John is anxious to have the explanation of some events considered a full explanation, since Steenie's story, although it may tend to Sir Robert's credit as an honest man, suggests doubts about his soul's health. "So, I think," Sir John says, "we had better lay the haill dirdum on that ill-deedie creature, Major Weir, and sae naething about your dream in the wood of Pitmurkie. You had taken ower muckle brandy to be very certain about onything."

We as readers were of course aware of the agency of the jackanapes in Steenie's affairs, perhaps as early in the tale as the account of the death of Dougal. It turns out, then, that the only events explained are events marvellous in the minds of persons in the tale, but not in the minds of its readers. The explanation, moreover, is discredited imaginatively because it is the way in which Sir John chooses to protect the memory of his father:

> Sir John made up his story about the jackanape as he liked himsell; and some believe till this day there was no more in the matter than the filching nature of the brute. Indeed, ye'll no hinder some to threap, that it was nane o' the auld Enemy that Dougal and my gudesire saw in the Laird's room,[11] but only that wanchancy creature, the Major, capering on the coffin; and that, as to the blawing on the Laird's whistle that was heard after he was dead, the filthy brute could do that as weel as the Laird himsell, if no better.

But if all the marvellous events in the Redgauntlet Castle on this earth seem to be explained away, nothing of Steenie's experience in Pitmurkie wood and in that Redgauntlet Castle elsewhere is naturally accounted for. No reader will feel that any mutchkin of brandy ever distilled can account for the quality of Steenie's strange experience. The receipt is the tangible sign of the mystery that remains, a mystery satisfying to the reader's innate, even if unformulated, conviction that not all experience is explicable, that we pretend to understand more than we know.

For "Wandering Willie's Tale," despite its comedy, is not a sportive use of preternatural materials. Even in the grotesque

mistaking of the jackanapes on the coffin for the devil, the creature seems an emblem of evil. The comedy inheres in Steenie's
relationships with men; his dealing with the invisible world is
awesome. Beyond Willie's delight in his skill, there is something
of bravado in his way of storytelling; and Scott uses the frame of
the tale to make Willie indicate how he connects the events of the
tale with his own misfortunes.

When a writer is able to use his narrator skillfully, he solves
the problem of his own relationship to the story. A few years ago
we were hearing a good deal about "the disappearing author"; in
"Wandering Willie's Tale" Scott disappears as completely as a
fiction writer can. The narrative methods of the tale are appropriate to Willie's character and seem to arise from it. Willie is a
practiced storyteller—even a conscious artist. He has, he says, in
the frame of the tale, "some fearsome" stories, which frighten
and delight old women and children. This tale is not one of
them; it is "a thing that befell in our ain house." He has
cherished—and polished—his gudesire's story and given it a
planned structure. As he moves through the five easily discerni-
ble sections of his tale, he varies the pace and makes calculated
changes in the method of his narration.

Beyond the advantage of making himself disappear, a writer
who uses a narrator with skill adds a quality of reality to his tale
that will hardly be attained by the use of any other narrative
point of view. The narrator's knowledge of the persons and
events with which he is concerned comes to him in the way our
knowledge of the experience of others comes to us—by observation, by report, by inference. His knowledge has the kind of
limits our own knowledge of others has; and those limits are
specified or clearly implied. Willie is avowedly retelling the story
his gudesire had often told, however much in Willie's retelling it
is adapted to his sense of form and modified by his sceptical view
of the behavior of his fellowmen. This naturalness is of special
importance to a tale of the preternatural that would win our
imaginative assent.

But a tale of the preternatural does not succeed by its
technique alone; the imagination works with materials. And evidently the best materials are beliefs once really held in the region
and the period of the tale. When Scott tries to work in the preternatural without such materials, as he does with the White

Lady of Avenel in *The Monastery*, he works with small success; he acknowledges as much in the Introductory Epistle to *The Fortunes of Nigel*. Moreover, the best materials are beliefs that were not only real, but once held by many or most persons. The "rapping spirits" and other psychic phenomena of the nineteenth century have furnished material for good stories, but not, I think, for great ones. They were firmly believed in by a good many persons, given some credence by more, ridiculed by many others. With such material a writer may have some success; but he is not likely to succeed with a preternatural that is largely the result of his own fancy.

The great writers of fiction who use material from popular belief are never controlled by it, but use it for their own purposes. Yet what seems to be required is the density of material that comes from a writer's familiarity with the records of a period, even though he may not use documents within them specifically as sources, even though he avoids the crudities and grotesqueries of the records, and even though his own imagination transforms some elements. Ideally the reader too will have some comparable familiarity, so that in his response to the tale there will be an element of recognition. A good many readers will have that recognition in "Wandering Willie's Tale." But even if a reader had no knowledge of the period of the tale, he would realize that Scott is dealing with beliefs once widely and sincerely held, and therefore with a historical reality—just as he would realize when a writer is writing from close observation, even if he had seen nothing of the pattern of life observed. The excellence of Scott's "Wandering Willie's Tale"—and the excellences of Hawthorne's "Young Goodman Brown" and Stevenson's "Thrawn Janet"[12] after Scott—depend upon their writers' control of their materials quite as much as upon any other quality.

NOTES

1. Introduction to *Short Stories by Sir Walter Scott*, pp. xvi–xvii.
2. Leslie Stephen, *Hours in a Library* (London, 1892), 2: 206.
3. C. S. Lewis, *Selected Literary Essays*, ed. Walter Hooper (London: Cambridge University Press, 1969), p. 217. Scott himself remarks in a discussion of *The Old English Baron* that in Clara Reeve's day no great attention to the accurate representation of period was required, but that "in the present day, more attention to costume is demanded, and au-

thors . . . are obliged to make attempts, however fantastic or grotesque, to imitate the manners, on the one hand, and the dress on the other, of the times in which the scene is laid." Scott must have realized as he wrote that he was himself primarily responsible for the change. See his *Lives of the Novelists*, p. 208.

4. Review of Whittier's *The Supernaturalism of New England*, rpt. in "Two Uncollected Reviews by Hawthorne," ed. Randall Stewart, *New England Quarterly* 9 (1936): 507.

5. See Coleman O. Parsons, *Witchcraft and Demonology in Scott's Fiction* (Edinburgh and London: Oliver and Boyd, 1964), pp. 180–81. Since we are concerned with Mary Russell Mitford in this book, it may be appropriate to notice that she suggests an anecdote about Swedenborg as a source for the matter of the receipt in Scott's tale. See *Our Village*, Bohn ed. (London: George Bell & Sons, 1880), 2: 292 n.

6. For Scott's account of Major Weir, see his *Letters on Demonology and Witchcraft* (London: George Routledge and Sons, 1887), pp. 265–67.

7. Darsie says: "In fact, Alan, my companion mimicked, with a good deal of humour, the flattering, conciliating tone of the tenant's address, and the hypocritical melancholy of the Laird's reply."

8. In his note to the tale, Scott remarks that he is drawing on an appendix to John Howie, *Account of the Lives of the Most Eminent Scots Worthies*, an appendix that is an account of the lives and deaths of persons considered "Apostates and Bloody Persecutors."

9. "Weel hoddled, Luckie" would mean something like "well waddled, old woman." Apparently some tunes were associated with witch meetings; King James I caused Geillis Duncan to play before him (on a jew's harp) a tune she had played at a witch meeting in North Berwick churchyard. See *Letters on Demonology and Witchcraft*, p. 253.

10. For the black man of popular belief in Scotland see *Letters on Demonology and Witchcraft*, pp. 233, 252, 258. Cotton Mather in *The Wonders of the Invisible World* (1693) tells us that in Massachusetts the devil showed himself "ordinarily as a small *Black Man*." See *Salem Witchcraft* (Salem, Mass., 1861), p. 395.

11. "Dougal and my gudesire" is of course a slip for "Dougal and Hutcheon"—the only instance in the tale, I believe, of Scott's typical carelessness.

12. Although the tone of "Thrawn Janet" is different from that of "Wandering Willie's Tale," Stevenson manages his narrator with quite as much skill as Scott does, and the narrator's conviction infects the reader in the same way that Willie's does. Stevenson thought "Thrawn Janet" one of his best works. See *Letters of Robert Louis Stevenson*, ed. Sidney Colvin (New York: Scribners, 1911), 2: 37 and 210; 4: 182.

6

A Very Lively Work

As he concludes *A Legend of Montrose* (1819), Sir Walter Scott says—prematurely indeed—that he retires from the representation of Scottish character and manners. He is "conscious that there remains behind not only a large harvest, but labourers capable of gathering it in," and "he would mention in particular, the author of a very lively work entitled 'Marriage.'" Scott is doing his best to promote the first novel of Susan Ferrier, the daughter of a friend and legal colleague. *Marriage* was published in 1818;[1] Scott's novels had prepared the way for it, and perhaps made its publication and success possible. But Miss Ferrier's novel had its inception as early as 1810,[2] and she cannot be considered a follower of Scott.

The reviewer of *Marriage* in *Blackwood's* thinks that Miss Ferrier "unites some of the best qualities of [Maria] Edgeworth and [Fanny] Burney."[3] I suppose we may agree. In her treatment of national character she shares with Scott an influence from Miss Edgeworth and, too, *Marriage* may be considered an "educational" novel. Like Fanny Burney's Evelina, Susan Ferrier's Mary Douglas in *Marriage* is an inexperienced girl thrust into a society different from any she had ever known. And in *Marriage* Miss Ferrier shares with other women novelists of the time a preoccupation with "love" marriages as against "prudent" marriages. Nevertheless, *Marriage* is interesting to consider in itself, for Miss Ferrier is very much her own woman, and her novel stands remarkably apart from novels that in one way or another it somewhat resembles.

The *Blackwood's* reviewer, who thinks highly of the book in general, finds it marked "with many failings characteristic of an

unpractised writer," and there is much in *Marriage* that will seem
amateurish to the reader today.[4] Yet Miss Ferrier's amateur
status is also a strength, for she depends upon her own and
recorded observation far more than do most novelists of her
time. The early nineteenth-century critics of *Marriage* all think it
lacks plot interest,[5] and probably many of her first readers did
too; it does lack such expected interests as the hero or heroine of
mysterious birth. Yet the reader today may think the representation of character and manners more consonant with the plot of
Marriage than with the plot of, say, *The Antiquary*—and that Scott
succeeds in spite of his plot.

In *Marriage* what difficulties Miss Ferrier has seem to arise
from her effort to carry out two intentions, not perhaps incom-
patible in themselves. One is a didactic intention that for her is
clearly primary; indeed she writes:

> I don't think . . . that 'tis absolutely necessary that the good
> boys and girls should be rewarded, and the naughty ones
> punished. Yet . . . where there is much tribulation, 'tis fitter
> it should be the *consequence*, rather than the *cause* of miscon-
> duct or frailty. . . . The only good purpose of a book is to
> inculcate morality.[6]

The other intention is indicated by the fine passage from Dr.
Johnson's *A Journey to the Western Islands of Scotland* that Miss
Ferrier uses as the epigraph for her novel:

> Life consists not of a series of illustrious actions; the greater
> part of our time passes in compliance with necessities—in
> the performance of daily duties—in the removal of small
> inconveniencies—in the procurement of petty pleasures;
> and we are well or ill at ease, as the main stream of life glides
> on smoothly, or is ruffled by small and frequent interrup-
> tion.

Unfortunately, Miss Ferrier is not always able to find a happy
means by which to carry out the intention her epigraph suggests,
nor always able to combine gracefully that intention with the
inculcation of morality.

But we need not much object to the structure of *Marriage*.
Although volume 1 seems to have been written as a unit and

volumes 2 and 3 have a different scene and a somewhat different temper, it does not seem to me that the novel falls apart. The
three volumes have a common theme—the importance of upbringing, especially as it affects a girl's choice of a husband—and
they are dominated by a single character, Lady Juliana, at once
comic and appalling.

In the first chapter of volume 1 we learn, in very rapid narration, that Lady Juliana at seventeen, avoiding the bad marriage
with an elderly duke that her father would force upon her,
makes another sort of bad marriage with the handsome, penni-
less Henry Douglas, an army officer. Henry is forced to take his
pregnant wife to Glenfern, his father's house in the Highlands,
where he has not lived himself since he was eight. Most of the
action of volume 1 goes on there. Lady Juliana, like a child
contemptuous of all that she is unused to, is the most difficult of
guests, although Henry's three aunts, five sisters, and the Laird
himself mean to be kind.

In due time Lady Juliana gives birth to twin girls, Adelaide
and Mary. Mrs. Archibald Douglas, Henry's sister-in-law and an
exemplary Christian woman, takes Mary to care for. Soon after
the birth of his daughters, Henry regains the favor of General
Cameron, his benefactor; and Henry and Lady Juliana, taking
only Adelaide with them, return to London. But they get into
debt, Henry is forced to serve in India (we learn of his death
there late in the novel), and at the end of volume 1 we leave Lady
Juliana, her little son Edward, and Adelaide living in the household of Lord Courtland, Lady Juliana's brother. Fifteen years
and a little more elapse between volume 1 and the central narrative of volume 2.

Nowadays students of the relationship between the influences
of heredity and environment are especially interested in twins
who have been separated early in life. Adelaide and Mary are
such twins. Miss Ferrier, by bringing them together in volumes 2
and 3, and by subjecting them to the same sort of matrimonial
opportunity and the same sort of pressure from Lady Juliana,
manages a fictional experiment the issue of which, of course, she
completely controls. Mary's behavior is made to represent a signal triumph for environment and the wise instruction of Mrs.
Douglas over heredity. The occasion of Mary's going to live with

her mother, now domiciled with Lord Courtland in the vicinity
of Bath, is Mary's ill health, which makes the milder climate of
England desirable.[7]

Mary is not made very welcome in Lord Courtland's household: her uncle, although good-natured, pays little attention to
her: her brother Edward, now a naval officer, is at sea; Adelaide
is cold and disdainful; and Lady Juliana, irritated that Mary is
there at all, puts no curb on her bad temper or her
selfishness—only Lady Emily, Mary's cousin, welcomes her with
cordial love. But Lady Juliana, despite her irritation, has yet an
interest in Mary's matrimonial prospects; she is convinced that
her own marriage is the sole cause of her every disappointment
and unhappiness, and she is determined that her daughters will
not repeat her mistake of marrying for love. Adelaide, although
she loves her cousin, Lord Lindore, accepts her mother's standards and marries the Duke of Altamont, a man much older
than she. She lives with him unhappily until she runs away with
Lord Lindore, with whom she lives in virtual exile abroad.

Mary is courted by William Downe Wright, whose suit Lady
Juliana favors; when he succeeds to a title and becomes Lord
Glenallan, she considers Mary undeservedly fortunate. Since the
young man has no great fault but dimwittedness, Mary's firmness in resisting both his suit and her mother's urging of it is to
be accounted the more virtue. Mary does finally marry a distinguished army officer, Colonel Lennox, a most admirable man
but of narrow means. In the fiction of Miss Ferrier's time, this
outcome is something of an affirmation.

As Scott concludes his review of Jane Austen's *Emma*, he admonishes fiction writers. They have, he thinks, too much exalted
the prudent marriage and depreciated romantic love; "we would
have them reflect," he says, "that they may sometimes lend their
aid to substitute more mean, more sordid, and more selfish motives of conduct, for the romantic feelings which their predecessors perhaps fanned into too powerful a flame."[8] Miss Ferrier
doubtless intended the proper balance. She makes Lady Emily,
pretending shock at Mary's ideas, satirically voice the doctrine of
the prudent marriage:

> "Love!" exclaimed Lady Emily; "can I credit my ears? Love!
> did you say? I thought that had only been for naughty ones,

such as me; and that saints like you would have married for
any thing and every thing but love! Prudence, I thought,
had been the word with you proper ladies—a prudent marriage! Come, confess, is not that the climax of virtue in the
creed of your school?" [P. 319][9]

But Mary follows the teaching of Mrs. Douglas. Though she
would avoid the passion that is "the result of indulged fancy,
warm imaginations, and ill regulated minds," she avers that she
would never marry until she could both love and respect the
man she was to marry. And she does refuse Lord Glenallan and
does marry Colonel Lennox. But Miss Ferrier allows her readers
the gratification of finding Mary's marriage both a love marriage
and a prudent marriage; the Colonel's last-minute succession to
a large estate makes it quite prudent enough.

The action of the novel and the development of its thesis have
a good deal more interest than a summary account suggests.
But, although some of the English women characters are very
much alive, it was the representation of Scottish character and
manners that struck Scott and Miss Ferrier's first readers. Her
success may depend to an extent on her use of actual persons as
the bases of some of her characters, persons who were apparently recognizable to readers in her own circle.

The Laird of Glenfern, however, is probably not based on any
one person; he is a recognizable type of simple, hardfisted,
well-meaning Scotsman. As John Gibson Lockhart points out,
the Scottish characters in Miss Ferrier's work have none of the
glamour we are used to in the Waverley novels, and they come in
a period when Highland "chieftains dwindled into imitation-
squires."[10] The Laird is bewildered by his son Henry and Lady
Juliana, and by the alien culture they represent; when Henry
rejects his offer of a farm because, Henry explains, farm life is
unfitting for one of Lady Juliana's education, the Laird says:

Edication! what has her edication been, to mak her different
frae other women? If a woman can nurse her bairns, mak
their claes, and manage her hooss, what mair need she do?
If she can play a tune on the spinnet, and dance a reel, and
play a rubber at whist—nae doot these are accomplishments, but they're soon learnt. Edication! pooh!—I'll be

> bound Leddy Jully Anie wull mak as gude a figure by and
> bye as the best edicated woman in the country. . . . Wait a
> wee till she has has a wheen bairns, an' a hooss o' her ain, an'
> I'll be bound she'll be happy as the day's lang. [Pp. 68–69]

The Laird, women-ridden in his household, is yet valiant, comic,
and likable—the only male character in the novel who emerges
convincingly.[11]

Lady Maclaughlan, the great lady of the region around Glenfern, is hardly a successful character for the reader today. The
Blackwood's reviewer enjoys her; she is, he says, "the pink of all
rough, rude, dogmatical, snuff-taking, doctoring, intolerable old
viragos"[12] (he might have added that she is unexpectedly generous). But her character will seem to us anomalous, however
much it is based upon actual persons; doubtless she was more
believable to nineteenth-century Scottish readers. Yet other
characters in the novel who, we are told, had prototypes in actual
persons are entirely believable for any reader. The best of them,
surely, are Henry's three long-chinned spinster aunts; of the
three Miss Grizzy is the most amusing.

Miss Jacky and Miss Nicky are a good deal more self-assured
than Miss Grizzy; they are all three naive, and all judge any
person by his own protestations; their ears, Miss Ferrier remarks, are "their only organs of intelligence" (p. 160). Miss
Grizzy is distinguished "by her simple good nature, the inextric-
able entanglement of her thoughts, her love of letter writing" (p.
41). Passages of her conversation are likely to turn on some such
transition as " . . . nobody can dispute that. At the same time . . ."
and are always beautifully inconclusive. The syntax of her letters
is a delight; here she is describing the suitor of one of Henry's
sisters:

> Betsy has, if Possible, been still More fortunate than her
> Sister, although you know Bella was always reckoned the
> Beauty of the Family, though some People certainly prefer-
> red Betsy's Looks too. She has made a Complete conquest of
> Major M'Tavish, of the Militia, who, Independent of his
> rank, which is certainly very High, has also distinguished
> himself very Much, and shewed the Greatest bravery once
> when there was a Very serious Riot about the raising the

Potatoes a penny a peck, when there was no Occasion for it, in the town of Dunoon; and it was very much talked of at the Time, as well as Being in all the Newspapers. This gives us all the Greatest Pleasure, as I am certain it will also Do Lady Juliana, and you, my dear Mary. At the same time, we Feel very much for poor Babby, and Beenie, and Becky, as they Naturally, and indeed all of us, Expected they would, of Course, be married first; and it is certainly a great Trial for them to See their younger sisters married before them. At the same Time, they are Wonderfully supported, and Behave with Astonishing firmness; and I Trust, my dear Mary, you will do the Same, as I have no doubt you will All be married yet, as I am sure you Richly deserve it when it Comes. [P. 369]

Miss Grizzy is everywhere amusing; but Miss Ferrier is so honest a novelist as to make clear that persons amusing to read about would be distressing to live with: the exemplary Mrs. Archibald Douglas finds the three aunts a strain on her charity, and when Mary goes about Bath with Miss Grizzy she frequently finds herself embarrassed by her.

On her journey to Bath, Mary is escorted by her uncle as far as Edinburgh (where Lord Courtland's carriage and servants meet her). In Edinburgh, Mary and Mr. Douglas call upon Mrs. Macshake. Mrs. Macshake is a bright and somewhat ungracious old woman of ninety-six, who tells Mary and us about the customs of her youth: of weddings; of the "crying," when, the day after the birth of a baby, the mother received her women friends at her bedside; and of the "cummerfeals," the grand supper after the mother's recovery. Mrs. Macshake, of course, has outlived her own world. She is very much a Scotswoman, but she stands, too, for old people everywhere who look back on their prime when all things had a realness and a rightness that they have somehow lost, and who feel a contemptuous pity for those too young to have experienced that right time. Yet readers today scarcely in their middle years will sympathize with her account of the changes in her own countryside:

"Impruvements! . . . what ken ye about impruvements, bairn?
A bonny impruvement or ens no, to see tyleyors and sclaters

leavin', whar I mind Jewks an' Yerls—An' that great glow-
rin' new toon there," pointing out of her windows, "whar I
used to sit an' luck oot at bonny green parks, and see the
coos milket, and the bits o' bairnys rowin' an' tummlin', an'
the lasses trampin' i' their tubs—What see I noo, but stane
an' lime, an' stoor an' dirt, an' idle cheels, an' dinket-oot
madams prancin'.—Impruvements indeed!"[P. 215][13]

Mrs. Macshake feels, indeed, that a time earlier than her own
had an order her own time lacked—and she is no feminist:

> "I' my grandfaither's time, as I hae heard him tell, ilka mais-
> ter o' a faamily had his ain sate in his ain hooss, ay! an' sat wi'
> his hat on his heed afore the best o' the land, an' had his ain
> dish, an' was aye helpit first, an' keepit up his owthority as a
> man sude du. Paurents war paurents than—bairnes dardna
> set up their gabs afore them than as they du noo. They ne'er
> presumed to say their heeds war their ain i' thae days— wife
> an' servants—reteeners an' childer, aw trummelt i' the pre-
> sence o' their heed." [Pp. 215–16]

The account of Mrs. Macshake is derived from the reminis-
cences of Elizabeth Mure, the aunt of a friend of Miss Ferrier.[14]
It is a high point of the novel, but Mrs. Macshake, like a number
of other characters, has no real connection with the action.[15]

Chapters 8 through 11 of volume 2, the chapters that are the
account of the journey of Mary and her uncle to Edinburgh and
their stay in the city, remind the reader of Tobias Smollett's
Humphry Clinker both in the progress of the narrative and the
characters represented.[16] But some of the character sketches in
volumes 2 and 3 of *Marriage* are "characters" in the long tradition stemming from Bishop Hall and Sir Thomas Overbury. We
shall be looking at the use of such "characters" in the sketches of
Miss Mitford's *Our Village*, where they are perhaps more at home
than they are in a novel. At any rate, Miss Ferrier gets them into
her novel a little awkwardly. Some are put into the mouth of
Lady Emily: Lady Placid (a combination of self-satisfaction and
small malice), Lady Wiseacre, and Mrs. Downe Wright (although
she later becomes an agent in the action). Others arise when
main characters call upon Lady Matilda Sufton, who parades her

fortitude in grief; a Mrs. Pullen, née Flora Macfuss (whose humour is domestic economy); and a Mrs. Fox, a philanthropist—she might be something out of a Dickens novel. But by far the most amusing of such accounts is that of the tea at Mrs. Bluemits's house, where Mary and Aunt Grizzy are among the guests.

The literary ladies at Mrs. Bluemits's tea are recognizable types even now, except that their contemporary parallels are more likely to be men than women. Mrs. Bluemits's guests are like the cocktail-party critics we know who prepare a comment on a chosen writer in the hope—too often fulfilled—of being able to work it into a conversation. Mrs. Bluemits is proud that "nothing but conversation is spoken in her house," and on the day of her tea her guests are well prepared. They can all repeat a few lines of some poem, and they have ready appropriate introductory statements, which elegantly avoid just naming the writers they talk about. "The sensitive poet of Olney [Cowper], if I mistake not," says Mrs. Dalton, "steers a middle course, betwixt the somewhat bald maxim of the Parisian philosopher [La Rochefoucauld], and the mournful pruriency of the Bard of Night [Young]." The ladies even make their farewells in quotation:

> "Fly not yet, 'tis just the hour," said Mrs. Bluemits to the first of her departing guests, as the clock struck ten.
> "It is gone, with its thorns and its roses," replied her friend with a sigh, and a farewell pressure of the hand.
> Another now advanced—"Wilt thou be gone?—it is not yet near day."
> "I have less will to go than care to stay," was the reply.
> *"Parto ti lascio addio,"* warbled Miss Parkins.
> "I vanish," said Mrs. Apsley, snatching up her tippet, reticule, &c. "and, like the baseless fabric of a vision, leave not a wreck behind,"
> "Fare-thee-well at once—Adieu, adieu, adieu, remember me!" cried the last of the band, as she slowly retreated. [Pp. 422–23]

For her part Miss Grizzy regrets not having repeated what she could remember of Allan Ramsay's "Lochabar no more" as her farewell; but Mary concludes "that people, who only read to talk of their reading, might as well let it alone."

Amusing as Mrs. Bluemits, her guests, and the other type characters are, Susan Ferrier's great gift is for firmly and completely imagined women characters, although her heroine may not be one of them. But Lady Emily and Lady Juliana are considerable achievements. Lady Emily is the more complex character, but with Lady Juliana the reader experiences a shuddering recognition, even though she lives in a society so different from any nowadays.

Lady Juliana is comic in her persistent, her entire unreasonableness. When, for instance, the word comes that Aunt Grizzy is to visit in Bath, Lady Juliana blames Mary: but for her she should have no connection with Miss Grizzy. Lady Emily gravely remarks to Mary that "there can be no doubt but that you are the origin of Lady Juliana's unfortunate connection with the family of Douglas," and Lady Juliana neither sees nor suspects any sarcasm: "Undoubtedly," she says (p. 371). A complete lack of sense of humor is the symptom—in her and in the sort of woman she represents—of an insensitivity which includes insensitivity to any need but her own.

Stupidity and ignorance are not in themselves moral faults; but their conjunction with a desire for power and a need for excitement makes them moral faults in effect. And it is in her need for excitement that Lady Juliana is most malicious; she requires always "something to excite a sensation, and give her something to complain of, and talk about, and put her in a bustle, and make her angry, and alarmed, and ill-used, and, in short, all the things which a fool is fond of being" (p. 446). Lady Juliana is given a trick of ridiculous superlatives which stands for this trait in her character; she even manages "excessively extraordinary" (p. 239).

Since Lady Juliana is in a dependent position, real danger from her is largely limited to her influence on her daughters. In her relationship with them she is supremely confident of her own excellence. When Adelaide has married the Duke of Altamont, she thinks: "Such as Adelaide is, I might have been, had I been blest with such a mother, and brought up to know what was for my good!" (p. 367). And when Adelaide runs away with

Lord Lindore, she blames, by turns, Adelaide's ingratitude, Lord Lindore's treachery, and the Duke's obstinate rule of his wife (p. 433). Her confidence in her own folly protects Lady Juliana from herself ever experiencing any great misery. But she does her best to make Mary miserable.

Mary's role in the action is largely passive. Her mother is her antagonist, and she tries to counter her mother by charity, patience, and obedience where obedience is possible. She does resist her mother's insistence that she marry Lord Glenallan, but she resists by meekly enduring abuse, and is even in some doubt that she ought to resist. She gains no real victory over her mother in the matter of her engagement to Colonel Lennox, for Lady Juliana loses interest in opposing her when Adelaide, unhappy in her liaison, invites her mother to live with her on the continent, where Lady Juliana imagines that she will find new social opportunities. Such readers as find Fanny Price in *Mansfield Park* an unsatisfactory heroine may also find Mary unsatisfactory.

But Mary is not, Miss Ferrier is careful to point out, "of the heroic cast" (p. 241), and she has "scarcely ever read a novel in her life" (p. 331). She acts, not by the standards of the fictional heroine, but by the religious principles instilled into her by Mrs. Archibald Douglas. I think we are almost always at fault in estimating the religious sentiments in novels of the period, and unable to separate the conventional from the deeply felt. A passage put into the mouth of Lady Emily is therefore helpful, for it summarizes Mary's character, we can be pretty sure, as Miss Ferrier would have us understand it. Mary's object, Lady Emily says, "is to *be*, not to *seem*, religious. . . . She is forebearing, without meanness—gentle, without insipidity—sincere, without rudeness. . . . She is . . . almost as much alive to the ridiculous as I am; but she is only diverted where I am provoked" (p. 288). Yet perhaps we do not apprehend Mary's character in just this way; our apprehension is at any rate curiously affected by the simultaneous representation of Lady Emily.

Lady Emily is an interesting character, the more interesting, it seems to me, because we cannot be sure of Miss Ferrier's intention with her. She may be called Mary's confidante; yet Miss Ferrier, who is quite willing to tell us what Mary thinks or feels

and constantly does so, has no real need for Lady Emily in the
technical function of confidante. On the other hand, Miss Ferrier takes pains that Lady Emily does not have much story: she
has become engaged to Edward, her cousin and Mary's brother,
before she enters the action of the novel, and Edward does not
appear until late in it; then Lady Emily and he are safely married. Since he is cheerful, good-hearted, and not very bright,
Lady Emily will doubtless manage with him well.

Lady Emily's environment has been much the same as
Adelaide's; Lady Juliana has been responsible for the early training of both, and they have had the same governesses. She is
therefore an exception to Miss Ferrier's thesis about the importance of a girl's early training, an exception Miss Ferrier is careful to point out.[17] Her conduct is admirable, but she will not say
she is admirable. Although one thinks of no duty she leaves
unfulfilled, she says, "O hang duties! they are odious things.
And as for your amiable, dutiful, virtuous Goody Two-Shoes
characters, I detest them. . . . They were ever my abhorrence, as
every species of canting and hypocrisy still is" (p. 259). And both
Miss Ferrier in authorial comment (p. 187) and Mary in reflection (p. 406) seem to fear for Lady Emily in her lack of seriousness and restraint.

Lady Emily, it is true, is not very religious, but never irrever-
ent. She does abhor "every species of canting and hypocrisy,"
and freely expresses her abhorrence. She delights in tormenting
Lady Juliana and Adelaide, the more when she torments them in
defense of Mary. A scene of feminine verbal warfare, carried on
within the limits of politeness, between Lady Emily and Mrs.
Downe Wright is a masterpiece of its kind (pp. 435–40). And it is
a matter of curious interest that the tags of quotation frequent in
Lady Emily's speech have a fine mock-heroic effect, when
somewhat similar quotation elsewhere is ineffectual, at times irritating.

Lady Emily functions both as foil for Mary and as a sardonic
chorus. She has that special sort of feminine cynicism that Mrs.
Oliphant attributes to Jane Austen, although to be sure she
never troubles to keep it from being obvious. Sometimes the
effect of her comments is to make Mary's scrupulousness seem
overstrained and her spirituality self-conscious—but one is

never sure that effect is quite Miss Ferrier's intention.

Yet some of the moral reflection in Lady Emily's speeches seems as surely to be what Miss Ferrier thinks as is anything that Mary says. Lady Emily remarks, for instance, that "even a noble nature may fall into a great error; but what is that to the ever-enduring pride, envy, malice, and conceit of a little mind. Yes—I would, at any time, rather be the fallen, as the one to exult over the fall of another" (p. 282). The remark would not seem convincing were it spoken by Mary—not quite appropriate to her moral purview. Or, in another instance, when the two girls have been calling on the blind and pathetic Mrs. Lennox and Mary speaks of sympathy as a consolation to the afflicted, Lady Emily says: "I don't quite understand the nature of that mysterious feeling called sympathy. When I go to visit Mrs. Lennox, she always sets me a crying, and I try to set her a laughing—Is that what you call sympathy?" (p. 268). Mary shakes her head, but the question is not resolved; often moral or spiritual issues between the two are not.

Lady Emily looks forward to her marriage determined to keep her independence of mind; her husband shall know and own, she says, that woman is a reasonable being. "All things that men ought to know better I shall yield," she continues; "whatever may belong to either sex, I either seize upon as my prerogative, or scrupulously divide" (p. 384). As the time of her marriage approaches, Lady Emily, perhaps only half-mockingly, professes a dread: "I feel myself turning into a fond, faithful, rational, humble, meek-spirited wife!" (p. 465). But Miss Ferrier does not fear, nor will the readers of *Marriage* fear, that Lady Emily will "dwindle into a wife."

Marriage is perhaps on some standards not a very good novel, yet if it fails to be so, it fails for admirable reasons. Miss Ferrier wanted to take her book out of what Scott calls "the land of fiction." In particular she did not want to portray a heroine who spends every moment not being in love with one man and being in love with another. But she was groping for what a later time would call realism very early and had to find her own way. The diversification of her narrative often depends upon devices to bring Mary into contact with figures outside the action who can be amusingly or strikingly portrayed. The devices are those of a writer on her way to a technique—one that she never quite attains.

And there is another consideration. The novel had become, especially for women writers, the dominant genre; and the dominant genre always draws into itself some talents that in another time might use another genre. Miss Ferrier may have had no more reverence for the novel as a genre than had Jane Austen when she wrote *Northanger Abbey*; indeed Miss Ferrier indicates her attitude by her epigraph, by her remark that Mary is not "of the heroic cast," and above all by "the shrewd and somewhat dry and caustic tone" that bothers the *Edinburgh Review* critic.[18] She does not make the genre she is using an important subject of her satire, as Jane Austen does in *Northanger Abbey*, but there is one touch of such satire. Lady Emily has been humorously complaining that no one at all opposes her marriage to Edward:

> "What! you had rather have been locked up in a tower— wringing your hands at the height of the windows, the thickness of the walls, and so forth," said Mary.
>
> "No: I should never have done any thing so like a washerwoman, as to wring my hands; though I might, like some heroines, have fallen to work in a regular blacksmith-way, by examining the lock of the door, and, perhaps, have succeeded in picking it; but, alas! I live in degenerate days. Oh! that I had been born the persecuted daughter of some ancient Baron bold, instead of the spoiled child of a good natured modern Earl! Heavens! to think that I must tamely, abjectly submit to be married in the presence of all my family, even in the very parish church! Oh, what detractions from the brilliancy of my star!" [Pp. 449–50]

But in general Miss Ferrier accepts the genre she works in, avoids most of what is absurd in its conventions, and uses it to do what she likes to do.

No great perception is necessary to see what Miss Ferrier enjoyed writing about: the tea at Mrs. Bluemits; that fine and acerb old lady, Mrs. Macshake; Lady Emily puncturing pretense with the hat pin of her sarcasm; the vicious absurdity of Lady Juliana; the clash of cultures when Lady Juliana is a guest at Glenfern; the conversation and the letters of Aunt Grizzy—the list is long and the order of its items hardly matters. And one delight of the book a short discussion can hardly illustrate: some of the chapter mottoes are chosen with a fine eye to their ironic contrast with the chapters they head, suggesting sly ironic reservation to their content—as the very presence of Lady Emily also sometimes suggests.

What Miss Ferrier enjoyed writing about is, of course, what we enjoy reading about. Her novel has, I would insist, its merits as a novel. But it is a vehicle for what she enjoyed, and the vehicle is not itself the most important thing, either to her or to us. When Scott praised *Marriage*, he chose his words; he did not say a very good novel but "a very lively work."

Notes

1. Susan Ferrier wrote but two other novels: *The Inheritance* (1824) and *Destiny* (1831).

2. Miss Ferrier had originally intended a collaboration with her friend Charlotte Clavering (later Mrs. Miles Fletcher), niece of the Duke of Argyll, but Miss Clavering's preference for sensationalism in novels made it impracticable. See Ian Jack, *English Literature, 1815–1832*, pp. 236–37. Miss Clavering retained an interest in the novel, however, and contributed to it the interpolated "History of Mrs. Douglas," a stilted narrative on the order of, say, "Mrs. Bennet's History" in Fielding's *Amelia*. She apparently also wrote some of the interpolated poems.

3. *Blackwood's Edinburgh Magazine* 3 (1818): 287.

4. Like other writers of her time—chiefly women writers— Miss Ferrier works a great many tags of quotation into her narrative and her authorial comment, often ineffectively. On various pretexts she introduces poems into the novel, some of which—particularly those that seem to be her own work or that of Miss Clavering—we could do without. Her style is not always adapted to her narrative purpose, as when she uses elaborately balanced sentences in an account of what is going on in a character's mind. And even allowing for her didactic purpose, a reader may feel he is too often supplied with moral judgments he is capable of making for himself.

5. The *Blackwood's* reviewer thinks "the plot is by no means excellent" (3 [1818]: 287); John Gibson Lockhart, in "Noctes Ambrosianae," lviii,

says that the plots of all three of Miss Ferrier's novels are "poor" and "their episodes disproportionate" (*Blackwood's* 30 [1831]: 533). The reviewer of Miss Ferrier's three novels as collected in Bentley's "Standard Novels" says, more perceptively, that *Marriage* has "no pretensions to rouse curiosity by a dexterously-constructed plot"; nevertheless he laments a lack of plot interest (*Edinburgh Review* 74 [1842]: 498 and 501).

6. Quoted in Ian Jack, p. 236.

7. The matter of getting Mary to England is poorly circumstanced and motivated. We are asked to believe that the sudden death of the Laird of Glenfern seriously disturbs Mary's health and spirits, and that the wise and prudent Mrs. Archibald Douglas thinks it well, therefore, to put her under the care of her selfish mother. The latest editor of *Marriage* points out as a major defect in the novel that in the fifteen years between the central narratives of volumes 1 and 2, except for Mary's growing up, "no visible change appears among the members of the Glenfern circle."

8. See *Jane Austen: The Critical Heritage*, p. 68. The last paragraph of the review is interesting also as it suggests that Scott is rather wistfully remembering his own youth.

9. Page references are to the Oxford English Novels edition of *Marriage*, ed. Herbert Foltinek (London: Oxford University Press, 1971)—an admirable edition.

10. *Blackwood's* 30 (1831): 533.

11. The *Blackwood's* reviewer of *Marriage* likes Dr. Redgill (3 [1818]: 294) and the latest editor of the novel does too. Dr. Redgill is a parasite in Lord Courtland's household, and a gourmet. He seems to me a stock comic figure not well handled.

12. *Blackwood's* 3 (1818): 294.

13. This passage is, I think, an example of Miss Ferrier's effort to reproduce dialect too completely, not only in its terms but phonetically. In passages of the speech of the Laird of Glenfern, of a post-boy, and of a servant at Glenfern, Miss Ferrier seems also to try for a too complete reproduction of dialect. In the 1841 edition of the novel in Bentley's "Standard Novels" the dialect is modified.

14. For an interesting account of some circumstances of Miss Ferrier's use of this reminiscence, see Nelson S. Bushnell, "Susan Ferrier's *Marriage* as a Novel of Manners," *Studies in Scottish Literature* 5 (1968): 220–22.

15. The account of Mrs. Macshake has been admired from the beginning: the *Blackwood's* reviewer reproduces it entire in his review; the reviewer of Miss Ferrier's collected novels thinks that Scott supplied Mrs. Macshake "with an elaborate and most appropriate *pendant*, in the

more stately Mrs Bethune Baliol of the 'Chronicles of the Canongate' "
(*Edinburgh Review* 74 [1842]: 502).

16. In particular Bailie Broadfoot of Edinburgh and the feckless Bob
Gawffaw and his affected, slattern life remind one of the Smollett novel.
The Gawffaws are a Lowland couple at whose house Mary and her
uncle spend a night. They have no connection with the action, but they
do serve as another example of a bad marriage. Nelson S. Bushnell,
"Susan Ferrier's *Marriage*," counts "some fifteen or sixteen examples" of
marriages good and bad.

17. "It sometimes happens, that the very means used, with success, in
the formation of one character, produce a totally opposite effect upon
another. The mind of Lady Emily Lindore had undergone exactly the
same process in its formation as that of her cousin; yet in all things they
differed. Whether it were the independence of high birth, or the pride
of a mind conscious of its own powers, she had hitherto resisted the
sophistry of her governesses, and the solecisms of her aunt" (p. 187).

18. *Edinburgh Review* 74 (1842): 499.

7

Mr. Balwhidder's Half-Century

"Annals of the Parish;/ or the/ Chronicle of Dalmailing;/ During
the Ministry of/ The Rev. Micah Balwhidder./ Written by Himself." So reads the title page of John Galt's best-known work—
best known, but even so not as well known as it deserves to be.[1] It
was perhaps a misfortune for Galt's reputation that his distinguished fiction appeared in the years 1821–23,[2] within the
period of Sir Walter Scott's great popularity, and that Scott's
prestige somewhat obscured Galt's work. Yet the *Annals of the
Parish* (1821), like Scott's best novels, is intended to make readers
aware of the changes in Scotland over the latter half of the
eighteenth century and to represent character and manners in
the recent past. The intention the two writers share Galt carried
out more minutely than Scott ever did. And he carried it out
before he could have been influenced by Scott's work, for he
undertook the *Annals* in 1813, although he could not find a
publisher until Scott had awakened an interest in Scottish settings.

Scott, we remember, acknowledges that he is emulating the
work of Maria Edgeworth; and *Castle Rackrent* may have
suggested to Galt the use of the vernacular and something of his
technique with his narrator, although he does not remark the
influence in his *Literary Life*. He does say there that when he was
young he "wished to write a book that would be for Scotland
what the Vicar of Wakefield is for England," but the connection
must be primarily the use of a naive clergyman narrator in both.
Probably both Miss Edgeworth and Goldsmith were influences;
Scott, whose insight is to be respected, groups Dr. Primrose,
Thady, and Mr. Balwhidder in a class of narrators.[3]

The *Annals of the Parish* is, Galt says, "void of anything like a plot," but it is not without connection and development. The *Annals* encompass the years 1760–1810 (Galt's dates are 1779–1839). As the Reverend Mr. Balwhidder makes clear at once, he is not one of "the chroniclers of the realm"; we have here, rather, the account of the year-by-year life of ordinary folk in Ayrshire in the southwest of Scotland. Galt spreads out before us a half-century of life, convincingly and with an imaginative completion that is easier to parallel in one's own memory—if one is old enough—than it is in the work of any writer.

The events and persons of Dalmailing we realize through the memory of the minister, and the selection in the book is of the sort the memory accomplishes by itself—or at least of the sort Mr. Balwhidder's memory might be expected to accomplish. Sometimes there is an amusing proportion: the finding of a toad in a stone, a surgical operation on a duck that has overeaten, the parish's first sight of a great turtle loom in the minister's memory. But his memory retains the significant things, too, and it is continuous. A number of his parishioners keep recurring in his record, and we come to know their histories and their children; they grow old and die. And year by year Dalmailing feels in one way or another the effect of the changes in the world outside it. Perhaps no other book gives its readers at once so full a sense of transience, change, and continuity in human experience.

Mr. Balwhidder is in himself a great achievement. He is naive, vain in ways that only interrupt his pervasive humility, intelligent without intellectual arrogance. He has a strain of eloquence that must appear even in such brief passages as will be quoted in this chapter. His language is that of a man educated at the Divinity Hall of Glasgow, but with an admixture of the vernacular—a decided admixture when he is emotionally concerned.[4] Indeed, the minister has a good deal of feeling for the Scottish inheritance: "I never could abide," he says in the record for 1789, "that the plain auld Kirk of Scotland, with her sober presbyterian simplicity, should borrow, either in word or in deed, from the language of the prelatic hierarchy of England." When he wants to be precise, he prefers the Scots expression: a book of moral essays is creditable, but lacks "birr and smeddum." And he has a special gift for metaphors extended through a sentence or two, metaphors always imaginatively coherent, often striking, and sometimes a little grotesque.

The minister has in his character inconsistencies of just the sort we know in persons of our own acquaintance. He has a considerable flexibility of mind and an ability to accommodate himself to most new ideas and conditions, but there is in him a residue of superstition, although it seems to appear only in the records of the first twenty years or so of his ministry.[5] Despite admirable qualities of sympathy and Christian charity, his attitude toward Jenny Gaffow and her daughter Meg, the "naturals" of the parish, is not much enlightened. At a dinner party during the time he is courting the third Mrs. Balwhidder, he caps a jest of the jocose Dr. Dinwiddie with a crudity that seems not quite ministerial.[6]

But some inconsistencies in the character of the minister may be lapses on Galt's part. After the death of the first Mrs. Balwhidder in 1763, the minister finds the planning of her monument and the composing of a ridiculous conventional epitaph for her "a blessed entertainment." But we cannot be convinced that a man with the feeling for language Galt has given his minister would ever write the epitaph ascribed to him; Galt seems to have been led astray by his own impulse to write a burlesque epitaph.[7] And the minister's account of his determination to write a great work, which comes about the same time, seems to some readers an inconsistency in him and a mistake on Galt's part. The minister considers whether "an orthodox poem, like Paradise Lost" or "a connect treatise on the efficacy of Free Grace" would be the more taking, and makes some beginnings in each. His projection of works he could never have managed is amusing, but, James Kinsley thinks, "wantonly reduced to farce by his throbs, thrills, and transports."[8] But here we need to realize that Galt is having fun with some conventional ways of talking about literary composition.[9] The poor minister's troubles with the servant lassies in his widower's establishment—an impediment to his literary designs—come in nice ironic contrast to his transports.

The Reverend Mr. Balwhidder is amusing in himself, and he has a gift for seeing sometimes and always for conveying what is amusing in others. The reader on occasion sees the minister in ways he does not see himself, and may be amused by the record when the minister is aware of nothing amusing in it. But in general the reader takes the account of the parish and its affairs as the minister intends it, and sees the citizens of Dalmailing as the minister apprehends them. Although it is not always agreed that Galt's handling of his narrator is entirely successful,[10] the objections to it seem not to allow—as I think we must—for the necessities of his intention. Indeed, the question of Mr. Balwhidder as narrator may be more complex than has been recognized.

What Galt is trying for, certainly, is a narrator who will seem self-consistent, but one who will enable him to fulfill his purpose, not hamper it. Galt wants to represent the history of a Scottish clachan in a period of change, to use his own estimate of the quality of that change, and to use the wealth of tradition, observation, and anecdote he has for the work.[11] But Galt is a writer of fiction, and so far an artist; and an artist's choices are choices of limits. It is a great pleasure for the attentive reader of the *Annals of the Parish* to watch Galt work within the limits that the choice of Mr. Balwhidder as narrator imposes, limits he seldom violates; and at the same time to watch the growth of Galt's own understanding, as the book goes on, of the minister as a humorous character.[12] Yet our interest in the minister is not allowed to overwhelm our interest in his record; as he is made to remark, "it would be a very improper and uncomely thing" for him to speak too much of his own affairs in a book intended to be a record of his ministry. But we get to know him thoroughly through that record and, although little space is given them, the three Mrs. Balwhidders emerge with great clarity.

Once complexity of narrative point of view in the *Annals* arises not so much from the minister's character as it does from the scheme of annals written in retrospect. The minister, except in the latter chapters, is writing long after the events he records, and when their results are at least partly apparent. If he sometimes attributes to himself at the time of the events a comprehension that he would not in actuality have gained until later, he is the more convincing figure thereby, for he is doing what we are all likely to do. But I think that it has not been sufficiently recognized that, although Galt is careful to make the minister remind us throughout that he is writing in retrospect, the interpretation of the events of his early years is really not much affected by his later attitudes. We are not aware of any prescience on his part—or of anything he takes as prescience—until late in the record. This may be a kind of accident in the development of Galt's scheme; at any rate the minister does not justify his insight on the basis of experience until late in the book.[13] Indeed, there is a kind of development in his judgments of men and events in the record year by year that may not be quite consistent with the assumption that the record is written in his last years.

For the continuity of the book, the sense of an ongoing life in Dalmailing, Galt wisely depends upon the minister's occasional recurrence to a small number of persons, so that the *Annals* simulates the quality of our own knowledge of the people around us, as their troubles or joys become apparent, and as their lives are interconnected. These persons emerge vividly, although our estimate of their characters is sometimes, as in our ordinary experience, the result of our own inference. We come to know Miss Girzie Gilchrist ("called Lady Skim-milk"), the sister of a Major who has made his fortune in India; the Lady Macadam, imperious widow of a general; Miss Sabrina Hooky, the schoolmistress, whose Glasgow experience gives her a position as tastemaker in the clachan; Lord Eglesham, a fine type of eighteenth-century nobleman; and several more. We get, too, a sense of the continuing life of the parish: the minister and his elders sometimes have to seek out the father of an apparently fatherless baby; the heritors are difficult and obtuse; the minister, sometimes by stratagem, accomplishes improvements to the church or to the manse.

Particularly the affairs of Mrs. Malcolm and her family recur. The widow of a Clyde shipmaster, she settles in Dalmailing in the year of the minister's placing, and lives through most of his tenure. She is the one person in the book upon whom the minister comments at any length; his feeling for her is like a spiritual love affair, and after the death of the second Mrs. Balwhidder in 1796, he had, he says, "a glimmer in my mind of speaking to Mrs Malcolm, but when I reflected upon the saintly steadiness of her character, I was satisfied it would be of no use to think of her."

We follow the fortunes of the Malcolm family as one might any family with which he had a long acquaintance. The eldest son, Charles, especially dear to the minister, goes to sea, is impressed into the Navy, finds a career there, and is killed in the Battle of the Saints. Robert, likewise a sailor, is, toward the end of the book, "in a great way as a shipmaster"; Kate, the protégée of the Lady Macadam, becomes, greatly to the old lady's initial displeasure, the wife of her son, the Laird of Macadam; Effie marries a naval officer, the friend of her brother Charles; and William, with the assistance of Lord Eglesham, becomes a minister and published author, and preaches from Mr. Balwhidder's pulpit in 1789. Surely there is in the Malcolms, perhaps especially in the relationship of Kate and Lady Macadam, a potential novel.

In the latter half of the book there is a recurrent interest, too, in the minister's relationship with Mr. Cayenne. Mr. Cayenne is a Tory expatriate from America; he comes to the parish in 1785 and becomes a partner in the cotton mill which so changed its life. The settlement which grows up around the mill is called Cayenneville and afterwards Canaille. (The minister sees no significance in the shortening of the name, and merely remarks that the country folk, "not used to such lang-nebbit words," had shortened it.) Cayenneville represents the new era, as Dalmailing continues to represent the old. Mr. Cayenne is irascible, ungodly, meddlesome—and capable, good-hearted, and shrewd.[14] The minister concludes that "though we thought him, for many a day, a serpent plague sent upon the parish, he proved . . . one of our greatest benefactors." Although we may not be so sure of the entire beneficence of industrialism as the minister sometimes seems to be, the development of Cayenneville has a representative significance and Mr. Cayenne is a striking figure; there are materials here that by themselves might have made a social novel.[15]

The persons who emerge so vividly may well be for many readers the chief interest of the *Annals of the Parish*. Certainly Galt deals with them with amazing economy of means; better than most writers, he knows how to trust his readers. And it would be hard to find another book in which a writer has been so generous with his materials. Even the persons who appear only once might have been developed at length. The story of the exposing of the hypocrisy of the Reverend Mr. Heckletext, told within two pages of the record for 1772, has both comic and pathetic possibilities and would admit of extended treatment. Or, in the record for 1801, there is the account of the poor widow's son, Colin Mavis, who becomes the poet of Dalmailing. Colin represents a kind of literary career possible perhaps only in the Scotland of Galt's time—although in Dalmailing the publication of Colin's first book angers "all those who had foretold he would be a do-nae-gude." In the *Annals* Galt uses up materials of experience, anecdote, observation, and printed sources that might furnish out a number of novels richly and well.

In the vivid representation of his persons, however, Galt is equaled by writers of his own time, and by writers before and after him. Galt's distinction, his great excellence, is in his representation of change as it comes to Dalmailing and of the effects of events outside the little clachan upon it. Galt carries out this representation with nothing of the heavy-handedness we are used to in the social novel.

What may be even more unusual, Galt seems never to fake a connection between a historical event and a Dalmailing result. The Gordon Riots of 1780, for instance, although they interest the citizens of Dalmailing, hardly affect them: "we spent our time," the minister says, "in the lea of the hedge." The only incident for Dalmailing is that "the two irreclaimable naturals," Jenny Gaffow and her daughter, hearing of "the luminations that were lighted up through the country, on the ending of the Popish Bill," and somehow gathering a score of candle ends, illuminate their house so successfully that their frightened neighbors think it afire.

But often the chronicles of the realm impinge upon the story of Dalmailing. The parish does not escape, for instance, the ills of smuggling that plagued eighteenth-century Britain. One realizes when he reads the *Annals* that his knowledge of that smuggling was mostly from once-aboard-the-lugger, muffled-hoofbeats-in-the-darkness boys' stories. What Galt does is to make the past seem immediate, and to make us see it from a point of view that belongs to it. Nowhere in the book does he handle his narrator better.

Mr. Balwhidder must of course disapprove of smuggling;

early in his ministry, in 1761, he preaches against tea as connected with it, and "sixteen times from the text, Render to Cæsar
the things that are Cæsar's"—with little effect. Smuggling makes
him immediate trouble: "we had," he says, "no less than three
contested bastard bairns upon our hands at one time, which was
a thing never heard of in a parish of the shire of Ayr, since the
Reformation." Smuggling is, he says and doubtless believes, the
"wicked mother of many mischiefs." Yet the excise man he admires is Robin Bicker, who is not "overly gleg, but when a job
was ill-done . . . obliged to notice it." In the record for 1778 he
tells an amusing story of one of the Paukie sisters, dealers in
smuggled goods. In order to protect her wares from the excise
man, she pretends to be "taken with a heart colic" and lies moan-
ing on a mattress stuffed with tea. When her ruse is discovered
and the officious companion of the excise man carries the mattress away as evidence, she pursues and overtakes him, and slits
the mattress just as he is crossing a burn on stepping stones, so
that the tea all floats away. "The story," the minister writes, "not
a little helped to lighten our melancholy meditations."

Other events of the realm and of the world beyond touch the
clachan. The minister's account of the ways in which the American Revolution and Britain's related struggle with France affect
Dalmailing stuck longest in my memory after a first reading of
the *Annals*; probably this portion will be of particular interest to
most American readers.

In 1768 Charles Malcolm is impressed from his merchant ship
to a man-of-war; he does well in the service; four young men of
the parish sail with him when he gets his first command. In 1769
the clachan gets its first knowledge of the growing revolt in the
colonies and realizes that it has something to do with the high
price of tobacco. In 1774 a soldier stationed near Dalmailing kills
a camp follower, one Jean Glaikit; her body is found by schoolboys, a "dark and awful event." In 1776 enlistment begins—first
a Thomas Wilson, who leaves his wife and children as the responsibilities of Session; then another lad, "a ramplor," whom
the parish thinks it will not much miss; and then "the listing"
becomes "a catching distemper." The minister preaches a sermon which leaves "a deep sob in the church, verily it was Rachel
weeping for her children."

By the next year the forebodings of the people of Dalmailing are fulfilled. The minister begins his record for 1777:

> This may well be called the year of the heavy heart, for we had sad tidings of the lads that went away as soldiers to America. First, there was a boding in the minds of all their friends that they were never to see them more, and their sadness, like a mist spreading from the waters and covering the fields, darkened the spirit of the neighbours. Secondly, a sound was bruited about, that the King's forces would have a hot and a sore struggle before the rebels were put down, if they were ever put down. Then came the cruel truth of all the poor lads' friends had feared.

The cruel truth that touches the minister most nearly does not come until the fighting in America is over; it comes with the news of the last major naval engagement of British and French forces before the Treaty of Paris.

In his record for the year 1782 the minister tells us, simply and with no attempt to heighten the irony, how the news of the British victory in the Battle of the Saints (12 April 1782) and the news of the death of Captain Charles Malcolm come together, and how Mrs. Malcolm hears from the minister of the death of her son while "the callants of the school" are shouting in triumph and the steeple bell is ringing. As the minister escorts Mrs. Malcolm home, the boys guess what has happened and throw away their banners and stand silent while Mrs. Malcolm and the minister pass. The next Sunday the minister tries to preach a sermon in celebration of the victory, but fails.

> I prepared a suitable sermon, taking as the words of my text, "Howl, ye ships of Tarshish, for your strength is laid waste." But when I saw around me so many of my people, clad in complimentary mourning for the gallant Charles Malcolm, and that even poor daft Jenny Gaffaw, and her daughter, had on an old black ribbon; and when I thought of him, the spirited laddie, coming home from Jamaica, with his parrot on his shoulder, and his limes for me, my heart filled full, and I was obliged to sit down in the pulpit, and drop a tear.

The minister's account of the sorrow that came to Dalmailing through the War of American Independence—so far away and so little understood in the clachan—is singularly arresting; it gives one's ancestral history implications which perhaps he had never realized, and allows one to see it from a point of view he could not by himself attain.

The minister remarks the occasional "Sabbath-years" of his ministry, but as we know well enough, no society ever has a very long holiday from stresses within it or those coming from outside it. The new industrialism and the ferment of ideas at the time of the French Revolution both affect Dalmailing. For the year 1788 the minister records his awareness of "an erect and out-looking spirit abroad that was not to be satisfied with the taciturn regularity of ancient affairs," and accompanying "signs of decay in the wonted simplicity of our country ways." The literacy and intellectual activity of the Cayenneville weavers and spinners are surprising things to him, remarked from time to time through the rest of the book.

The minister tries to use his influence for good in a disrupted time. Seeing a spiritual danger in the new prosperity, he preaches a series of sermons in 1791 against avarice, and is by his own heritors taken for "a black-neb," but he is successfully defended the next year by the Dalmailing embodiment of capitalism, Mr. Cayenne. "The sad division of [his] people into government-men and jacobins" disturbs the minister, but he endeavors not to exacerbate it. In 1794 he preaches that the new doctrine of utilitarians like Jeremy Bentham is only another and new way of designating the doctrine of Christian charity that the Church has always taught. In 1793 he preaches a sermon against the regicides of France, yet by 1800 he believes that he has seen a gradual lessening of infidelity, and that "the elements of reconciliation were coming together throughout the world." But he cannot prevent the rise of sectarianism in his own parish; indeed a sermon preached in 1806 against it results in a seceding church. Yet he believes that among the old families, if not perhaps among the weavers, there is a renewal "of the sense of the utility, even in earthly affairs, of a religious life," which, he trusts, is "in some . . . more than prudence, and really a birth of grace."

In general the minister accommodates himself well to a period of rapid and disturbing change—perhaps a little more easily than is quite convincing. But Galt is careful not to make him do so in any way that will seem really inconsistent with his nature and profession. It is, indeed, his professional attitudes that he can hardly change or modify. His soul is, he says, shaken within him when he learns that a Father O'Grady, confessor to some Irish workmen, has brought the Mass—"with all its mummeries and abominations"—into Cayenneville. The minister calls the Session together with an intent toward some rigorous measure of suppression. But he is convinced as he writes his record of 1804 that the judgment of the Session that no action be taken is right, that it is "a comfort to see mankind cherishing any sense of religion at all, after the vehement infidelity that had been sent abroad by the French Republicans." However, when in 1809 on the first Sunday there is a meeting in the seceded church, he cannot refrain in his "remembering prayer"—although he regrets it afterwards—from entreating the Lord "to do with the hobbleshow at Cayenneville" as he sees fit in his displeasure.

Despite the persistence of Mr. Balwhidder's convictions, there are subtle differences in his attitudes over the years—one of the indications that the records year by year reflect the attitudes of the minister at the times of the experiences recorded. We find that he becomes more than a little infected by the new spirit of the latter years of the eighteenth century and that, without his realizing it, his belief in Providence changes into something very like a faith in the Idea of Progress. It is a change that must have taken place in the minds of many men in the minister's time and in somewhat the same way that it does in the minister's mind.

In the records of the early years of his ministry, Mr. Balwhidder finds the "hand of Providence" visible in his own affairs and in the life of Dalmailing very much as we should expect a Scottish country clergyman to do. He not only believes in Providence; he tends to consider himself its special representative. When in 1761, for instance, he becomes aware of some women engaged in the surreptitious drinking of smuggled tea—doubtless laced with smuggled "conek"—he disperses them, he says, by giving "a sign by a loud host [cough], that Providence sees all." Or he believes that the toothache which had prevented

his preaching on a Sunday in 1772 and led him to invite Mr.
Heckletext to occupy his pulpit "had been instrumental in the
hand of a chastising Providence . . . to bring the hidden hypocrisy of the ungodly preacher to light."

Nor in the records of the early years of his ministry is Mr.
Balwhidder at all likely to assume that change is necessarily improvement. In his record for the year 1768, when he is discussing changes that seemed to the parish then "a great advantage,"
he has his doubts: "For with wealth come wants, like a troop of
clamorous beggars at the heels of a generous man, and it's hard
to tell wherein the benefit of improvement in a country parish
consists, especially to those who live by the sweat of their brow."
But, he concludes, it is not for him to make reflections: "my task
and my duty is to note the changes of time and habitudes." As
the *Annals* proceed, he is more likely to feel that it does belong to
him to make reflections.

By the time of his record for the year 1779, the minister's
reflection has decidedly a new cast. He is still speaking, to be
sure, of the hand of Providence, but with a significant alteration
of the metaphor. Although the minister does not so intend it,
this passage may make an instructed Christian uncomfortable:

> The rest of the year was merely a quiet succession of small
> incidents, none of which are worthy of notation, though
> they were all severally, no doubt, of aught somewhere, as
> they took up both time and place in the coming to pass, and
> nothing comes to pass without helping onwards some great
> end; each particular little thing that happens in the world,
> being a seed sown by the hand of Providence to yield an
> increase, which increase is destined, in its turn, to minister
> to some higher purpose, until at last the issue affects the
> whole earth. There is nothing in all the world that doth not
> advance the cause of goodness; no, not even the sins of the
> wicked, though through the dim casement of her mortal
> tabernacle, the soul of man cannot discern the method
> thereof.

This indication of a Tennysonian belief in some far-off divine
event toward which an ineluctable Progress moves becomes
more explicit in the record of the last year of his tenure.

At his retirement, the church that had seceded from his own gives Mr. Balwhidder a silver service as a retirement gift. The minister remarks that the inscription thereon had been "written by a weaver lad that works for his daily bread"—a thing that would have been a prodigy in the early years of his ministry. But, he goes on, "the progress of book learning and education has been wonderful since, and with it has come a spirit of greater liberality than the world knew before," so that "by the mollifying influence of knowledge, the time will come to pass, when the tiger of papistry shall lie down with the lamb of reformation, and the vultures of prelacy be as harmless as the presbyterian doves." It is a subtle passage on Galt's part: the minister's metaphors betray the persistence of his ingrained feeling about the Roman Catholic Church; at the same time he foresees an ecumenical outcome for the divisions of Christianity. But the basis of his hope seems hardly a trust in Providence, but a trust in the un-questioned benefits of education as the mainspring of Progress. The minister seems no longer to be saying that "the soul of man cannot discern the method thereof."

Mr. Balwhidder's reflections on Providence and Progress are historically representative and a considerable interest in the book. But the *Annals of the Parish* transcends history; the wonder of the book is the way in which the mystery of time emerges from it—no less a mystery to the minister because almost all his time stretches out behind him. And part of the wonder is that Galt, who was about thirty-four when he wrote the *Annals*, could so fully know that mystery as it presents itself to an old man. The reader of the *Annals* is often aware of the interplay of transience and continuity, for it inheres in the whole and arises from the very record of events. But his awareness of the mystery of time is curiously and poignantly pointed up by the minister's own kind of retrospective metaphor.

With an accurate insight, Galt makes the minister reflect on the mystery of time particularly as he records from long retrospect the early and middle years of his tenure. When he comes to the twenty-fifth anniversary of his placing (1785), he says: "The bairns, that were bairns when I came among my people, were ripened into parents, and a new generation was swelling in the bud around me." For him, as for all of us, the experience is commonplace, inevitable, and inexplicable. Again, he looks back on the pleasant year 1784 "as on a sunny spot in a valley, amidst the shadows of the clouds of time." In another passage—one in which the special quality of his imagination emerges strikingly—the minister, concluding his account of the events of 1783, writes that "the year flowed in a calm, and we floated on in the stream of time towards the great ocean of eternity, like ducks and geese in the river's tide, that are carried down without being sensible of the speed of the current."

And when Mr. Balwhidder is at the brink of eternity, and is preaching his farewell sermon (which Galt has him record in the introduction to his book) he says: "As for you, my old companions, many changes have we seen in our day, but the change that we ourselves are soon to undergo will be the greatest of all." The minister's book, which is so fully a record of the manifold changes of this world as they came to Dalmailing, cannot record the greatest change, or time's last manifestation.

The *Annals of the Parish* has not had its due place in the history of fiction, perhaps because it came so long before there was any movement that called itself realism. But John Galt did find an entirely adequate technique for his purposes; he achieved what Susan Ferrier could not quite manage. Galt himself regretted that his public took the *Annals* as a novel, thinking, evidently, that it would suffer if his readers tried to fit the book into their preconceptions about what a novel should be. When, years after its publication, he reconsiders the *Annals* in his *Literary Life*, he says that he is surprised to find that "it affords so many exact specimens of the kind of art which I have indifferently studied," and "in almost every page, proofs of those kind of memorials to which I have been most addicted—things of which the originals are, or were, actually in nature, but brought together into composition by art." Our definitions of realism are notoriously unsatisfactory; certainly there is implicit in Galt's remark a definition as good as any we have.

When we speak of the reality of the *Annals* we know what reality we are talking about. It is not precisely the reality of life in Dalmailing in the years 1760–1810; it is that life as known, understood, remembered, and recorded by the Reverend Micah

Balwhidder, the reality of experience as it is known to a single mind, the only way it can be known. And Galt did not fear to have his Mr. Balwhidder record characters "of which the originals are, or were, actually in nature," just because they exhibit such surprising variety, because they seem too strange for fiction. As an early American critic, defending some striking characters in Scott, asks: "If nature did not furnish the study, how came the picture so spirited and consistent, yet at the same time so peculiar?"[16]

The *Annals of the Parish* is a remarkable achievement. Galt shares with Scott the feeling for period, but Scott himself never accomplishes such precise and subtle distinctions of period as we find in the *Annals*. And Galt handles the long time span in a way satisfyingly consonant with our experience. Our response is preeminently recognition: this is right, we say, this is the way a half-century of life in a Scottish clachan must present itself in retrospect when selected by the memory of Mr. Balwhidder, whose qualities of mind and heart we thoroughly know.

NOTES

1. The 1975 *Books in Print* lists only the volume in an expensive reprint of *Works*, ed. D. S. Meldrum and W. Roughead (New York: AMS Press, 1936), and *Annals of the Parish*, ed. James Kinsley (London: Oxford University Press, 1967). Page numbers in the footnotes to this chapter refer to Professor Kinsley's excellent edition, which reprints the pages from Galt's *Literary Life* that have to do with the *Annals*. The dates within the text make a way of reference to any edition.

2. *The Ayrshire Legatees, Annals of the Parish, The Provost*, and *The Entail*, as well as other works, all appeared within these years.

3. *The Lives of the Novelists*, p. 376.

4. See for example the minister's account of a sermon preached in 1776, pp. 81–82.

5. Some of the minister's remarks suggest a lingering belief not in the present but in the past reality of witchcraft (see pp. 12, 18 and compare pp. 38–39). His second marriage is hurried a little to avoid a marriage in May (p. 32). His parishioners believe that Mungo Argyle (who afterwards murders Lord Eglesham) is fay; and the minister, when he sees him "so gallant and gay" and notes "his glowing face and his gleg e'en" agrees that there is "something no canny about him" (p. 104).

6. 1796, pp. 155–56.

7. There are other lapses, in which Galt, like the minister when he thinks of his proposed great work, seems to be thinking about what might be "taking" instead of what is consistent with his intention. The reader might consider the "tale of this pious and resigned spirit," the widow Mirkland (pp. 85–87); the account of the minister's Assembly Sermon (pp. 97–100); and the account of the minister's dream (pp. 142–43). These, like the epitaph, all have an unhappy air of being labored set pieces.

8. *Annals of the Parish*, ed. Kinsley, p. xvi.

9. In his *Literary Life*, Galt himself, in reference to the *Annals*, tells us that on a Sunday walk to the village of Innerkip, "while looking at various improvements around, my intention of writing a minister's sedate adventures returned upon me, as if the mantle of inspiration had suddenly dropped upon my shoulders" (Appendix, p. 208). The minister's transports are perhaps only appropriately more extravagant than Galt's.

10. See Kinsley's introduction, pp. vii–viii.

11. In his *Literary Life* Galt gives a number of examples of his materials; Kinsley reprints them in his notes.

12. This change of attitude on the part of a writer toward a character is the sort of thing that happened to Cervantes in writing *Don Quixote* and to Dickens in writing *Pickwick Papers*. See Dickens's retrospective Preface to *Pickwick Papers*.

13. See 1800, p. 170, and 1802, p. 175.

14. The minister is much troubled by Mr. Cayenne's irreligion and is almost overwhelmed in 1793 when two young weavers are brought before Mr. Cayenne in his capacity as justice of the peace on a suspicion of high treason. The young men deny that they are traitors, but admit that they are reformers. The minister records this dialogue: " 'Was not,' they said, 'our Lord Jesus Christ a reformer?'—'And what the devil did he make of it?' cried Mr Cayenne, bursting with passion; 'Was he not crucified?' " (p. 144). It may not have been noticed that Galt is here borrowing a story told of a famous Scottish judge, Robert MacQueen, Lord Braxfield (1722–99): "When [Joseph] Gerrald ventured to say that Christianity was an innovation, and that all great men had been reformers, 'even our Saviour himself,' Braxfield chuckled in an undertone, 'Muckle he made o' that, he was hanget' " (quoted from Henry, Lord Cockburn's *Memorials of His Time* [1856] in the entry for Braxfield in *Dictionary of National Biography*). Cockburn's *Memorials* is not, of course, Galt's source for the anecdote.

15. The account of Mr. Cayenne represents the near identification of

loyalty to the established government with Christianity. The minister, after recording Mr. Cayenne's remark to the weavers, says: "I never, from that day, could look on Mr Cayenne as a Christian, though surely he was a true government-man" (p. 144). And Mr. Cayenne himself, just before his death, says: "I am however no saint, as you know, doctor; so I wish you to put in a word for me, doctor; for you know that in these times, doctor, it is the duty of every good subject to die a Christian" (p. 191). But Mr. Cayenne makes a better ending than might have been expected.

16. John Gorham Palfrey, *North American Review* 5 (1817): 263.

8

Miss Mitford's Village Sketches

In his *Annals of the Parish* John Galt was content to portray the people of an obscure village, very ordinary folk indeed. And ordinary folk are among the most memorable of Sir Walter Scott's host of characters; perhaps it is the Mucklebackits and Douce Davie Deans and his daughters that we remember best of all. But the novels written in England in the same period had little interest in commonplace persons and experience. William Hazlitt in "The Dandy School" complains that the novels of his time are failing to extend their readers' experience, that "they are narrowed to a single point, the admiration of the folly, caprice, insolence, and affectation of a certain class;—so that with the exception of people who ride in their carriages, you are taught to look down upon the rest of the species with indifference, abhorrence, or contempt." Not all novels written in England in the period were "fashionable novels," of course, but those that were not were likely to have even more exotic subject matters. The portrayal of simple rural English men and women by the means of fiction was pretty well left to Mary Russell Mitford.

In the introduction to the last series of sketches that make up *Our Village*,[1] Miss Mitford says: "For ten long years, for five tedious volumes, has that most multifarious and most kind personage, the public, endured to hear history, half real and half imaginary, of a half imaginary and half real little spot on the sunny side of Berkshire." When the sketches came out in the *Lady's Magazine* and other publications, and then every two years in successive volumes (1824–32), their first readers doubtless enjoyed the reappearance of a familiar narrator, familiar scenes, and familiar persons; and they doubtless enjoyed an increasing at-homeness with them—a pleasure that Miss Mitford expected and fostered in the introductory pieces and in the sketches themselves.

The reader today who encounters the sketches all together may agree a little more fully than Miss Mitford would quite have liked with her own complaint that "a country village . . . does, I confess, occasionally labour under a stagnation of topics."[2] But she should not be thought of as a charming old maid who happened to write village sketches. Although in *Our Village* she was purposely keeping to a woman's point of view, she was a highly professional writer,[3] hard driven to support her fatuous father. The best evidence of the professionalism of her sketches is her complete confidence that she can interest her readers in any commonplace she chooses to write about. She made the most she could of the literary capital her life in the village of Three Mile Cross (near Reading) afforded her. Perhaps she tried to make too much of it; the wonder is that so much of what she did with it is successful.

Our Village is part of the movement, clear in English poetry if not in English fiction, in which, as Emerson says in "The American Scholar," "the near, the low, the common, was explored and poetized." Miss Mitford has a pervading and very feminine interest in her persons; she writes of them with sympathy and love, and probably with no feeling of essential superiority to them. But she speaks of herself as "a country gentlewoman of small fortune," who has lived much among poor people and feels "an unaffected interest in their health and comfort";[4] and she recognizes that she describes her persons from without. She delineates, she says in her preface, "country scenery and country manners," but the manners, at least, are described from the distance inherent in her status as a gentlewoman: in "Lucy" she remarks, "There is always great freshness and originality in an uneducated and quick-witted person, who surprises one continually by unsuspected knowledge or amusing ignorance." Even the country scenes are realized by an imagination developed and trained by a knowledge of the visual arts and of literature.

Miss Mitford is before all a literary person, and there are literary analogues for *Our Village*; indeed she points out the most important of them. She intends, she says, to write "essays and characters and stories, chiefly of country life, in the manner of the 'Sketch Book,' but without sentimentality or pathos—two things which I abhor."[5] One can see a resemblance to *The Sketch Book*, but more to *Bracebridge Hall* in the "characters" and in the confined locality. "Even in books," Miss Mitford writes in her first sketch, "I like a confined locality, and so do the critics when they talk of the unities. . . . Nothing is so delightful as to sit down in a country village in one of Miss Austen's delicious novels . . . or to ramble with Mr. White over his own parish of Selborne."[6] Yet Miss Mitford's interests and her style are her own.

The confined locality of *Our Village* is quite as confined as that in any of Jane Austen's novels, but it is very differently populated. Miss Austen restricted herself to the class of English gentry to which she belonged. Miss Mitford, as Mrs. Oliphant points out, belonged to the same class (with somewhat higher connections) but she "recognizes a big world about her, even though she only draws it within the limited proportions of 'Our Village,' " and her heart "takes in all the Joes and Pollys and Harriets of a country-side"—her world is "twice as full as Miss Austen's . . . overflowing with life, like a medieval picture."[7]

The style of *Our Village* is disciplined and calculated: "What looks like ease in my style," Miss Mitford wrote to Thomas Noon Talfourd, "is labour."[8] Some passages will seem to us overexclamatory, even irritatingly so; but there is hardly any other mannerism that will much trouble readers familiar with early nineteenth-century writing—we must understand Miss Mitford's term "ease" in the context of her time. Although she exhausts her restricted topics, she is distinguished for a precision of statement. And apparently she does not try to make the "I" of the sketches emerge as especially a striking or a charming person; she seems content that the "I" appear everywhere likable and unpretentious. Charles Lamb's essays and Miss Mitford's sketches were making their first appearances in the same years, and there is high contrast between them.

But what will strike the reader today in the style of *Our Village* is the wealth of literary allusion and quotation. We have noted Susan Ferrier's fondness for quotation in *Marriage*; and Mary Lascelles acutely points out that the writers of the period have

"the impulse (it is deeper-rooted than a mere fashion) to introduce quotations from familiar literature into all kinds of writing," and that often the impulse manifests itself awkwardly:
"they cannot get quietly past a quotation or an allusion."[9] Nor
can Miss Mitford.

In *Our Village* many of the quotations, not identified except by
quotation marks, are worked into the text. Most of them one
recognizes as tags from well-known writers, often from Shakespeare; those one does not recognize may be from writers better
known in Miss Mitford's time than in ours. Yet although this
persistent literary reference is a feature of her style, its importance is more than stylistic; it indicates something of her attitude
toward her subjects and her readers. She is assuming a literary
experience in common with her readers, and it is within this
shared experience that the village experience is to be realized.
The effect is often playful. Sometimes a quotation is given a
twist: the clergyman in "An Old Bachelor" is "not only *dull* in
himself, but the cause of *dullness* in others." Or, to take another
sort of example, "The Talking Lady," one of the "characters,"
begins this way:

> Ben Jonson has a play called *The Silent Woman*, who turns
> out, as might be expected, to be no woman at all—nothing,
> as Master Slender said, but "a great lubberly boy"; thereby,
> as I apprehend, discourteously presuming that a silent
> woman is a nonentity. If the learned dramatist, thus happily
> prepared and predisposed, had happened to fall in with
> such a specimen of female loquacity as I have just parted
> with, he might, perhaps, have given us a pendant to his
> picture in *The Talking Lady*. Pity but he had! He would have
> done her justice.

Although quotations and allusions do come into the sketches in
ways that seem a bit forced—as perhaps the passage just quoted
does—we hardly think of them as pedantry. One suspects that
they are used primarily to allow the readers Miss Mitford envis-
aged the gratification of recognition.

Another stylistic interest in *Our Village*—perhaps a little at
odds with the pervasive literary reference—is the frequent use
of a country word or expression. Sometimes Miss Mitford re-

marks her use of a colloquialism, as she does when she uses "so much lissomer," "they fall so deedily," and "tongue-banging." More often she uses her colloquialisms just as they happen in context: "betweenities," "beaten us hollow," "and that's a bold word," "at tide-times," "they ratted [deserted] to a man," "the wind . . . played us booty [false]" and (of her greyhound) "five years old this grass." A mischievous boy is always "a pickle" ("he's a sad pickle, is Sam"); and since she is charmed by mischievous boys, the word keeps recurring.

Other feminine attitudes emerge in the sketches, often wittily. Of a "most determined bachelor" in "A Country Apothecary," who is "as uncivil as his good nature would permit" to all unmarried women, Miss Mitford writes: "but they got used to it—it was the man's way; and there was an indirect flattery in his fear of their charms which the maiden ladies, especially the elder ones, found very mollifying; so he was forgiven." Or she remarks in "A Christmas Party": "For my part, I . . . hold it very hard that an innocent woman cannot entertain a little harmless aversion towards her next neighbour without being called to account for so natural a feeling." And in "A Parting Glance at Our Village" she says of the pretty daughter of the shoemaker, "She is my opposite neighbour, and I have a right to watch her doings—the right of retaliation."

Miss Mitford is perhaps more amused at masculine assumptions of superiority than resentful of them. In "The General and His Lady" she remarks that all men have at least a slight shade of contempt for women's intellects, but that "the clever ones discreetly keep it to themselves"; in "The Visit" she says that all males are "sticklers for dominion; though, when it is undisputed, some of them are generous enough to abandon it," so that discreet wives manage their husbands with "no better secret than this seeming submission." A bit later in the same sketch Miss Mitford tells how a teamster helps her and a woman friend in a difficulty on the road, helps them with great good-humor, but "with a certain triumphant, masterful look in his eyes, which I have noted in men, even the best of them, when a woman gets into straits by attempting manly employments." And she remarks in "The Cowslip Ball": "We went on very prosperously, *considering*—as people say of . . . a woman's tragedy, or . . . of any performance which is accomplished by means seemingly inadequate to its production"—a reference to her own tragedy, *Julian*.

Although Miss Mitford can speak for herself incisively, her persons do not speak with any particular vividness, and indeed there is little dialogue in the sketches; she was probably right in believing that she did not handle dialogue nor action well.[10] Those of her sketches that come closest to what we should call a short story are of little merit. But she does have a neat hand with anecdotes; those of the old French émigré in "A Country Apothecary" and of Mr. Sidney's Sunday evening in "An Old Bachelor" are fine examples.

The full title of Miss Mitford's book is *Our Village: Sketches of Rural Character and Scenery*. Although "sketch" in early nineteenth-century literary use is a word often difficult to tie down, it makes little trouble here. In many of her pieces, in all of the better ones, Miss Mitford is doing with words something closely parallel to what the landscape painter or the portrait painter does in his medium. But she would not say "pictures" in her title; the word "sketch" carries here the suggestion it often does in nineteenth-century titles: a modest depreciation of what it designates. The best of Miss Mitford's sketches fall into two genres—"country walks" and "characters."

The "country walk" seems to be Miss Mitford's own genre. "The Fall of the Leaf" illustrates it in its simplest form. As the "country walks" often are, it is dated (Nov. 6th); it describes a walk on a mild autumn day, with careful attention to just what territory is transversed and to elapsing time. It uses one of Miss Mitford's ways of including the reader; the pronoun is "we" although the "I" has no companion: "We must bend our steps towards the water-side. . . . We must get on." There is a paragraph on a post-boy and a group of children—"quite a group for a painter"—who function like the small figures in landscape paintings. The sketch concludes as evening comes on and the walk turns homeward.

The "country walks" may be a little more elaborate than this example and include descriptions of persons and general accounts of the quality of their lives, but without the use of the techniques of the "characters." In "The Dell," for instance, the account of Farmer Allen and his wife on their little farm—"an order of cultivators now passing rapidly away"—becomes part of the scene, and our interest in them is largely pictorial. All the "country walks" benefit by Miss Mitford's extensive and precise knowledge of flowers and growing things, and her precision of description keeps the appreciative passages from being merely tasteful gush. But the "country walk," obviously, is a genre in which success largely depends upon control and style.

Miss Mitford's "characters" have, of course, a long tradition behind them—the same tradition out of which Miss Ferrier writes her "characters." But Miss Mitford's "characters"—they seem to be drawn from life—are first of all individuals, although they may have highly typical qualities, and are most interesting when they do. The barber in "A Country Barber"[11] (who is a little like old Jacob Caxon in *The Antiquary*) stands for a human predicament that constantly recurs; his skill has become obsolescent, and from the care of the wigs of dignitaries, even the wig of a bishop, he is reduced to winding trout flies. He was a friend from Miss Mitford's childhood, and she writes of him in affectionate retrospect. But perhaps the "characters" that sharpen toward satire, like "The Talking Lady," are better examples of Miss Mitford's skill. The Talking Lady is not only talkative and typical; she is a complete person, and the reader feels her overwhelming presence. Yet in this sketch, and even better in "An Old Bachelor," Miss Mitford manages the difficult trick of the representation of a bore without allowing the representation itself to become boring. She may manage it better than Jane Austen does with Miss Bates in *Emma*.

Mr. Sidney, the clergyman in "An Old Bachelor," whose youth and middle years passed in the eighteenth century, could have existed only in his time and place and is so far typical; yet we come to know, "under all his polish, well covered, but not concealed, the quiet selfishness, the little whims, the precise habits, the primness and priggishness of [his] disconsolate condition." His one accomplishment is his skill at whist, and he fully respects no persons but other capital whist players; his commentary on the errors of ordinary players is made in "the calm tone of undoubted superiority with which a great critic will sometimes take a small poet . . . to task in a review." His whole career has a sort of foolish irony. Although he has been ordained, he has never functioned as a clergyman; people forget that he is one and neglect to ask him to say grace when he is their guest. He has rejected living after living in the expectation of a particular rectory he had early taken a fancy to. At last its occupant dies at a great age, and Mr. Sidney takes possession. "He had waited for this living thirty years," the sketch ends; "he did not enjoy it thirty days." Yet this footling clergyman is, among the many persons in *Our Village*, the chief representative of early nineteenth-century Anglicanism.

"The Touchy Lady"[12] is one of the best of the "characters." Although one has known touchiness like hers in persons of both sexes, one has scarcely encountered just her "ingenuity of perverseness"; nor understood so well how it must have been fostered by silly parents. That ingenuity is so great that with her no topic is safe:

> Even the Scotch novels, which she does own to reading, are no resource in her desperate case. There we are shipwrecked on the rocks of taste. A difference there is fatal. She takes to those delicious books as personal property, and spreads over them the prickly shield of her protection in the same spirit with which she appropriates her husband and her children; is huffy if you prefer Guy Mannering to the Antiquary, and quite jealous if you presume to praise Jeanie Deans; thus cutting of his Majesty's lieges from the most approved topic of discussion among civilized people, a neutral ground as open and various as the weather, and far more delightful.

But neither the Touchy Lady nor any one of Miss Mitford's other "characters" repels us. Some of them we like, some of them we are a little sorry for; all of them amuse us. She envelops them all with her charity. And since in developing them she does not face the exigencies of plot, they are likely to be more convincing representations of persons than the characters we know in the general run of novels.

Some of the "characters" are not types except as they represent country occupations—"Tom Cordery" (former poacher), for instance, or "The Mole-Catcher."[13] And within the sketches there is often a sort of miniature "character" done in a paragraph or so. Mr. Simon Shuter, the predecessor of the "Country Apothecary," is a good example. A more vivid example, in "A Christmas Party," is old Timothy, fiddler and parish drunk, who in his youth was discharged from the army in consequence of a saber cut on his skull, a cut which was thought to have left him infirm of mind—but not so infirm that he does not realize his scar makes him a privileged person, protecting him from "justice and constable, treadmill and stocks," and even from all serious disapproval. These miniature "characters" are sometimes offered as interesting in themselves, as Mr. Simon Shuter is; sometimes they have a part to play in the slight story of one of the sketches, as old Timothy does.

In some sketches the techniques of Miss Mitford's two principal genres are combined, or otherwise modified. "The Bird-Catcher," for instance, seems as it begins to be a "country walk" but then to become a "character." "Wheat-hoeing," however, dated and proceeding as a "country walk," has its final interest preempted by an account of a love affair. But a "character" as well as a "country walk" may have a love affair as its final interest: "The Rat-Catcher" seems wholly a "character" for its first six pages, but ends with the amusing love-troubles of the rat catcher and a widow. A number of the sketches are primarily accounts of simple love affairs; "Hannah" and "The Old Gipsy" are pleasant specimens of sketches that convey something of Miss Mitford's own delight in young lovers.

In all these sketches, Miss Mitford's great excellence is pictorial; as she remarks, she gets on best when she sticks to "landscape and portrait painting." Now of course literary history has much to say about the influence of the visual arts on literature in the eighteenth and early nineteenth centuries; and there is a rather wearisome convention of *Tours to* one and another scenic region and of disquisitions on the picturesque. Jane Austen, we remember, makes fun of the Tilneys, who cannot look at the countryside without deciding "on its capability of being formed into pictures." Miss Mitford had been subjected to much the same influences as the Tilneys had, but her effort is to be aware of the beauty of her own countryside and to make others aware. Yet her excellence in "landscape and portrait painting" may not be entirely accessible to us. We are generally uninterested in description *qua* description, and we do not even read it well.

Literary description once filled a need later satisfied by photography and in other ways; indeed in Miss Mitford's own time the new steel engravings in the annuals presage the displacement of descriptive writing. We need to make some effort of the historical imagination if we are to recognize and understand the pleasure that descriptive writing once gave. Miss Mitford's sketches offer a special opportunity for that imaginative effort.

Miss Mitford constantly sees the scenes and persons of *Our Village* as pictures, or makes them into pictures. In the first sketch, when she is concerned with the topography of the village, she says of her little friend Lizzy and her greyhound Mayflower playing together, "What a pretty picture they would make; what a pretty foreground they do make to the real landscape!" But within the next long sentence that landscape becomes a picture: "over every part of the picture, trees so profusely scattered that it appears like a woodland scene, with glades and villages intermixed." Mrs. Oliphant rightly thinks of the whole impression of *Our Village* as a series of "descriptions of the pretty, luxuriant, leafy landscape, in which her little pictures are enclosed."[14] Yet this persistence in describing the ordinary rural scenery of England must have required a kind of literary courage, for Miss Mitford knew that the imaginations of many of her readers had been nurtured on the portentous scenery in Mrs. Radcliffe's novels.

Miss Mitford's descriptions of persons are quite as pictorial as her descriptions of landscapes. Here is the baker's daughter in "The Two Valentines":

> Sally walks round the parish every morning, with her great basket, piled to the very brim, poised on her pretty head—now lending it the light support of one slender hand, and now of another; the dancing black eyes, and the bright blushing smile, that flash from under her burthen, as well as the perfect ease and grace with which she trips along, entirely taking away all painful impressions of drudgery or toil. She is quite a figure for the painter, is Sally North—and the gypsy knows it.

Miss Mitford often writes in painter's terms: as we have seen, persons at a distance are figures in a landscape; in "The First

Primrose" there is "a long piece of water letting light into the picture."

And, more than that, Miss Mitford, influenced by both Mrs. Radcliffe and Scott, sees scenes and persons as like the work of particular artists. Readers of Sir Walter Scott may remember how often he associates scenes in his novels with the artists appropriate for them.[15] The habit is even more persistent in Miss Mitford: "A deep, woody green lane [is] such as Hobbema or Ruysdael might have painted"; "Titian or Velazquez should be born again" to paint a young woman; a mother is like "the small Madonnas of Raphael"; a "little parlour seems made for Hogarth's old maid and her stunted footboy"; a group in a stagecoach on a hot day is "a companion picture to Hogarth's 'Afternoon' "; an assemblage of country people at a Maying is like a genre painting by Teniers.[16] Particularly when the scene described has a composition like a painting, a reference to the appropriate artist may be effective: in "The Old Gipsy" the broken banks of "a dark deep pool . . . have an air of wildness and grandeur that might have suited the pencil of Salvator Rosa." Of course to the student of literature who has had solemn instruction about the influence of certain painters on eighteenth-century sensibility the reference may seem hackneyed; but to Miss Mitford's first readers, who retained the sensibility, it was doubtless evocative enough.

Such reference to painters is comparable to literary reference in effect, and the two are sometimes used together. In "The Young Gipsy," for instance, the gipsy girl has a face like those Sir Joshua Reynolds often painted and is as artless as Shakespeare's Miranda. And a literary allusion may appear where a reference to a painter would hardly serve: A description in "The Bird-Catcher" of a valley emerging from fog moves in time and is therefore not really like a painting, but the literary allusion at the end makes for the same sort of aesthetic distance that references to painters do elsewhere.

> It was curious to observe how object after object glanced out of the vapour. First of all, the huge oak, at the corner of Farmer Locke's field, which juts out into the lane like a crag into the sea, forcing the road to wind around it, stood forth

like a hoary giant, with its head lost in the clouds; then Farmer Hewitt's great barn—the house, ricks, and stables still invisible; then a gate, and half a cow, her head being projected over it in strong relief, whilst the hinder part of her body remained in the haze; then, more and more distinctly, hedgerows, cottages, trees, and fields, until, as we reached the top of Barkham Hill, the glorious sun broke forth, and the lovely picture lay before our eyes in its soft and calm beauty, emerging gradually from the vapour that overhung it, in such manner as the image of his sleeping Geraldine is said to have been revealed to Surrey in the magic glass.

The literary allusion in the last sentence is somewhat out of the way,[17] but it makes for an evocative image, enforcing the sense of strangeness in the revelation of a familiar scene as the fog lifts. Miss Mitford's descriptions of "country scenery" are carefully done.

But Miss Mitford intends to delineate "country manners" as well as "country scenery": she shares with Scott and John Galt the impulse to record manners and customs, but she records for the most part what is immediately before her eyes, much less often what is in the span of her memory.[18] Although in "The Incendiary" there is a vivid account of the dread attending the disorders of 1831,[19] usually national events impinge very little upon the life of her village. But we know her time the better for her "characters," and her anecdotes of country people ring true and seem surely to have had their origin in life. Her accounts of farm activities, although written always from a spectator point of view, are sometimes vivid. An account of sheep-washing in "Lost and Found"[20] is a good example, and an account of women working at bean-setting in "Violeting" shows a surprisingly modern sort of sympathy for stoop-laborers.[21] Miss Mitford's record is unsystematic, and governed only by her own interest; for the most part the observation and the record come close together in time.

Miss Mitford has no great antiquarian interest, but she recognizes that her time is one of transition,[22] and that many of the customs she records are survivals that will soon pass out of use.

In her village, for instance, Valentine's Day is kept "as simply and confidingly as [by] our ancestors of old," she tells us in "The Two Valentines"; and it is still held that the first unmarried and unrelated man a maiden sees on Valentine's Day is to be her valentine—a belief which may force her to sit with her eyes closed half the morning listening for an expected voice. But Miss Mitford records old customs only in the mode in which they have survived. A reference at the beginning of "Bramley May-ing" to Irving's "delightful but somewhat fanciful writings" suggests both his influence and the different quality of her record.[23]

In "Bramley Maying" and in the later "Our Maying" Miss Mitford records the survival of a custom we know in song and story. A Maying as she knows it is "a meeting of the lads and lasses of two or three parishes," who build May-houses, "covered alleys built of green boughs," and decorated with garlands and flowers, for a dance. In "Our Maying" it is "an honest English country dance (there had been some danger of waltzing and quadrilling)." But at the Bramley Maying some young men without coats are "excluded from the dance by the disgrace of a smock-frock." "Who would have thought," Miss Mitford asks, "of etiquette finding its way into the May-houses!" There are fiddlers, a Punch and Judy show, a Frenchman with dancing dogs, and various stalls, so that the Maying has taken on some of the attributes of a fair. In "Our Maying" a cricket match is a feature of the entertainment. There is no maypole at either Maying, and the Maying in "Our Maying" is "held between hay-time and harvest"—but we remember that the rites of May were often celebrated in later months.

Perhaps surprisingly, one of the liveliest pieces in *Our Village* is "A Country Cricket Match"—and there is a good deal about cricket and the boys and young men who play it scattered about in other sketches. The cricket Miss Mitford describes is not the gentlemen's game; it is "a real solid old-fashioned match be-tween neighbouring parishes, where each attacks the other for honour and a supper, glory and half a crown a man." Her sketch is an excellent piece of sports reporting, with the slight sugges-tion of the mock-heroic that belongs to the best sports writing. Quite as lively is the account, in "A Great Farm-house," of cours-

ing with greyhounds. Miss Mitford describes that unattractive
sport with what seems an intimate and technical knowledge,
both of the dogs and of the sport itself, and without any sign of
squeamishness.

Another, and quite different interest, is the account in "The
Visit" of the estate of "a rich country gentleman of high descent
and higher attainments," who had made what had been ordinary
countryside into "a mimic forest," with laboriously constructed
eminences, prospects, "green glades, and impervious recesses,
and apparently interminable extent." "Never," Miss Mitford
says, "was the 'prophetic eye of taste' exerted with more magical
skill than in these plantations"; and our profit in her account is
that we see this "triumph of landscape gardening" through the
eye of taste of such a person as it was intended to please, see it
have "a striking air of natural beauty, developed and heightened
by the perfection of art."[24] But for all that, the admiration of
wealth and birth implicit and explicit in the sketch is a little
embarrassing to encounter; in writing it Miss Mitford was very
much a woman of her time.

Although "The Visit" picks up the vogue of landscape gardening, Miss Mitford's sketches are generally not much influenced
by the affectations of her time. But "Rosedale" ridicules one of
them amusingly. Rosedale cottage—"the very name," Miss Mitford says, "smacks of the Minerva Press"—is rented by two
young women, Londoners, one of whom has read Anna Seward's letters, and has persuaded the other to retire with her from
the world in order to live a life of simplicity, sensibility, and
independence from the other sex. They succeed but poorly in
their aims, and are the happier therefore. Miss Mitford does not
ordinarily go in for either literary or social satire, but the intent
in "Rosedale" to ridicule a fake pastoralism is natural enough to
a country gentlewoman who in the long series of sketches that
make up *Our Village* records many of the actualities of pastoral
life.

Our Village has an interesting position in literary history. Miss
Mitford lived through the period we have been used to call the
English Romantic Era. But it will hardly occur to anyone to use
the term "romantic" in reference to her sketches. She wrote

those sketches, she says in her preface, "in nearly every instance, with the closest and most resolute fidelity to the place and the people." But she adds that "if she be accused of having given a brighter aspect to her villagers than is usually met with in books," she has done so "under an intense and thankful conviction that, in every condition of life, goodness and happiness may be found by those who seek them." With that bias of selection, and with the persistent allusion to literature and the visual arts that provides a sort of aesthetic distance in *Our Village*, we cannot say that the sketches look forward to any later development we call realism. Yet they are written from no visible social theory; and the record, although highly selected, is not distorted.

Miss Mitford's bias of selection everywhere controls her subject matter, and little of sorrow, danger, or evil is allowed to enter the sketches; the notes of pain in them, Mrs. Oliphant says, "sound no harsher than a sigh."[25] The sorrow that attends our mortality of course Miss Mitford recognizes, but she does not exploit it; the death of little Lizzy, for instance, is reported in one paragraph in the introduction to the third series of sketches.[26] Miss Mitford quotes George Crabbe—"the most graphical of our poets," she calls him—with respect,[27] but she feels free to select as Crabbe could not. Her "resolute fidelity" is a fidelity only to what she chooses to represent in the life of her village.

But she is resolutely unsentimental; once, in "The Copse," after a nostalgic sentence she pulls herself up with, "But we are not to talk sentiment . . . that maudlin language." She wanted to write, she says, "without sentimentality or pathos," and if we will understand the words as the early nineteenth century understood them, we will probably agree that she succeeded. She manages to avoid self-exploitation—perhaps better than did any writer with whom she might reasonably be compared. And in a time when the novel had become the dominant literary form, she did not allow her talent to be preempted by it, but used those means of fiction that were under her control for her own purposes. The circumstances of her life gave her only limited opportunities for the observation of men and events, yet she made her "confined locality" a strength, and interested readers in it throughout five series of sketches which were reprinted in selected volumes throughout her century and into ours.

No considerations of literary history, however, will explain the interest her sketches have had for so many readers for so long a time; her readers, for the most part, have been unconcerned with literary history. They have found her a writer both sensible and sensitive, one who seemes unaffectedly to enjoy her experience. "I think that we delight to praise what we enjoy," C. S. Lewis once wrote, "because the praise not merely expresses but completes the enjoyment; it is its appointed consummation."[28] Miss Mitford praised what she enjoyed, often with skill and grace; generations of readers, starting with the praise, recovered the enjoyment.

NOTES

1. The Everyman edition of *Our Village* uses this introduction as the concluding piece of its selection of the sketches. Unless otherwise indicated, the sketches quoted or referred to in this chapter are in the Everyman edition.

2. *Our Village*, Bohn ed. (London: George Bell & Sons; vol. 1, 1879, vol. 2, 1880), 1:464. The Bohn edition in two volumes is the most nearly complete edition after the first.

3. Miss Mitford's work includes three successful tragedies and a number of volumes of verse, as well as other work in the vein of *Our Village*. She contributed to magazines and annuals, and edited the annual *Finden's Tableaux*. She ought to be remembered in American literary history for her two collections of American writing (each of three volumes) which appeared in 1830 and 1832, and her two series of children's stories by American writers in 1831 and 1832. See the bibliography in Ian Jack, *English Literature, 1815–1832*, pp. 585–86. Miss Mitford retained her interest in American writing; in the early 1850s James T. Fields was writing to her about what Hawthorne was working on. See Randall Stewart, *Nathaniel Hawthorne* (New Haven: Yale University Press, 1948), pp. 104, 123, 134. Hawthorne was pleased by her interest in his work, and wrote to Fields: "Her sketches, long ago as I read them, are as sweet in my memory as the scent of new hay" (Fields, *Yesterday with Authors* [Boston, 1872], p. 61).

4. Everyman ed., p. 333; Bohn ed., 1:417.

5. Quoted in Ian Jack, p. 339.

6. Miss Mitford quotes *The Natural History of Selborne* appositely (see Everyman ed., p. 22; Bohn ed., 1: 204), and she has so considerable an interest in natural history that she sometimes attaches a note on some

natural phenomenon to a sketch with which it is only tenuously connected (see Everyman ed., pp. 57 and 211). There is also reference of a rather general sort to Isaac Walton.

7. See [Margaret Oliphant], "Miss Austen and Miss Mitford," *Blackwood's Edinburgh Magazine* 107 (1870): 293–97.

8. Quoted in Ian Jack, p. 340.

9. *Jane Austen and Her Art*, p. 10. It is worth noting that Miss Lascelles's examples—Mrs. Grant's *Letters* and the novels of Mrs. Radcliffe, Fanny Burney, and Maria Edgeworth (and later of George Eliot)—are all the work of women writers.

10. Miss Mitford once wrote: "I have begun two [novels] and got on very well as long as I stuck to landscape and portrait painting; but when I was obliged to make my pictures walk out of their frames and speak for themselves, when I came to the action, I was foundered" (quoted in Ian Jack, p. 342).

11. Bohn ed., 2: 31–40.

12. Bohn ed., 1: 366–72.

13. John Masefield remembered the occupation of mole-catcher persisting to the time of his youth. See *Grace Before Ploughing* (New York: MacMillan, 1966), pp. 36–38.

14. "Miss Austen and Miss Mitford," p. 307.

15. Readers may recall such instances as these: in *Guy Mannering*, the gipsies whom the Laird of Ellangowen expels "would have been an excellent subject for the pencil of Calotte" (chap. 8); in *The Antiquary*, the funeral of Steenie Mucklebackit is "a scene, which our Wilkie alone could have painted"; in the Mucklebackit cottage, old Elspeth's face is "illuminated, in the way that Rembrandt would have chosen" by the light from an opened window (chaps. 31 and 32).

16. Everyman ed., pp. 13, 112, 307, 6, 91, 236.

17. In an episode in Thomas Nashe's *The Unfortunate Traveller* (1594), Surrey and Jack Wilton are said to have seen a representation of Geraldine in Cornelius Agrippa's magic glass. See *The Unfortunate Traveller*, ed. John Berryman (New York: Putnam's, 1960), pp. 76–77.

18. In "The General and His Lady" there is an amusing retrospective account of the military excitement at the time of the threat of a French invasion. It reminds one a little of the account of Ballie Littlejohn in *The Antiquary*.

19. Bohn ed., 2: 318–24.

20. Bohn ed., 2: 132–33.

21. "What work bean-setting is! What a reverse of the position assigned to man to distinguish him from the beasts of the field! Only think of stooping for six, eight, ten hours a day, drilling holes in the earth with a little stick, and then dropping in the beans one by one!

They are paid according to the quantity they plant: and some of the poor women used to be accused of clumping them—that is to say, of dropping more than one bean into a hole. It seems to me, considering the temptation, that not to clump is to be at the very pinnacle of human virtue."

22. See "Ghost Stories" in Bohn ed., 2: 291–93.

23. Bohn ed., 1: 142. See "May-Day Customs" and "May-Day" in Irving's *Bracebridge Hall*.

24. To say that an estate had been developed so that its natural beauty was heightened by art was the proper praise. Compare a passage in Jane Austen's account of Elizabeth's visit to Pemberley: "A stream of some natural importance was swelled into greater, but without any artificial appearance. Its banks were neither formal, nor falsely adorned. Elizabeth was delighted. She had never seen a place for which nature had done more, or where natural beauty had been so little counteracted by an awkward taste." See *Pride and Prejudice*, ed. R. W. Chapman (Oxford edition), p. 245.

25. "Miss Austen and Miss Mitford," p. 308.

26. Bohn ed., 1: 462–63.

27. Bohn ed., 1: 386; 2: 193–94.

28. C. S. Lewis, *Reflections on the Psalms* (New York: Harcourt, Brace and Company, 1958), p. 95.

9

Fiction in a New Nation: The Naturalization of Legend

The British writers we have been considering were all imaginatively at home in their regions; and in their new attempts with the means of fiction they worked out from conventions long and comfortably established. Fiction writers in the United States in the same period, although intensely conscious of their status as American writers, still had no conventions to work with or to work out from but British conventions. The problem was, of course, that British fictional conventions had developed in a society quite different from that of the new nation. Indeed, there was a respectable body of opinion which held that the United States was too young a country to have an imaginative literature, and even that it could hardly develop one. The best of our early writers felt the difficulty, and in essays, addresses, and periodicals the matter was gravely discussed.[1]

In the third of his "Lectures on Poetry," William Cullen Bryant considers the resources for literature in the United States. It is contended, he recognizes, that the new nation lacks, among other things, "the national supersitions which linger yet in every district of Europe, and the legends of distant and dark ages and of wild and unsettled times of which the old world reminds you at every step." But he points out that whenever literature has successfully used such material, it has used for the most part "those superstitions which exist rather in tradition than in serious belief"; and that "it is especially the privilege of an age which has no engrossing superstitions of its own, to make use in its poetry of those of past ages; to levy contributions from the credulity of all time."[2] Bryant is speaking in 1826, and he seems to be suggesting a resource to American writers. But it

must have occurred to him that the best pieces of short fiction by Americans before 1826 were examples of the successful use of the very resource he was suggesting.

Everyone knows that both Washington Irving's "Rip Van Winkle" and his "Legend of Sleepy Hollow" (*Sketch Book*, 1819–20) have German legends at their cores, although the legends are so thoroughly acclimated to the Hudson River region and adapted to its history that in reading the tales we hardly distinguish their cores. We here consider two tales in which the adaptation of legend is more obvious and the borrowed legend—that of the *Flying Dutchman*—better known. One of them is Irving's own "The Storm-Ship"; the other, "Peter Rugg, the Missing Man," is by William Austin, who—for this tale only—exhibits a remarkable skill. Irving says of his Squire Bracebridge that "whenever he read any legend of a striking nature, he endeavored to transplant it, and give it a local habitation among the scenes of his boyhood." Irving and Austin are doing in our early literature what the Squire did in his little domain: they are transplanting a legend and supplying American places and experience with legendary associations thereby.

The *Flying Dutchman* legend has had a long history and a wide appeal. It must have had its origin in the conviction of sailors that they saw a phantom ship in storm clouds around the Cape of Good Hope. Our writers come to the legend before it had been overelaborated,[3] and they start with the legend itself. Our two tales, however different they are in tone and setting, are versions, not perversions, of the legend, and each of them brings it to American experience.[4]

"The Storm-Ship" is a fine little tale, a few pages in the best vein of Knickerbocker's *A History of New York*. But since it is an interpolated tale in the little-read "Dolph Heyliger" (*Bracebridge Hall*, 1822), not everyone who would enjoy it knows it. It has a most complicated frame. When in *Bracebridge Hall* it becomes Geoffrey Crayon's turn to tell a story, he instead reads a manuscript which, he says, was found among Diedrich Knickerbocker's papers. The manuscript begins with an introductory piece in which Diedrich ascribes the tale he is about to record, "Dolph Heyliger," to one "John Josse Vandermoere, a pleasant gossiping man, whose whole life was spent in hearing and telling the news of the province," and he avers that he is setting it down, as well as he can, in Vandermoere's own words. Within "Dolph Heyliger," after Dolph has been rescued by Antony Vander Heyden, the conversation turns to mysterious difficulties in the navigation of the Hudson River, and Vander Heyden undertakes to tell the story of the Storm-Ship, as far as he can "in the very words in which it had been written out by Mynheer Selyne, an early poet of the New Nederlandts." Mynheer Selyne (or Selyns) is the name of a real personage, the first settled minister of Brooklyn. He did write some poems, and Irving knew them.[5]

As we have seen in his mysterious portrait tales, Irving delighted in putting his tales in complex frames, and positing narrators behind the one he is using to tell the tale. Here there is imaginative point in so doing, for the frame and the succession of narrators represent the transmission of a legend. Perhaps Irving as author does not quite disappear, but he is at least pretty well obscured behind his five narrator-figures. And if Irving had written only this one tale in the Knickerbocker vein, as Scott wrote only one tale with Wandering Willie as narrator, we might think of it as seeming to have an existence quite apart from Irving.

The tale opens with an account of a tremendous thunderstorm in New Amsterdam and with homely detail about it: the Dutch housewives put a shoe on the iron point of every bedpost; Garret Van Horne's chimney is struck by lightning; Doffue Mildeberger is struck speechless from his bald-faced mare. According to the Aristotelian principle, this is the sort of detail that, instinctively taken as truth by the reader, carries the marvellous along with it into imaginative credence.

Just after the storm there appears a mysterious ship. The sentinel who first sights her says it is "as if she had come out of the bosom of the black thunder-cloud." She stands up the bay, and the citizens at first suppose she is their yearly ship from Holland, a little out of the time in which she was expected. But it is soon apparent that the ship is more mysterious than that. The old seamen fall into a dispute about her; and the harbor master, Hans Van Pelt, "the nautical oracle of the place," will at first give no opinion. The alarm is so great that a gun is brought to bear upon the ship, but when it is fired the shot seems to pass through her harmlessly. With all sails set, she sails "right against wind and tide."

Hans Van Pelt orders out a boat, but his oarsmen somehow cannot get to the ship; some cynical persons say that it is because they are too fat and short-winded. They get close enough, however, to see that she is manned by a crew dressed in the Dutch fashion, all standing still as statues. She keeps up the river until she fades from sight, "like a little white cloud melting away in the summer sky." The governor—he is Wouter Van Twiller, known as the Doubter, whom we remember from Knickerbocker's *History*—is thrown into "one of the deepest doubts that ever beset him in the whole course of his administration." But his doubt is not much greater than that of the citizens. Continual reports of sightings of the mysterious ship on the Hudson only deepen the mystery. She suddenly appears, always sailing against the wind. Her appearances are always "just after, or just before, or just in the midst of, unruly weather." Skippers and voyagers on the Hudson come to call her the Storm-Ship.

The behavior of the Storm-Ship, from her first appearance as if from a storm cloud to her appearances on the Hudson, seem to identify her as the *Flying Dutchman*; and indeed the nautical oracle, Hans Van Pelt, "who had been more than once to the Dutch colony at the Cape of Good Hope," comes to insist that she must be that specter ship which had long haunted Table Bay. But so that the legend may be the more thoroughly naturalized, Irving is careful to suggest alternate possibilities. Some recall the legends of ships off the New England coast manned by witches and goblins. Another explanation which, although it has little weight with the governor, has wide acceptance is that the ship must be the specter of the *Half-Moon*, Hendrick Hudson's ship, which had, it is remembered, run aground in the upper part of the river; indeed, "it had already been reported, that Hendrick Hudson and his crew haunted the Kaatskill Mountain"—as we, who have read "Rip Van Winkle," well know. But the *Flying Dutchman* legend is returned to at the end of the tale; Vander Heyden says in conclusion that his source, Selyne, affirms that the Storm-Ship came "from some old ghost-ridden country of Europe."

The Storm-Ship continues to be a matter of popular belief and marvellous anecdote even down to the time of the capture of New Amsterdam by English forces, and her appearances just before that time are taken as omens. It is said by persons who live along the Hudson that she still appears, and though the narrator doubts that, he is certain that mysterious things do happen on the Hudson, things that are connected in many minds with the old story. In particular there are the doings "of a little bulbous-bottomed Dutch goblin, in trunk hose and sugar-loafed hat, with a speaking trumpet in his hand, which they say keeps about the Dunderburg." He and his crew plague the Dutch river captains with grotesque practical jokes but, apparently, do them no real harm. As he had in "Rip Van Winkle," Irving here enjoys suggesting a continuing local habitation for his legend. And in that William Austin in his "Peter Rugg, the Missing Man" follows him.

"Peter Rugg, the Missing Man" was first printed in 1824 in Joseph T. Buckingham's newspaper, the *New England Galaxy*. It appeared anonymously, and apparently Buckingham himself did not know its authorship for some time. But it was familiarly alluded to soon after its first printing, and reprinted in other periodicals (there was even a spurious sequel) and, by 1827, in two gift books. "This article," Buckingham wrote in his *Personal Memoir*, "was reprinted in other papers and books and read more than any newspaper communication that has fallen within my knowledge." William Austin's authorship was established in 1841 when the tale was reprinted and ascribed to him in *The Boston Book*, edited by George S. Hillard. After that the tale was at least five times reprinted by 1884, although in 1888 Colonel Thomas Wentworth Higginson, in an article he called "William Austin: A Precursor of Hawthorne,"[6] seems to consider himself a rediscoverer of Austin's tale. In a letter of 1888 Higginson urged Edmund Clarence Stedman to include it in the Stedman and Hutchinson *Library of American Literature*, which Stedman had already done.[7] With its appearance there in 1889 it in some sort entered the canon of American literature, although it remains, I believe, less well known than a good many tales much inferior to it.

William Austin (1778–1841) was a successful Boston lawyer and legislator. As a young man he had written *Letters from London*

(1804), a record of his observations as a law student at Lincoln's Inn, which was apparently well received. After "Peter Rugg" he wrote a not-very-successful continuation of the tale, and five other tales.[8] None of them is now much remembered nor much deserves to be. It is not easy to account for "Peter Rugg." I suspect that we could find a number of young New England lawyers in Austin's time with literary ambitions which they abandoned as their professional responsibilities increased—William Howard Gardiner is an example. But Austin's tales were printed and doubtless written in his maturity, and apparently as a recreation; there is no sign that he attached any great importance to them. Yet we cannot say that "Peter Rugg" is just a fluke; so skillful and calculated a tale does not come by happy accident. Possibly a professional writer would not quite have dared, as Austin does, to bring the *Flying Dutchman* legend to land; yet it is a great literary skill that accomplishes the transshipment, and that makes it imaginatively acceptable.

The tale professes to be a report by one Jonathan Dunwell of New York to a Mr. Hermann Krauff—rather a formal report. Austin gives to Jonathan Dunwell's narrative an air of the dispassionate presentation of evidence without seeming to urge it that may remind us a little of Daniel Defoe's "True Relation of the Apparition of one Mrs. Veal." And Dunwell is made to take the greatest care with topography, so that Austin's first readers would have known the highways upon which Peter Rugg was encountered, and would have been familiar with such taverns and hotels as those in which conversations about him took place. Austin is busy about supplying legendary associations for a wide region, and the precision of reference does much to give his tale an air of authenticity.

Jonathan Dunwell, however objective his account, still emerges for us clearly. He is a Yankee; Austin probably chose his first name to suggest his Yankee nature. He is hard-headed, or would like to think himself so. He has a Yankee curiosity, and even an unacknowledged appetite for the marvellous. Since he is man of good address, he moves easily through his investigations. But he is a little embarrassed by the wonders they turn up. The matter-of-fact efficiency of his report, although appropriate to his nature and, we infer, to his relationship with Krauff, seems also defensive. He is highly literate, but Austin makes sure that he does not write with any particular grace; he is not a literary person.

Our information about Peter Rugg comes to us partly through Dunwell's account of his own observations, partly through his record of the testimony of his informants, so that the method simulates the way in which we combine information in our actual experience. Although Austin does not separate them, the tale develops in four clearly distinct sections. Each successive section builds upon the one preceding, confirming and extending our knowledge of Rugg. Together the four sections are an account of an inquiry that moves forward through more than three years,[9] but which moves backward into Rugg's history until at last we have the text of the "fatal oath," so closely parallel to that of the skipper of the *Flying Dutchman* that the connection must be entirely clear. But it would be an inattentive or an uninformed reader who, in reading the first section and learning that Rugg was never seen except in storms, did not suspect some connection with the *Flying Dutchman* legend.

Dunwell opens his report with an account of a journey from Providence to Boston in the summer of 1820. He was sitting with the driver of the stage, he says, when, about ten miles out of Providence, "the horses suddenly threw their ears on their necks, as flat as a hare's." Although there was not a cloud in the sky, the driver explained that the horses were aware of what he called the "storm breeder." It is a skillful choice of initial incident, for the horses may be supposed to have acted from instinct (later we learn that a peddler's horse had acted just in the same way). "Presently," Dunwell continues, "a man with a child beside him, with a large black horse, and a weather-beaten chair, once built for a chaise body, passed in great haste, apparently at the rate of twelve miles an hour." A storm cloud followed the carriage as the driver had predicted, and he affirmed that "every flash of lightning near its centre discovered to him distinctly the form of a man sitting in an open carriage drawn by a black horse." But Dunwell does not accept that: "It is a very common thing," he remarks, "for the imagination to paint for the senses, both in the visible and the invisible world"; here, as often, the testimony recorded is partially discredited, although it yet may affect the reader.[10] When a little later the stage stopped at a tavern, Dunwell heard a peddler say that he had encountered the man and his carriage in four different states within a fortnight, that each time the man had asked the way to Boston, and that each time he had himself been caught in a thunder-shower. The man and his horse did not look to him, he said, "as if they belonged to this world."

In the second section of his report, Dunwell recounts events more than three years later than his first sight of the mysterious figure and his equipage. He was standing one day at the doorstep of a hotel in Hartford and heard a man say: "There goes Peter Rugg and his child! he looks wet and weary, and farther from Boston than ever." Dunwell, who realized that the man was speaking of the figure he himself had seen on the Providence-Boston road (it is the first time the name Peter Rugg appears in the tale), took the opportunity to accost him. Rugg asked to be directed to Boston, and told Dunwell that he lived on Middle Street there, and that he did not quite know when he had left Boston: "I cannot tell precisely," he said, "it seems a considerable time." Rugg had supposed, it became clear, that he was in Newburyport, Massachusetts, and that he had been following the Merrimack River. "Have the rivers, too," Rugg asked, "changed their courses, as the cities have changed places? . . . Ah, that fatal oath!" And his impatient horse carried him away. We may guess the nature of that oath; we are not yet told what it was.

Dunwell now had one clue to Rugg's past, and a hint of the inception of his troubles. Soon after his interview with Rugg in Hartford, Dunwell went to Boston: the third section of his report recounts his investigations there. He found an elderly Mrs. Croft, who had lived for twenty years in the Middle Street house once occupied by the Rugg family. Only the summer before a stranger, accompanied by a little girl and driving a black horse, had inquired of her about Mrs. Rugg and about persons and places of which she knew nothing; she had assured him, for instance, that there was no King Street in Boston. "City of Boston it may be," the stranger had concluded, "but it is not the Boston where I live"; and he had let his impatient horse—which he seemed never fully to control—take him away. Mrs. Croft sent Dunwell to the ancient James Felt, antiquarian of the neighborhood, who remembered Rugg and his disappearance, which he placed about the time of the Boston Massacre in 1770. Dunwell, although he seems to accept the 1770 date, thinks Felt in his dotage and his testimony undependable.

Now to this point in his report, Dunwell has seemed not at all a credulous person. The reader accepts fully what he records of his own immediate knowledge of Rugg, and is aware that the testimony of his informants seems generally to agree, and that, indeed, from all the knowledge he has, a pattern is emerging— although Dunwell carefully refrains from pointing it out. What the reader knows, or thinks he knows, seems to require a preter- natural explanation, but when Dunwell comes to it in the con- cluding section of the tale, he merely records, without comment or interruption, the story of a gentleman designated only as "one of the company" with whom Dunwell had spent the evening after his interview with Mrs. Croft. This gentleman repeats what his grandfather used to tell "as though he seriously believed his own story"; his way of narration is much more vivid than Dun- well's. The device works; the story seems to corroborate the preternatural explanation that has already emerged in the reader's mind.

This informant's grandfather had known Rugg as "a good sort of man," but subject to ungovernable and terribly profane fits of passion. One autumn day, Rugg and his little daughter "in his own chair, with a fine large bay horse" (not, be it noted, a black horse) had driven to Concord, and on their return had been overtaken by a storm "in Menotomy (now West Cambridge)." Rugg was strongly urged by a friend to stay the night, but an- swered in a passion: " *'Let the storm increase,'* said Rugg, with a fearful oath, *'I will see home tonight, in spite of the last tempest! or may I never see home.'* " Rugg drove away, and never reached home. Thereafter for a while his neighbors fancied they heard on stormy nights the familiar tread of Rugg's horse, and once, watching with lanterns, saw Rugg passing his own house, vainly trying to rein in his horse. Later they heard rumors of him at widely separated places in New England. It was known, too, that the toll-gatherer at Charleston bridge, exasperated by the fre- quent passage on stormy nights of an equipage that went over the bridge in utter contempt of toll, had thrown a stool directly through the appearance of a horse, presumably Rugg's. But the toll-gatherer would never say whether or not he had seen the equipage again.

"This, sir," Dunwell concludes his report, "is all that I could learn of Peter Rugg in Boston." Like Irving and like Hawthorne, Austin knows how to let the distinctly preternatural come into a tale only by unvouched-for report.

The literary history of "Peter Rugg, the Missing Man" has two striking features. One is, of course, the currency and the persistence of the tale without the attention of its author or the support of his other work, and without the promotion of a publisher; the tale persisted in itself. The other is the way in which the tale assumed the status of a piece of folklore. As early as 1842 Hawthorne uses the figure of Peter Rugg in his "Virtuoso's Collection" as if he were confident that all his readers would recognize it. Perhaps the tale did in some sense become folklore; indeed Amy Lowell tells us that she knew an oral version of the story of Peter Rugg long before she had ever heard of William Austin.[11] Miss Lowell and Louise Imogen Guiney have used the story much as they might have used a folk tale, although the reader may find their poems disappointing.[12] And there is, too, a fine tale by the historian of American journalism, Frank Luther Mott, in which Peter Rugg travels Kansas roads in a Model T Ford.[13] "Peter Rugg, the Missing Man" is not folklore, but a conscious adaptation of a European legend to American experience; yet it may not be altogether inappropriate that it is reprinted in such collections as B. A. Botkin's *A Treasury of American Folklore*.

That the tale is a successful adaptation of a legend to American experience helps to account for its literary history. Although readers may not quite formulate what they sense in it, the tale is highly representative. Rugg's experience seems to stand for the restless movement and the rootlessness that from the beginning have been qualities of American life. Dunwell is made to say: "If Peter Rugg, thought I, has been travelling since the Boston massacre, there is no reason why he should not travel to the end of time. If the present generation know little of him, the next will know less, and Peter and his child will have no hold on this

world." Austin was writing for a generation that, however shrilly
confident some its members now seem to us, knew itself cut off
from its past and its cultural home.

"Peter Rugg, the Missing Man" and "The Storm-Ship," along
with "Rip Van Winkle" and "The Legend of Sleepy Hollow," are
the masterpieces in this kind. Irving does naturalize another
European legend in "The Devil and Tom Walker" (*Tales of a
Traveller*, 1824), a tale which also purports to be part of the
Knickerbocker papers. The excellence of the tale is primarily in
the narrator, for whom a character emerges clearly. He is at
once delighted with his material and sceptical of it; aware of the
way in which he is relocating the Faust story in the region of
Boston in the second quarter of the eighteenth century, and
amused by what he is doing. Nathaniel Hawthorne, too, has one
tale in this kind; his "Drowne's Wooden Image" (1844) is, at least
by its publication date, a very late example. In it Hawthorne
adapts the Pygmalion story to the Boston of the 1770s and, with
an admirable literary tact, makes it at home there.[14] The wonder
is, it seems to me, how thoroughly a part of their new environment all the old stories seem, how much a part of American
imaginative experience they become.

But this early response to the demand for a national literature
is of course a very limited one, incapable of much development
or of satisfying American readers very long. Even before the
publication of *The Sketch Book*, indeed soon after the appearance
of Scott's *Waverley*, literary thinkers had begun to discuss the
resources in American history and experience (including indigenous American legends) available to American writers, and to
urge their use. The discussion was widespread in periodicals, but
most significant in the *North American Review*, which more than
other publications gathered a school of critics—relatively young
men for the most part, some of whom we know for their later
accomplishments. One of them, Willard Phillips, compares "the
author of any literary work, upon a subject peculiar to ourselves,
and truly American" to the pioneer who opens up new territory
for homes and farms; such a writer "peoples the regions of fancy
and memory" (18 [1824]: 314). And the pioneering was often
the joint effort of fiction writers and critics.

William Tudor, the first editor of the *North American Review,*
may be said to begin the discussion of American materials in
1815, the *Review*'s first year. The materials for an American
literature, Tudor thinks, will come out of the period from the
close of the sixteenth century to the middle of the eighteenth
century. Although he thinks Indians will be the classic subject
for American writers, he does not think they will be the only
subject, and indeed makes suggestions from Puritan history.
"Perilous and romantick adventures, figurative and eloquent
harangues, strong contrasts and important interests," Tudor
writes, "are as frequent in this portion of history, as the theatre
on which these events were performed is abundant in grand and
beautiful scenery" (2: 28–29).

Tudor's sentence illustrates not only the influence of Scott,
but that of the Associationism of Archibald Alison, which held
that the interest of scenery depends not only on color and con-
formation, but particularly upon the associations that the reader
can bring to it. Many Americans had felt that the beauty of
American scenery was "the beauty of a face without expression,"[15] that it lacked connection with human life and history.
The *Review* critics contended that place and story might easily be
connected, that American experience was after all a rich experience.

The *Review* critics, therefore, took it as particularly their function to point out what in American experience was usable for the
fiction writer, sometimes specifically what incidents and persons
he might use. John Gorham Palfrey, for instance, contended
that American materials were in at least one respect better than
those Scott had used: "We had the same puritan character of
stern, romantic enthusiasm of which, in the Scottish novels, such
effective use is made, but inpressed here on the whole face of
society, and sublimed to a degree which it never elsewhere
reached" (12 [1821]: 480). And Palfrey suggests a number of
personages from the history of the Bay Colony that should
interest the fiction writer, some of whom Hawthorne did use
more than a decade later.

But the publication of James Fenimore Cooper's *The Spy* in
1821 seemed the first clear proof that the literary doctrines of
the *North American Review* could come to successful practice; Irv-

ing's use of American materials was not, apparently, quite convincing to the *Review* critics. It is in his review of *The Spy* that William Howard Gardiner makes his famous statement of the three epochs of American history useful to the fiction writer: "the times just succeeding the first settlements—the æra of the Indian wars, which lie scattered along a considerable period—and the revolution" (15 [1822]: 255). But this division of history had been at least implicit in previous discussion; and there had been questioning about which epoch furnished the best material: Tudor, for instance, thought the Revolution too recent for literary use. Although Gardiner still thinks "our earlier history" more prolific for the fiction writer, Cooper, he believes, has succeeded with material from the Revolution (p. 281).

Gardiner, to be sure, finds a great deal to object to in *The Spy*. But Cooper has nevertheless "laid the foundations of American romance, and is really the first who has deserved the appellation of distinguished American novel writer" (p. 281). Consequently there is much to hope for, and Gardiner uses much of his space, not on *The Spy*, but on the resources in American experience that the fiction writer might use. "What," he asks, "would not the author of Waverley make of such materials?" (p. 257). Some of the *North American Review* critics, and indeed other Americans, came close to defining fiction by the characteristics of the Waverley novels.

By 1830 the *North American Review* critics had turned to other interests, but the influence of their discussion of American materials persisted. We shall be considering that influence as it manifests itself in the short fiction of William Leete Stone and of Nathaniel Hawthorne in the 1830s, and later—in curious ways—in Hawthorne's romances.

NOTES

1. This discussion is represented in Robert E. Spiller, ed., *The American Literary Revolution, 1783–1837* (New York: Doubleday, 1967).

2. Bryant, *Prose Writings*, ed. Parke Godwin (New York: Appleton, 1901), 1: 24–31.

3. Captain Marryat's *The Phantom Ship* was published in 1839; Richard Wagner's *Der fliegende Holländer* was produced in 1843.

4. The legend has had other literary uses in America. Irving himself

has a minuscule version of it in a paragraph of "A Chronicle of Wolfert's Roost." Hawthorne, in "The Canal Boat," makes his Story Teller fancy that a rusty old scow is the Erie Canal equivalent of the *Flying Dutchman*. Mark Twain has a fine little anecdote in which the legend is transshipped from the *Flying Dutchman* to a river boat (*Life on the Mississippi*, chap. 17).

5. Henricus Selyns (1636–1701) was minister of Brooklyn 1660–64 and minister in New York 1682–1701. He was an active and apparently an admirable man, who faced many difficulties in his ministries. A selection of his poems in Dutch with English translations and a memoir appear in Henry C. Murphy, *Anthology of New Netherland*, Bradford Club Series (New York, 1865). Irving borrowed the manuscript volume of Selyns's poems from its owner while he was writing Knickerbocker's *History of New York*. See a letter from Irving quoted in Murphy, pp. 14–15. Selyns's name may appear as Selijns.

6. *Independent* 40 (1888): 385–86; rpt. in Walter Austin, *William Austin: The Creator of Peter Rugg* (Boston: Marshall Jones Company, 1925), pp. 121–26.

7. See Walter Austin, pp. v, 116–20, 126–28, and 318.

8. Walter Austin reprints "Peter Rugg, the Missing Man," its continuation, "Further Account of Peter Rugg," and three other tales: "The Late Joseph Natterstrom," "Martha Gardner, or Moral Reaction," and "The Man with the Cloaks."

9. Since we are told that Dunwell's first sight of Rugg was in 1820 and that his inquiries extended over more than three years, the first readers of the tale in 1824 could be expected to suppose that they were getting Dunwell's report as soon as it could be printed.

10. It is in this quality that Higginson thinks Hawthorne most resembles Austin.

11. *Legends* (Boston: Houghton Mifflin, 1921), p. xiii.

12. Miss Lowell's "Before the Storm: The Legend of Peter Rugg" is in *Legends* and is reprinted in Walter Austin, pp. 153–59. Miss Guiney's "Peter Rugg the Bostonian" appeared in both the *Independent* and *Scribner's Magazine* in 1891 and is reprinted in Walter Austin, pp. 146–52.

13. *Saturday Evening Post Stories, 1950* (New York: Random House, 1951), pp. 155–65.

14. "Drowne's Wooden Image" is, Hawthorne says, the tale of "a modern Pygmalion in the person of a Yankee mechanic"—that is, in the person of a woodcarver who does ships' figureheads.

15. The expression is Bryant's as he sums up the attitudes of those who despair of an American literature. The idea emerges, for instance,

even from Irving, who in "The Author's Account of Himself" in the *Sketch Book*, writes: "I visited various parts of my country; and had I been merely a lover of fine scenery, I should have felt little desire to seek elsewhere its gratification. . . . But Europe held forth the charms of storied and poetical association. . . . Her very ruins told the history of times gone by, and every mouldering stone was a chronicle."

10

Templeton,
Late December 1793
–October 1794

William Howard Gardiner's exultant review of *The Spy* was the high point of the discussion of the possibility of fiction in the new nation, and, what was more important to James Fenimore Cooper, the success of *The Spy* (1821) was a clear indication that he could become a professional writer of fiction. It might have been expected, therefore, that Cooper in his next novel would try to repeat his success in the same kind. But the unpredictable Cooper took a different tack and wrote *The Pioneers*, he asserts in his preface, exclusively to please himself. Yet Cooper's change of direction was not mere whim, and Gardiner himself approved it.[1]

Precaution (1820), Cooper's first novel, was an attempt to portray English social life, and it was a failure, even in Cooper's own estimation. But the failure pointed Cooper toward the discovery of his great resources in American social history. His third novel, *The Pioneers* (1823), is a novel of American character and manners, and in it he uses the materials of his own boyhood experience in Cooperstown, New York, setting the date of the action back somewhat to the early days of the settlement, but only a little before the time of his own memories of the place.

Like many another novelist, Cooper has his greatest success in the use of his own early experience. He uses it extensively and with some literalness; he wrote to John Murray, his London publisher: "Perhaps [I] have confined myself too much to describing the scenes of my own youth. . . . If there be any virtue in truth, the pictures are very faithful."[2] Fortunately Cooper's early experience came on the New York frontier where the American character was still fluid and forming. More than that, in setting the action at a time when the new settlement was about seven years old, Cooper fixes upon the significant period in which what had been a hunter's and trapper's frontier was just becoming a farming frontier—but had not quite become one, for in the novel the settlers' money income still is largely from forest products: maple sugar, lumber, potash. *The Pioneers* has a feeling for period comparable to that in the best of the Waverley novels.

Cooper, whatever he lacked of the equipment of a great novelist—certainly he never learned to write with grace—had an eye for subject matter. Before William Cullen Bryant affirmed in his review of *Redwood* the advantages for fiction of the variety in the life, character, and national origins of Americans, Cooper had realized them. On his title page, he designated his novel "A Descriptive Tale," and he used as an epigraph some verses from James Kirke Paulding's *The Backwoodsman* (1818):

> Extremes of habits, manners, time and space,
> Brought close together, here stood face to face,
> And gave at once a contrast to the view,
> That other lands and ages never knew.

The verses are entirely appropriate to Cooper's intention, an intention that may be obscured for us because the novel introduces Natty Bumppo, and because it became the fourth novel in the Leather-stocking epic series, so that we tend to think of it in a context Cooper had not yet imagined when he wrote it.

Cooper's novel of American character and manners is curiously influenced in its inception by Washington Irving's narrative of the Christmas visit to the Bracebridge family and the church service during it in *The Sketch Book* (1818–20), and perhaps within the time of its composition by *Bracebridge Hall* (1822), of which Cooper seems to have had an advance review copy.[3] Squire Bracebridge is an English landed proprietor whose values and interests are largely obsolescent in his own day; Judge Temple is an American landed proprietor very much the product of his time and place. One can sense Cooper considering the likenesses and differences between the two. Even the names Temple and Templeton seem to have been suggested by the name of Squire Bracebridge's ward, Julia Templeton. And for one of his major characters, Cooper has an indebtedness to

Irving that almost amounts to imitation. Although Richard Jones, Judge Temple's busy cousin, has a prototype in Richard Smith of Cooperstown, in the early chapters of the novel he is clearly also patterned on Mr. Simon Bracebridge, the Squire's "factotum," only given a much larger measure of conceit, and made a broadly comic figure. This time Cooper seems not to have been writing in rivalry with another book; he seems, rather, to have been drawing on Irving and, even though Irving writes of so different a society, trying to use his ways of making character and manners emerge in fiction.

This relationship to Irving's work is clearest early in *The Pioneers*. The first nineteen chapters (out of forty-one) recount the events of the day before Christmas, Christmas Eve, Christmas day, and the day thereafter of 1793. They are busy chapters and full of incident. They do adumbrate—Cooper would have liked the word—the mystery of the identity of the young man called Oliver Edwards; and chapter 2 tells us of Marmaduke Temple's early history and his friendship with Edward Effingham and business relations with him—a preparation for the denouement. Beyond that, there is little concern in these early chapters for what is to be the plot of the novel. What Cooper is busy about is representing to us (by my count) twenty named characters, all of whom emerge clearly enough, and all of whom are to appear in subsequent action. Could he have succeeded in what he seems to attempt and managed to make their speech convincing, his achievement would be comparable to that of Scott or Maria Edgeworth. But American dialects in such a community as Templeton offered problems different from any they had to cope with, and far more difficult.

Cooper endeavors to represent Templeton as a community, or at least to represent the men of Templeton in a community, for beside the two young women among the leading characters, one remembers only two other women who are particularized. He has therefore what he calls a motley dramatis personae—all of whom have origins elsewhere, of course, in northern Europe, in New England, and for the solid core of citizens, in the middle states. They make up a community of hopeful people; they live in a rude abundance; the settlement is young and prosperous. In his commemorative address for Cooper, Byrant remembered

The Pioneers as idyllic, and Cooper in it as "the poet of rural life in this country—our Hesiod, our Theocritus, except that he writes without the restraint of numbers, and is a greater poet than they."[4] And the account of the progress of the seasons which marks off the progress of the action of the novel does have some analogy with James Thomson's *Seasons*.[5] But the citizens of Templeton, although they have their virtues, are not characters in an idyl. They are often contentious, often suspicious of one another, always bent on gain; and in them what we have been taught to think of as frontier self-reliance manifests itself as an endemic boastfulness.

Cooper in *The Pioneers*, and particularly in chapters 1–19, conveys a sense of community largely by the way in which he moves his characters about and groups them. They are moved and grouped in a firmly drawn world; we see the surrounding landscape from several vantages; we move through new streets and past new structures thoroughly realized. Cooper knows the representative value of places and things. The description of the furnishings and art objects in the Temple house[6] has, I think, no rival in American fiction until Huck's description of the Grangerford house in *Adventures of Huckelberry Finn*. And within these first nineteen chapters there are set pieces with which Cooper takes particular care. By far the most interesting of them is the account in chapter 11 of Mr. Grant's service of Evening Prayer on Christmas Eve for a congregation unused to liturgy. The account is, we are told, a reflection of the efforts of Cooper's father to establish an Episcopal church in the early days of Cooperstown.

Although Richard Jones and Hiram Doolittle, who passes for an architect, are collaborating on a church building to be called the "New St. Paul's,"[7] the edifice is unfinished, and the service is held in the "Academy," a cheerless hall made ready as best may be for the occasion. The whole of the various population of Templeton—including representatives of "half the nations of northern Europe"—attend, dressed in their various best. They look on and listen respectfully in an atmosphere of painfully reserved judgment, while Mr. Grant has certain liturgical difficulties. Jones is to serve as clerk, but "something unfortunately striking the mind of Richard as incomplete," he tiptoes out of the hall, leaving Mr. Grant without responses until his daughter Louisa and Edwards come to his rescue. The congregation cannot be brought to kneel; they belong to what Remarkable Pettibone, the spinster housekeeper in the Temple household, calls "the standing order" of Christians, "all sitch as don't go on their knees to prayer" (p. 166).[8] They are, however, used to sermons and experienced judges of doctrinal differences, and much more at ease when Mr. Grant preaches. The whole account reminds one in its technique of Irving's sketch of the Christmas service in the Bracebridge church, and is therefore the more striking for its differences in scene and congregation.[9]

The account of the church service is followed in chapters 13 and 14 by a piece of genre painting of the company at the Bold Dragoon tavern late Christmas Eve, interesting not only for its representation of frontier conviviality and of what really seems—with the single exception of Judge Temple—a classless society, but for the way in which we become aware in it of the tensions of the community. And while the company at the Bold Dragoon drink heartily, Remarkable Pettibone and Ben Pump, another servant, drink as heartily—or at least Ben does—in the main room of the Temple house and from its sideboard (chapter 15). The burden of Remarkable's concern on this occasion is her resentment of Judge Temple's insistence that she address his daughter as Miss Temple and not Betsy. Cooper makes the dialogue go on too long, but it is striking in its representation of that refusal of servility in American servants that Alexis de Tocqueville was to record some years later, a trait most marked, doubtless, on the frontier.

Another of these set pieces is of quite a different kind: the remarkable description of an ice storm as Elizabeth Temple sees it on the morning after Christmas from her bedroom window, looking westward over the lake and to forest-covered hills beyond (chapter 19). Cooper feels the impulse, as did Byrant in a comparable description of an ice storm in his "A Winter Piece," to give literary embodiment to the splendor of American scenery, splendor that up to their time had had so little record. There are analogies between the work of the Hudson River painters and descriptive passages in both Bryant and Cooper, and Cooper often takes such high vantage points in his descriptions as we are familiar with in the paintings of Asher B. Durand and Thomas Cole.[10] Such delight in description belongs to the time, of course, and we have seen something like it in Miss Mitford's work; but American writers had their own impulse—to complete American experience by its expression. Ralph Waldo Emerson, speaking in celebration of Bryant's seventieth birthday, said:"It is his proper praise that he first, and he only, made known to mankind our northern landscape"; but Cooper deserves to share that praise.

These set pieces and the characters grouped within and around them reward the adult reader more than the later exciting action. Many of the characters have little connection with the plot, although Cooper arranges that almost all have some, as he does for Major Hartman and even for Monsieur Le Quoi,[11] who are in the novel primarily to represent immigrant types in frontier populations. The background and career of Dr. Elnathan Todd is recorded at some length, not because he has much connection with Cooper's story, but so that we will know what a frontier physician might be like. Jotham Riddel, who in the latter chapters assumes the role of a minor villain, is in the scene in the Bold Dragoon the representative of a kind of American common on the frontier and persisting far beyond frontier times: a man who, Judge Temple remarks, "changes his county every three years, his farm every six months, and his occupation every season!" (p. 325). Benjamin Pump, former English sailor now servant, is at first a pretty stagey type-figure, although he improves with his later involvement in the action.

But these figures, and well over half the figures in the novel, are comic within their representative quality, comic as distinguished from humorous. They are more or less successful comic figures, yet the reader is a little uncomforatble with them. He feels sure that Cooper intended at least some of them as humorous characters, intended that we like or love them while we are smiling or laughing at them, intended to be a good deal more like Irving than he succeeds in being. But a humorous character is not within his gifts.

Some of the major characters have representative qualities separable from their roles in the plot, notably Indian John, Natty Bumppo, and Billy Kirby. Indian John Mohegan in *The*

Pioneers is hardly Chingachgook, the Great Snake; he is heroic
only in the memory of his fallen greatness. His rhetoric (all too
influential in fixing a convention in fiction) often seems in ironic
contrast to his powers and circumstances. Stripped of his possessions, childless, drunken, except for his basket-weaving dependent on Natty, he is the emblem of the Indian exploited and
corrupted by white man; in the tavern scene his song of his
exploits is understood by none but Natty, and it ends in drunken
stupor. Natty Bumppo himself, until late in the novel, represents
the woodsman getting too old for his occupation and surviving
in a region in which he is obsolescent. But he is also representative in a larger way—as a garrulous old man who compensates
for his feeling of the inadequacy of age by recalling former
exploits, and boasting of them more naively than his urbane
counterparts would allow themselves to do.

Billy Kirby is the representative of the settlers who are
supplanting Leather-stocking. Billy is a woodchopper, not a
woodsman. He comes from Vermont, a young powerful man,
the possessor of several outdoor skills, good-natured and hearty,
but with no more intelligence than his activities require, and
carelessly insensitive—the type of thousands of frontiersman.
His delight is the felling of trees, but he will admit no superior
"for boiling down the maple sap; for tending brick-kiln; splitting
out rails; making potash, and parling [?pearl ash] too; or hoeing
corn" (p. 226). We meet him first as a contestant in the turkey
shoot on Christmas day, a frontier sport that Cooper describes at
length in chapters 16 and 17.

Now to deal with so many characters interesting in and for
themselves and still to manage a plot is a difficult matter. And
Cooper was no John Galt; he was no more likely to disregard his
readers' expectations in the matter of plot than were most
novelists of his time. To say that he should have done so, as some
critics seem to say, is to take the discussion out of time. But in
this one regard Cooper does better, not only than his American
contemporary Catharine Maria Sedgwick does in *Redwood*, but
better than Miss Edgeworth in *The Absentee* or Scott in *The Antiquary*.[12]

Cooper works in an ingenious manner to assure his readers
that he has a plot, yet to continue writing "A Descriptive Tale"

through twenty-four chapters. From time to time there are suggestions of mysteries to be resolved: Cooper makes sure that we note the curiosity of the community about the relationships among Edwards, Leather-stocking, and Indian John Mohegan. And he makes apparent to us the resentment Edwards feels toward Judge Temple and the tension in the attitudes of the Judge and his daughter toward Edwards. But even after chapter 18 when Cooper has managed the employment of Edwards as a sort of secretary to the Judge—which, however unconvincing, is a convenience to his storytelling—Cooper continues to suspend the development of his plot.

In the meantime, Cooper devotes himself to accounts of the spring activities at Templeton. The transition from the account of Christmastime to the account of springtime comes at the end of chapter 19 and in rapid summary narration, so that spring is gradually approaching at the beginning of chapter 20. Chapters 20–24 record typical spring activities of the settlement. There is first the visit to Billy Kirby's sugar bush, interesting for Judge Temple's reproof of Billy for the "dreadful wounds" he makes in tapping the maples, "the growth of centuries." Part of Billy's reply suggests that there is here too an influence from *Bracebridge Hall*: "I have heern the settlers from the old countries say, that their rich men keep great oaks and elms, that would make a barrel of pots [potash] to the tree . . . just to look on." Judge Temple has something of the feeling of responsibility that Squire Bracebridge has for the growth of centuries.

The account in chapter 22 of the shooting of pigeons—"a flock that the eye cannot see the end of"—we read with the fascinated horror with which Cooper wrote it. The people of Templeton slaughter pigeons, far beyond the possibility of any use, for the excitement of the killing. It is not a sport; it requires no skill and offers no difficulty: Richard Jones and Ben Pump use a small cannon loaded with duck-shot. The account of the seining of bass in the next chapter is a companion piece, an appalling narrative of heedless wastefulness. What is arresting in both accounts is the infectious excitement of destruction. The Judge himself kills pigeons "in common with the rest," although he has later regrets. Edwards, Natty remarks, is "as bad as the rest of them." Even Elizabeth Temple and Louisa Grant are "greatly excited and highly gratified" by the great haul of fish. Only Natty, who lives by hunting and fishing, is revolted by the slaughter at the time it is going on.

Chapters 20–24 will be the most memorable part of the novel for many readers today, yet they have very little to do with the plot. During the bass seining, it is true, Natty saves Ben Pump from drowning[13]—which will account for Ben's loyalty to Natty in later action. There is some foreshadowing in the Judge's account of his first encounter with Leather-stocking and Edwards's suggestion that the Judge has a doubtful right to his land, and some speculation on the part of Elizabeth and Louisa about Leather-stocking's unwillingness to allow anyone in his cabin.

One incident in chapter 21, however, does have a plot interest beyond foreshadowing, although it does not look forward to the resolution of any mystery. On a ride through the forest, Edwards saves Louisa from a falling tree, and in her gratitude she comes close to revealing the love she feels for him. Throughout, Cooper treats Louisa's love for Edwards with surprising delicacy. Once he describes Louisa as sighing so low as to be "scarcely audible to herself" (p. 286). And Louisa seems not to have been very audible to critics of *The Pioneers*, to have been thought of, if at all, as a foil to Elizabeth. Yet she is far more appealing than the young women in Cooper's novels commonly are: she has a timid charm and capabilities for love and loyalty. But also she has the anomalous social position that so often a clergyman's daughter occupied in the nineteenth century: she is a young gentlewoman by virtue of her father's calling, and a poor young woman as a result of it.

Chapter 25, which brings us to the heats of summer, is pivotal in the structure of *The Pioneers*. After it Cooper turns from a primary concern with the ordinary life of Templeton to a rapidly developing action; in it he prepares for the denouement of his novel. Judge Temple receives a ship-letter; its contents are withheld from us, but it disturbs him greatly, and he does some letter-writing and consults a lawyer. There is, too, a renewed interest on the part of Elizabeth and Louisa in Edwards's identity. Yet the next events, those of July—and exciting events they are—do not, seemingly, point toward denouement.

Those fortunate readers who read *The Pioneers* when they

were young will remember what happens in chapters 26–35:
how Natty shoots a panther that threatens Elizabeth and Louisa;
how he kills a buck out of season and resists the service of a
search warrant; how he burns down his cabin and then gives
himself up; how he is tried and convicted for his resistance to the
warrant; how Judge Temple sentences him, and how he escapes
from jail, assisted by Edwards and even by Miss Temple. The
comic scenes within all this excitement may not be remembered
so well—scenes involving Hiram Doolittle, Jotham Riddel, and
Richard Jones as Natty's opponents and Ben Pump as his ally.

Yet this exciting action is a dramatic representation of the
conflict between the ways of life of two epochs—between Judge
Temple as he stands for the new farming frontier and Leather-
stocking as he stands for the hunter's frontier that the region of
Templeton so lately was. Leather-stocking is given the eloquent
speeches and he breaks out of the jail to which the Judge has
committed him; but inevitably the "civilized restraints" that the
Judge reluctantly upholds in sentencing him and that the
Judge's authority represents will make impossible the sort of
individual freedom that Natty has experienced in the forests and
that he still desires. With an irony Cooper may have intended, it
is Natty's jail break that imperils Elizabeth and brings about the
death of Indian John in the next episode. Elizabeth has come to
the mountain to bring Natty gunpowder, and the forest fire has
started from the carelessly discarded torches of the searchers for
Natty the night before.

The episode of the forest fire in chapters 36–38 threatens
catastrophe and includes the tragic death of Indian John, but as
a matter of plot structure it merely leads toward the denouement.[14] When Elizabeth comes to the place Natty has arranged
to meet her, she finds Indian John wearing ceremonial orna-
ments and paint; the suggestion is that he has determined his
time to die. Her colloquy with him is interrupted by the approaching fire and the arrival of Edwards. Edwards fails to lead
her to safety, but Natty arrives in time to carry Indian John, who
has been badly burned, and to guide Elizabeth and Edwards
through a water course to a rock platform over a cave where the
fire cannot reach them. There Indian John dies, reverting to the
faith in which he was born. The episode ends when a thun-

derstorm has so subdued the fire that Elizabeth can leave the platform and be found by searchers.

Cooper apparently intends in chapter 39 to make the preparatory action to his denouement an exercise in the mock heroic—perhaps in an effort to recover the comic tone of the novel. Richard Jones, acting on the rumor that Edwards and Natty had set the forest fire, determines to attack the cave and calls out the militia, the Templeton Light Infantry, twenty-five strong, commanded by Captain Holister, landlord of the Bold Dragoon. The possibilities of a good mock heroic treatment are there, but Cooper is not the man to carry them out, and the action becomes low comedy—hardly suitable as preparation for a revelation scene precarious in effect at best.

The comic action comes to an end when Judge Temple arrives to halt the attack and Edwards promises that "all shall be revealed." Edwards and Major Hartman carry out in a chair a very old man, who, Edwards announces, is his grandfather, Major Oliver Effingham. He is the father of Edward Effingham, Judge Temple's friend and silent partner; it was the news of Edward Effingham's death that so disturbed Judge Temple in chapter 25. Major Hartman, we learn, once served under Major Effingham.

Major Oliver Effingham is the former owner of the land Judge Temple now holds; it was granted to him by John Mohegan (whose life he had saved) and the Delaware tribe. But Major Effingham is a loyalist and former King's officer; and his son Edward, to whom he had conveyed his whole estate, had served in the British forces as a colonel. When the Effingham lands were sold at auction as the confiscated lands of loyalists, Judge Temple had purchased them. Latterly, Major Effingham has been living in concealment and in the care of Natty Bumppo, who had years before served in his campaigns, and, since Edwards's arrival in Templeton, in the care of Edwards—or, as we now know him, Edward Oliver Effingham.

The mysteries of Edwards's identity and of his relationship with Natty and John Mohegan are now resolved. But we have more to learn. Judge Temple had not only bought up the Effingham lands; he had used large sums of money Edward Effingham had left with him when he joined the British forces.

The Judge had always intended that Edward Effingham have his fair share when political events made that possible.[15] On learning of his death, the Judge had willed his entire estate to his daughter and to Edward Oliver Effingham—who has only to marry Elizabeth to attain ultimate control of all.

As Cooper begins his last chapter he tells us that the novel concludes "in the delightful month of October"; he has chosen not to represent directly the events of August and September. Major Effingham is now dead; Edward Oliver Effingham and Elizabeth are married. Both are determined to care for Natty. But one day they find him at the graves of Indian John and Major Effingham, who are buried at the site of Natty's burned-down cabin. There he refuses all their offers. He is "form'd for the wilderness"; his "time has come at last" and he must go; he calls his dogs and heads westward, the representative of a great movement, and to become, when Cooper returns to him, the major figure in a great myth.

Bryant, in his commemorative address for Cooper, says that in *The Pioneers* the "scenes of rural life, drawn, as Cooper knew how to draw them, in the bright and healthful coloring of which he was master, are interwoven with a regular narrative of human fortunes, not unskilfully constructed."[16] The statement is inaccurate—the scenes of rural life are hardly interwoven with a regular narrative of human fortunes— but it is critically instructive. Bryant is speaking of the novel as the impression made by it has remained in his memory; and Bryant's impression is a testimony to Cooper's success in suspending his plot while he writes his "descriptive tale." In *The Pioneers* Cooper *is* skillful in construction, but his success is just that he is able to use the materials it pleases him to use, to interest us in them, and not to let the expectation of "a regular narrative of human fortunes" hamper him—indeed, to seem to fulfill that expectation.

If Cooper's first readers sought a single moral in *The Pioneers*, they found themselves at fault, as we should if we sought some single overriding theme. What we do find, as in other Cooper novels, are a number of ideas dramatically represented—and in this novel ideas pertinent in Cooper's time and in ours. Cooper complained in *A Letter to His Countrymen* (1834) that, although his novels had been well received, the ideas that he had represented in them were rejected when he presented them as principles in his social criticism.[17] But Cooper could deal with ideas dramatically far more adroitly than he could state them in general terms.

In Judge Temple we can see the beginning of an interest in the idea of the American gentleman, an idea that becomes explicit in Cooper's social criticism, particularly in *The American Democrat*.[18] Cooper shies away from the word "aristocracy," but he is concerned with the development of an aristocracy of worth in the United States. Although Judge Temple, by his situation, is an extreme example of that separation of the American gentleman from his kind that Cooper points out in *Gleanings in Europe: England*,[19] in general he fulfills his responsibilities well and gracefully. In the "starving time" in the very early days of the settlement, his decisive action had saved the lives of the settlers (pp. 234–35). His influence is great; he is therefore careful not always to exercise it: in the matter of the denomination of the new church, he had "declined all interference" when he might easily have had his way (p. 111).

Cooper's development of the Judge is surprisingly restrained. When, despite his gratitude to Natty for his rescue of Elizabeth from the panther, the Judge must sentence Natty, there are no heroics—even though the Judge's dilemma is one that a novelist might be tempted to exploit. And although Cooper would have us accept the Judge's principle that "society cannot exist without wholesome restraints" (p. 394), he allows our sympathies to go to Natty. Cooper's representation of a particular American gentleman is a good deal more attractive than his later definitions of the American gentleman in his social criticism.

Elizabeth Temple may be a more interesting character than her father. She has abounding health, "sweet but commanding features," lips that "at first sight, seemed only made for love," and "a form of exquisite proportion, rather full and rounded for her years" (pp. 55–56)—Cooper makes her as sexually attractive as the convention of the time allowed. As the novel opens she is returning from four years at school, the most highly educated woman in Templeton. Her mother has been dead for more than three years; Elizabeth is now the mistress of the Temple household. She is fearless, supremely self-confident and indeed imperious—partly by her own self-sufficiency and partly from her consciousness of her position as Judge Temple's daughter. She could not have been quite such a heroine as Cooper's first readers expected. But she is one—possibly the first—of a long line of heroines who represent their authors' interest in portraying new types of American young women.

In Elizabeth's position as Miss Temple, the only daughter of Judge Temple, she represents the feminine side of the problem of the separation of American aristocrats from their kind. The only woman of wealth and exalted social status in Templeton, Elizabeth is, she says, "a nun, here, without the vow of celibacy" (p. 286); before Edwards's identity is known, there is no possible husband for her in Templeton. Although she suspects that Edwards is her social equal, she makes him keep his distance until she is quite sure; and since the girls are always together, makes him keep his distance from Louisa too. She is aware of Louisa's feeling for Edwards, and indeed thinks of her as a rival,[20] but she has no doubt of her prerogative and no hesitation in exercising it.

The social status of Judge Temple and his daughter depends primarily upon the Judge's great landholdings. Readers today, with the renewed interest in the relationships of Indians and white men, may find a special interest in the consideration in *The Pioneers* of the right by which landholders in the United States hold their lands. The implications of that consideration go far beyond the mere matter of the Effinghams' rights. "I own that I grieve," Elizabeth says, "when I see old Mohegan walking about these lands, like the ghost of one of their ancient possessors, and feel how small is my right to possess them" (p. 285). Her father hardly feels his right is small: "The Indian title," he says, "was extinguished so far back as the close of the old war; and if it had not been at all, I hold under the patents of the Royal Governors, confirmed by an act of our own State Legislature, and no court in our country can affect my title" (p. 238).

But Cooper makes occasion, at least, for the reader to reflect on the moral title of all white landholders, and the clause with which chapter 7 begins suggests a question about that moral title on Cooper's own part: "Before the Europeans, or, to use a more significant term, the Christians, dispossessed the original owners

of the soil . . ." (p. 74). And although Mr. Grant admonishes
Edwards under the misapprehension that he is of Indian descent, what he says may represent Cooper's own moral adjustment to the problem: "the sin of the wrongs which have been
done to the natives is shared by Judge Temple, only, in common
with a whole people" (p. 137). At any rate, the acceptance of a
fractional responsibility on the part of one's ancestors is a common moral adjustment with us today.

The matter of the ultimate right of ownership is closely connected in *The Pioneers* with the conflict, perennial in a democ-
racy, between the social order and individual liberty, as it is
represented by the conflict between Judge Temple and Natty,
under the special conditions of a region to which the social order
is new. Judge Temple combines the roles of great landholder
and of judge; Natty stands quite apart from the purposes of the
community. In the first chapter, Natty, speaking of a privilege
that Judge Temple has granted him, complains: "There's them
living who say, that Nathaniel Bumppo's right to shoot in these
hills, is of older date than Marmaduke Temple's right to forbid
him" (pp. 11–12); "might often makes right here," Natty thinks,
"as well as in the old country" (p. 8). When Natty departs in the
last chapter, he realizes that he cannot have the liberty he desires
in a social order. His defeat comes to him from what we recognize as historical forces. Nevertheless, his rights have been invaded; and Judge Temple, although he has no malice toward
Natty, is the representative of the social order that invades them.
Natty will, of course, in pioneering westward, prepare the way
for the extension of the social order; ironically he is part of the
social forces that defeat him.

The social order, or at least society, also invades the natural
order; Cooper's thinking about the conservation of natural resources will seem to us prophetic.[21] In his first chapter, he remarks of the population of the state of New York that eventually
"the evil day must arrive, when their possessions will become
unequal to their wants." And from the Judge's irritation when
he finds sugar-maple burning in his own fireplace at Christmastime to his decision that even Natty must be punished for a
violation of the game laws, we find him concerned about the
ways in which his own people use their abundance. With his

"bias to look far into futurity" (p. 329), he grieves "to witness the extravagance that pervades this country, where the settlers trifle with the blessings they might enjoy," where they strip the forests "as if a single year would replace what [they] destroy" (pp. 229–30).

No one of the other characters can feel with the Judge, or even understand him. Richard Jones has a simple, an idiotic delight in the number of pigeons killed or the number of fish taken. Natty has his own solution for all the problems of ecology—sound enough from his point of view. The waste the Judge deplores "comes of settling a country" (p. 247); if he wants to save the woods and the pigeons, "put an ind, Judge, to your clearings" (p. 249). But it is Billy Kirby's attitude that will most matter; it is men like Kirby who will thwart the Judge's hopes. Billy can see no reason for husbanding what seems to him in endless abundance. Moreover, in the destruction of forests—which is his primary trade—he is clearing land for farms; he calls "no country much improved, that is pretty well covered with trees" (p. 230), and indeed he thinks that whatever interferes at all with the settlers' first business deserves destruction. The problems of ecology present themselves to us in increasingly complex shapes, yet it is easy to identify in our time the intellectual descendents of each of these four spokesmen.

But it is Cooper's literary thinking that makes possible the representation of his social ideas in *The Pioneers*, and it is his literary thinking that most deserves our respect. In writing a novel of character and manners in the United States, Cooper was doing, we need to remember, what critics had said and were saying could not be done—indeed, what he himself came close to saying later in a famous passage in *Notions of the Americans* (1828) could not be done.[22] There was scarcely anything in the fictional use of American experience to show Cooper the way. Perhaps there was Catharine Maria Sedgwick's *A New-England Tale* (1822), but that appeared when Cooper was well along in writing *The Pioneers*. Cooper may have found in the work of Maria Edgeworth, as well as in *The Vicar of Wakefield* and in the Waverley novels, some suggestions of ways to treat ordinary life; we have seen that he did profit by Irving's accounts of Squire

Bracebridge and his domain. But Cooper's ingenious design for a novel that would fulfill his readers' expectations about what a novel should be and yet allow him to use the materials of his experience as he pleased and to represent a set of interesting ideas was quite his own accomplishment. Indeed, no other novel in the period of our concern so much extends the uses of the means of fiction into the representation of general social ideas immediately pertinent to the lives of its first readers.

NOTES

1. In Gardiner's forty-eight-page review of *The Last of The Mohicans* and *The Pioneers*, he gives all but five pages to *The Last of the Mohicans* since it is the newer book. But he seems to prefer *The Pioneers*. Since Cooper has said in his preface that he wrote *The Pioneers* to please himself, Gardiner "presumes" that it has Cooper's own preference; "and on this point," he says, "we have the pleasure to agree with him." The characters are drawn "with great spirit and originality"; the Natty Bumppo of *The Pioneers* is superior to the Natty Bumppo of *The Last of the Mohicans* (*North American Review* 23 [1826]: 195).

2. *The Letters and Journals of James Fenimore Cooper*, ed. J. F. Beard (Cambridge: Harvard University Press, 1960), 1: 85. This letter also shows Cooper quite conscious of the unusual structure of *The Pioneers*: "I know that the present taste is for action and strong excitement, and in this respect am compelled to acknowledge that the first two volumes are deficient, I however am not without hope that the third will be thought to make amends."

3. See Thomas Philbrick, "Cooper's *The Pioneers*: Origins and Structure," *PMLA* 79 (1964): 582–84.

4. *Prose Writings*, 1: 307.

5. See Philbrick, pp. 584–87.

6. "Here all is literal," Cooper says in the 1850 preface to *The Pioneers*, "even to the severed arm of Wolfe, and the urn which held the ashes of Dido" (reprinted in *James Fenimore Cooper: Representative Selections*, ed. Robert E. Spiller [New York: American Book Company, 1936], p. 282).

7. This name is an amusing detail. Richard Jones wants to call the new church "St. Paul's," but compromises with Hiram Doolittle, who is willing that it be named after a building but not after a saint.

8. Page references to *The Pioneers* are to the Rinehart edition (New York: Rinehart & Company, 1959). The Rinehart edition reprints the edition of 1825, which is a reprint of the first edition with a few corrections.

9. Mr. Grant's sermon is a curious example of a Cooper lapse. Although Cooper affirms that Mr. Grant is "admirably qualified" and that he well understands "the character of his listeners," who are "mostly a primitive people in their habits," he makes Mr. Grant use in his sermon a complex syntax and such terms as "promulgated," "sophist," and "corollaries." One supposes that Cooper wanted to try his hand at an eloquent sermon, and was willing to offend against the "keeping" which he says in his preface he will try to observe. We expect Cooper to be frequently inept, but this is not the ineptitude of heedlessness, for Cooper obviously wrote that sermon with great care.

10. A remarkable example is Leather-stocking's description of prospects from the Catskills as he remembers them (pp. 297–300). Even when Cooper has Judge Temple describe his first full view of what was to become his domain, he has the Judge specify his vantage point: he had climbed a tree on the summit of a mountain, the pinnacle of which had been largely burned off so that the view was unobstructed (p. 236). A recent discussion of the pictorial in our early national literature is Donald A. Ringe, *The Pictorial Mode* (Lexington: University Press of Kentucky, 1971).

11. In the last chapter of *The Pioneers* Cooper remarks that "Monsieur Le Quoi . . . has been introduced to our readers, because no picture of that country [frontier New York] would be faithful without such a Gaul" (p. 466). In the novel Monsieur Le Quoi has the same name that his prototype had in Cooperstown. See *Cooper: Representative Selections*, p. lxxviii.

12. There is some likeness between Lovel in *The Antiquary* and Edwards in *The Pioneers*. Both seem to have as a chief characteristic a petulant pride along with a kind of helplessness in their own behalf. I do not think, however, it is a matter of influence; each writer is using a conventional hero, and neither can get interested in him.

13. Mark Twain does not use Natty's rescue of Ben Pump in "Fenimore Cooper's Literary Offenses," but it is quite as remarkable a Cooper incident as those he does use. Ben, as a result of Billy Kirby's awkwardness, falls overboard. Since he is the stock comic English sailor, he cannot swim. But instead of thrashing about in a effort to save himself, he sinks quietly, and is seen, by the aid of Indian John's fishing torch, "lying, about half way to the bottom, grasping with either hand the bottoms of some broken rushes" (p. 276), a position which makes it convenient for Natty to save him by twisting the tines of his fish spear in his queue and the cape of his coat and hauling him out thereby.

14. The denouement is twice foreshadowed within the episode. Indian John nearly reveals Edwards's identity, but is interrupted by the approaching fire (pp. 418–19). Edwards himself, just before Natty ap-

pears, speaks of forgetting his wrongs, name, and family in his love for Elizabeth (p. 428).

15. There is an aspect of Judge Temple's ethics that neither Cooper nor most readers of *The Pioneers* seem to notice. As James Grossman points out in his fine study, the Judge is saying (p. 458) that "he has held the land on a secret trust for [the Effinghams] which he has never declared openly because his declaration might prevent their obtaining compensation from the British Crown for their loss; in short, he has been trying to cheat the Crown and not them" (*James Fenimore Cooper* [New York: W. Sloane Associates, 1949], p. 31).

16. *Prose Writings*, 1: 307.

17. See a passage quoted in *Cooper: Representative Selections*, pp. xxxix–xl.

18. See *The American Democrat* as reprinted in *Cooper: Representative Selections*, pp. 197–205.

19. Many of the peculiarities of America, Cooper says, are to be accounted for by "the disproportion between surface and numbers." See a passage quoted in *Cooper: Representative Selections*, pp. xlviii–xlix.

20. Even after Elizabeth's marriage, she considers Louisa both friend and rival. By persuading her father to secure a call for Mr. Grant in one of the older cities, she both provides matrimonial possibilities for Louisa and manages to get her away from Templeton. The dialogue within which she informs her husband of her plans for Louisa is done with much more subtlety than we expect from Cooper; it ends with his saying that he did not know Elizabeth was such a manager (pp. 468–69). His apprehension has been somewhat behind that of the reader.

21. A good extensive discussion is E. Arthur Robinson, "Conservation in Cooper's *The Pioneers*," *PMLA* 82 (1967): 564–78.

22. It is striking that Cooper, who had so succeeded with American materials, wrote so vigorous a statement of their inadequacy for the fiction writer: "There are no annals for the historian; no follies (beyond the most vulgar and commonplace) for the satirist; no manners for the dramatist; no obscure fictions for the writer of romance; no gross and hardy offenses against decorum for the moralist; nor any of the rich artificial auxiliaries of poetry." Cooper here finds inadequate even such materials as he used in *The Pioneers*: "No doubt, traits of character that are a little peculiar, without, however, being either very poetical, or very rich, are to be found in remote districts; but they are rare, and not always happy exceptions." See Letter 23 in *Notions of the Americans*, as reprinted in *Cooper: Representative Selections*, pp. 15–16.

11

Redwood and Bryant's Review

Catharine Maria Sedgwick's *Redwood: A Tale* (1824) is dedicated to William Cullen Bryant, and he reviewed it in the *North American Review* for April 1825 (20:245–72). Since reviews were of course unsigned, Bryant could write about the novel without embarrassment, and his careful and elaborate review is doubtless evidence of his friendship for Miss Sedgwick and the Sedgwick family. But Bryant seized the opportunity to make his review the vehicle for literary theory of more importance than what he says specifically of the novel, and indeed of more importance than the novel itself.

Yet *Redwood* is important in Miss Sedgwick's effort to write fiction about her own time, an effort she defends in a somewhat labored introduction. There she says that it is "the peculiar province" of fictional narrative "to denote the passing character and manners of the present time and place. There is but one individual (whom it would be affectation to call *unknown*) who has had eminent success in the delineations of former periods, or what is called historical romance" (1:vii–viii).[1] Regarded historically, that is a startling statement. Many Americans and almost all fiction writers and critics thought Cooper's *The Spy* had proved, at the least, the possibility of success with American historical romance. In 1825 when Jared Sparks reviewed ten new American novels (most of them published in 1824), he found almost all of them "acknowledged copies" of the pattern of the Waverley novels.[2] Miss Sedgwick herself soon went to historical romance in her *Hope Leslie, or Early Times in the Massachusetts* (1827).[3]

Furthermore, Miss Sedgwick is denying a received critical dictum. Scott in his review of *Emma* remarks that "he who paints a scene of common occurrence, places his composition within that extensive range of criticism which general experience offers to every reader." The *North American Review* critics writing before Bryant's review of *Redwood* erect that obvious difficulty into a bar, and seem to assume that of course the American fiction writer cannot succeed with material from the American present. William Howard Gardiner in his review of *The Spy* is happy to find that, since the new country had gone through very rapid changes, writers need not "revert to any very remote period of antiquity to rid us of this familiarity, which forever plays about present things with a mischievous tendency to convert the romantic into the ludicrous."[4] Cooper in *The Pioneers,* as we have seen, reverts only to the last decade of the eighteenth century, but he is dealing with a region of especially rapid change. Before *Redwood* there were few or no American critics to recommend, and few fiction writers to attempt, the representation of their own present.

Miss Sedgwick's first novel, *A New-England Tale: or, Sketches of New-England Character and Manners* (1822), is dedicated to Maria Edgeworth, and *Redwood* too is a tribute to her, not only in its several references to her novels, but in a clear emulation of them. The didactic intention of *Redwood* is as persistent as is the didactic intention in Miss Edgeworth's work generally (although in *Redwood* it has the sanction of a Christian faith). Yet in one regard, *Redwood* is also curiously like Susan Ferrier's *Marriage*.

In *Marriage*, we remember, Adelaide and Mary are twins, brought up in very different ways. In *Redwood*, Caroline Redwood and Ellen Bruce (as the heroine is known) prove to be half-sisters, Ellen a year or two the elder. Caroline has been brought up in South Carolina by her aristocratic and foolish maternal grandmother, and has turned out both frivolous and vicious. Ellen has lived in Massachusetts, brought up by turns by Mrs. Allen, a fine woman of yeoman stock and Puritan inheritance, and by Mrs. Harrison, a fine woman of considerable cultivation and an Episcopalian. Ellen's upbringing, we are to take it, combines the best in the New England tradition and results in making Ellen a paragon of virtue.

Miss Sedgwick seems to think that in her emulation of Miss Edgeworth she has separated her heroine from the convention. When Ellen Bruce must ride in an old-fashioned chaise, Miss Sedgwick hopes that her "romantic readers will not regret that our heroine could not be accommodated with a more poetical or dignified vehicle" (2:3); when Ellen is hungry she does not regard her food "with the indifference of a true heroine" (2:111). We may be reminded of remarks about Catherine Morland in *Northanger Abbey*; but if, as Jane Austen says, a criterion of the true heroine is "to be disgraced in the eyes of the world . . . while her heart is all purity," Ellen qualifies.

The mystery of Ellen's birth constitutes the chief plot interest, and is fully elucidated only in the next-to-last chapter of the two volumes. As the novel opens, Henry Redwood, a Virginian, who with his daughter Caroline has been on a northern tour, suffers a road accident in Vermont, and is forced to stay with the family of Mr. Lenox, with whom Ellen is staying. As Bryant remarks, it is "not a little extraordinary" that the father and a daughter unknown to him should be brought together in so Edgeworthian a coincidence (pp. 268–69).

As soon as Miss Sedgwick has brought Redwood and Ellen together, she goes back in chapters 3 and 4 for a summary account of Redwood's early life. This history virtually but not explicitly assures the reader that Ellen is a legitimate daughter of Redwood and prepares for the dramatic irony that pervades the novel and is often exploited. Ellen's distresses arise from her own doubts of the legitimacy of her birth and her unwillingness to become engaged while they persist, and from the enmity of Caroline. It looks as if Miss Sedgwick hopes to get a greater interest out of the plot element of the heroine of mysterious birth than Miss Edgeworth had in *The Absentee*; there is significant reference to that novel and to the mystery of Grace Nugent's birth (1:257). But there is an interesting moral difference in the two novels. Lord Colambre never thinks it possible that he could marry Grace should she be illegitimate; Miss Sedgwick's hero, Charles Westall, says that if Ellen prove illegitimate, "it should be the business, the happiness of his life to make her forget it" (2:10).

Yet to the reader today the explanation of the mystery of

Ellen's birth may seem pretty flat. When Ellen was an infant, her mother, just before her death, had left a box containing evidence that she had been married to Redwood, with directions that Ellen open it when she became twenty-one or when she became engaged. Ellen is persuaded to open it before she is twenty-one in order to give an answer to her suitor.

In its main plot, Redwood has some likeness to an English "fashionable novel"— an aspect of the book that Bryant rather obscures in his review. Redwood and Caroline and Westall and his mother are Southern aristocrats. Miss Sedgwick manages to introduce into the main plot—or at least to connect with it—a group of Northerners of social standing, for one of whom, Miss Grace Campbell, a romance is provided. Much of the action of the second volume goes on at Lebanon Springs, a watering place, which for the purposes of the novel seems a kind of substitute for Bath.

Miss Sedgwick's intention with Grace Campbell may be in doubt. The romance provided for her is too obviously contrived; her connection with the main plot is awkwardly managed. But she is herself striking. She is assertive, unconventional, outspoken, and witty (or at least we are supposed to find her witty). One might think that readers who are expected greatly to admire Ellen should not be expected to admire Grace. But Miss Sedgwick clearly admires a lack of conventional femininity in her.[5]

The subplot has much more permanent interest than the main plot; and in the Shakers Miss Sedgwick discovers striking American materials.[6] The subplot has to do with the rescue of Emily Allen, daughter of the Mrs. Allen who had cared for Ellen, from her connection with the Shakers. Some time before Ellen had come to live with them, all the Allens except Mr. Allen's mother had been Shakers, and all had abandoned their connection except Susan Allen, Mr. Allen's sister. Susan has recently been able so to influence Emily that she lives in the Shaker community at Hancock, Massachusetts, and is about to commit herself entirely.

The accounts of Shaker life and ceremonies in the novel are vivid and, so far as my reading allows me to judge, accurate.[7] Here, as an instance, is an account of a ritual dance that was part of Shaker worship:

The assembly, without any visible external direction, but apparently in obedience to a common impulse, broke up their ranks,—arranged in pairs, the elder taking precedence of the younger, and the sisters of the brethren, they made in a dancing procession the circuit of the two apartments. A small knot of brethren and sisters remained in the center of each room, shouting strange music for the dancers, and slowly turning so as to keep their faces always towards the procession, which moved on with a uniform shuffling step, as if it was composed of so many automatons, their arms rising and falling mechanically. [2:43]

But we have such accounts elsewhere. What the reader today may value is the representation of the tragedy of lovers and of families torn apart by the Shaker requirement that converts break all ties with the world.

The scene in which Susan and Emily come too late to the Lenox house to see Emily's brother Edward before he dies, with the colloquy between them and grandmother Allen, rightly impressed Bryant, who reproduces its several pages. The old grandmother, even in her grief for Edward, almost fiercely throws off the restraint Ellen would put upon her. "Are we not," she asks Ellen, "to pluck out the right eye, to pluck off the right arm, if thereby we may save the soul? Ellen, I will speak to [Emily]; and if she is not dead to natural affection, the light of that pale face will send my words home to her heart" (1:87).

Susan and Emily bear the old lady's remonstrances meekly; but Susan's influence over Emily is such that her admonition in the terms to which Emily has been conditioned is sufficient to keep Emily to the Shaker faith for the time being. "Come my child," Susan says, "we wait for you, be not like a silly dove without heart; take up your cross, a full cross though it may be, and turn your back upon the world" (1:101). Old Mrs. Allen can say only: "They were my children, but they have gone out from me, and are not of me" (1:91).

Susan is the most memorable character in the novel; with her Miss Sedgwick surpasses herself. Susan's connection with the Shakers goes far back, and a deep impression of the founder of the sect in the United States, Mother Ann Lee, abides with her.

She tells Emily:

> There was a celestial melody in mother's voice in the gift of
> speaking, and a weight in all her words, and though I gave
> no outward sign, they sunk deeply into my heart. She said
> no more to me at that time—she was never forward to
> speak. In her looks there was a boldness and innocence that
> seemed, as it were, like the truth and gentleness of the gos-
> pel she preached, written for testimony in every line of her
> face. [2:29]

Susan had renounced the love of a fine young man (she tells
Emily how his life had come to ruin thereby) and she remembers
her inner conflict even yet:

> Oh Emily! you know not how the natural man can talk—and
> oh, my innocent child, be thankful; you know not how the
> unregenerate heart goes forth in what the world calls
> love—how the breath of the body and the life of the soul
> seem bound up in the life and breath of another; how cheap
> the sacrifice of earth—yea heaven, to the idol seems. [2:30]

But, although Susan as she speaks has not realized it, Emily had
herself known that conflict; and Susan at last acquiesces in Emily's decision to leave the Shakers and to marry James Lenox.

Miss Sedgwick's dealing with the Shakers is the most successful
portion of her effort to represent "the passing character and
manners of the present time and place." Yet in the problems of
the literary portrayal of religious enthusiasm, Miss Edgeworth's
example could not have been of much help. Miss Sedgwick
catches the accents of her Shaker speakers, and of grandmother
Allen, with somewhat the same sort of convincingness that Scott
attains with his Covenanters in *Old Mortality*. She is more convincing with the Shakers, I think, than with her ordinary New
Englanders.

Miss Sedgwick says in her introduction: "Whenever the course
of our narrative has thrown opportunities in our way, we have
attempted some sketches of the character and manners of this
country" (1:x). But the statement does not describe the novel
with entire accuracy. With the Shakers the material of Miss
Sedgwick's observation is primary, and she devises a subplot to

use it. With her dealing with the Redwoods, Ellen, and her suitor the plot is primary, and the statement in the introduction is more or less accurate: from time to time sketches of the character and manners of ordinary New Englanders are introduced.

It is to Bryant's purpose in his review to cite what he can as evidence of Miss Sedgwick's skill with New England character and manners. He admires the account of the funeral of Edward Allen (1:111–16), and indeed it is a competent piece of genre painting; the comparison with Scott's account of the funeral of Steenie Mucklebackit that may arise in the reader's mind is perhaps not quite a fair one. Bryant also admires the portrayal of Mr. Lenox, though he is directly represented only in the role of Yankee question-asker (1:239–40) and made to embody the "busy spirit of investigation [that] pervades the mass of society in New-England" (1:247); even in that role he is made to question Redwood about his family relationships for the effect of dramatic irony induced by the questions.[8] And Bryant admires the old Shaker gardener—not a very consistent Shaker, but a good New England type—who advises Emily to "go home to your friends, get a good husband, and 'guide the house' " (2:54–57).

Miss Debby Lenox is, Bryant says, "a great favorite of ours, an ancient maiden of Amazonian stature, and a very strikingly drawn and original character" (p. 260). She is clearly Miss Sedgwick's favorite. Her stature, masculine appearance, independence, and eccentricity keep her from being a typical New England spinster. She is a very busy character, important to the action of the subplot, and present and vocal in most of the episodes of the main plot. "I don't wish," she says to Westall, "to speak my own epitaph, 'logium, or whatever you call it, but to my mind, a lone woman that no one notices, no one praises, that is not coaxed into goodness, that envies no one, minds her own affairs, is contented and happy—such a woman is a sight to behold!" (1:230). Debby seems an early manifestation of what became for Miss Sedgwick a major interest and the theme of her last novel, *Married or Single?* (1857): the place of unmarried women in American life.[9] Perhaps it is surprising that her feminism emerges in the treatment of a comic character in this early novel.

What happened in the composition of *Redwood* is clear

enough. Miss Sedgwick did have an impulse to represent common life, and did carry it out; but she was unwilling to carry it
out without the support of such a plot as she believed her readers wanted and as had successfully served many writers. Even in
the subplot she feels it necessary to provide an abduction and
threatened forced marriage for Emily, and so far to take even
the Shaker material into what Scott calls "the land of fiction."
But in her representation of the common life of her contemporaries, she is ahead of her time; and Bryant is right in celebrat-
ing the new impulse he sees in her novel.

Bryant is apparently troubled, however, by a number of instances of the machinery of accident in the novel, although he
says what he can to condone them: Miss Edgeworth's *Ennui*, he
points out, has such unconvincing accidents; and "as for the
Waverley novels . . . they abound with licenses of this sort. After
all, the plot of a novel is little more than a convenient contrivance to introduce interesting situations and incidents, well
drawn characters and fine sketches from life and nature" (p.
269).[10] The reader of *Redwood* today will hardly be convinced.
The plot of this novel is not—to borrow an expression from
Irving—merely a frame on which to stretch materials; much of
the time the plot preempts the attention, and the constant concern with the mystery of Ellen's birth and with the troubles for
her that attend it mitigates the effect of the occasional representation of character and manners.

Before he comes to the specific consideration of *Redwood*,
Bryant devotes almost twelve pages to literary doctrine.[11] Indeed it is clear that in structure and approach his review is intended to parallel Gardiner's review of *The Spy*. Bryant's doctrine is new to American literary thinking, but he is nonetheless
writing as a *North American Review* critic. The somewhat superior
tone of his review is not so much his tone as that of the journal;
he presents his doctrine as a development of the *Review's* doctrine. The conventional "we" pronoun sometimes really does
have its reference to his colleagues on the *Review* and to a collec-
tive doctrine developed by them—a doctrine which, Bryant says,
has had its vindication in Cooper's success:

On more than one occasion, we have already given somewhat at large our opinion of the fertility of our country, and its history, in the materials of romance. If our reasonings needed any support from successful examples of that kind of writing, as a single fact is worth a volume of ingenious theorising, we have had the triumph of seeing them confirmed beyond all controversy, by the works of a popular American author, who has shown the literary world into what beautiful creations those materials may be wrought. [P. 248]

"In like manner," Bryant goes on, "we look upon the specimen before us as a conclusive argument, that the writers of works of fiction, of which the scene is laid in familiar and domestic life, have a rich and varied field before them in the United States." *Redwood* may not seem to us a conclusive argument; but it was what Bryant had to illustrate his thesis.

The notion that American writers cannot successfully deal with the American present is, Bryant thinks, only an unconsidered inference from the fact that no American writer had done so; if no writer had, the most "comfortable way" of accounting for it was that no writer could.[12] Bryant realizes the difficulty of dealing in fiction with life the reader knows about: "We have seen the original, and require that there be no false coloring or distortion in the copy. We want to be delighted with the development of traits, that had escaped our observation, or of which, if observed, we had never felt the peculiar significance" (p. 247). But that is a difficulty skill and effort can surmount; and ordinary life everywhere, Bryant eloquently argues, is rich in material for the fiction writer who is able to use it.

Bryant is careful not to suggest that he is calling for a literary revolt, nor questioning the prestige of Sir Walter Scott. Confronting the notion that successful fiction about the American present is impossible, he affirms that no one can predict what "a writer of genius" may accomplish. "Twenty years ago," he asks, "what possible conception could an English critic have had of the admirable productions of the author of Waverley, and of the wonderful improvement his example has effected in that kind of composition?" (p. 248). It is after all Scott, Bryant says, who has taught fiction writers how to deal with characters from all walks of life, to engage our interest in them as "beings of our own species": "It is here that James First, and Charles Second, and Louis Ninth, and Rob Roy, and Jeanie Deans, and Meg Merrilies are, by the great author of the Waverley novels, made to meet" (p. 252).

Nor does Bryant's plea that the American fiction writer find "objects of sympathy and interest" (p. 250) in his present really call into question William Howard Gardiner's three epochs of American experience available to the fiction writer.[13] Bryant would but add a fourth: the epoch of the writer's own time. Fiction had discovered the resources of the American past and used some of them; the present was ready to its use. *Redwood*, Bryant says as he concludes his review, confers "a sort of public benefit" in showing "what copious and valuable materials the private lives and daily habits of our countrymen offer to the writer of genius. It is as if one were to discover to us rich ores and gems lying in the common earth about us" (p. 272).

Miss Sedgwick does, to be sure, discover some interesting and useful American materials, notably in the Shakers. But *Redwood* illustrates only a little of Bryant's vision. His plea is nationalistic and perhaps influenced by his political convictions as a Democrat in 1825; he is confident of the superiority of American institutions. He is at his best in his sardonic consideration of the contention that American society is too undeveloped for the fiction writer's purposes:

> It has been objected, that the habits of our countrymen are too active and practical; that they are too universally and continually engrossed by the cares and occupations of business to have leisure for that intrigue, those plottings and counterplottings, which are necessary to give a sufficient degree of action and eventfulness to the novel of real life. . . . But will it be seriously contended, that [the novelist] can have no other resource but the rivalries and machinations of the idle, the frivolous, and the dissolute, to keep the reader from yawning over his pictures? [P. 251]

Yet the contention Bryant here opposes persisted long, and still persists. We shall return to it in a consideration of Hawthorne's romances; one can find it argued today in academic criticism.

Bryant's vision of the social field for the fiction writer is of a field far larger than just the society of the rich and leisured. The fiction writer will find "objects of sympathy and regard," Bryant insists, "abundantly in the characters of our countrymen, formed as they are under the influence of our free institutions, and shooting into a large and vigorous, though sometimes irregular luxuriance" (p. 253). And he proceeds to the discussion of the particular interests that American experience offers the fiction writer. There is first of all the variety of worship in a land where Jews, Christian bodies of European origin, and some indigenous sects coexist and exercise "their unnumerable and diverse influences upon the manners and temper of our people" (pp. 253–54). It is in this regard that *Redwood* best illustrates Bryant's literary doctrine, and he is careful to speak especially of the Shakers.[14]

But American experience offers the fiction writer other kinds of particular interests. There are, Bryant says in a passage which seems to predict the regional novel as we now know it, those "differences of character, which grow naturally out of geographical differences," often reinforced by ethnic differences from region to region (pp. 254–55). And there is an interest which is peculiar to the United States: a new nation where some considerable numbers of the population are persons whose characters were formed in Europe and who are now fitting into American life as they can. "We shall feel little pride," Bryant declares, "in the sagacity or the skill of that native author, who asks for a richer or wider field of observation" (p. 256).

Bryant's review of *Redwood* seems prophetic, and the reader today thinks ahead to things Emerson was to say in "The American Scholar" and in "The Poet," to Walt Whitman's celebrations of the diversity of American life, to the realistic movement in the last third of the century. The reader today sees that much of what William Dean Howells was to say in *Criticism and Fiction* is explicit or implicit in Bryant's review. But Bryant's thinking, so far as it was new, seems to have had no great immediate influence. Miss Sedgwick was not that "writer of genius" whose work could really exemplify Bryant's doctrine, nor were others at hand to do so. Indeed the ideal for fiction in the review has never been as nearly realized as we should like to think. But novelist and critic together make a beginning; and Bryant's review of *Redwood* is a significant document in American literary thinking.

NOTES

1. Parenthetical page references to *Redwood* are to the first edition: *Redwood; A Tale*, 2 vols. (New York: E. Bliss and E. White, 1824).

2. *North American Review* 21 (1825): 80.

3. Miss Sedgwick returns to a novel of her present in *Clarence; or, A Tale of Our Own Times* (1830), and goes back to the time of the Revolution in *The Linwoods; or "Sixty Years Since" in America* (1835)—a title in clear allusion to the title *Waverley; or, 'Tis Sixty Years Since.*

4. *North American Review* 15 (1822): 255.

5. Bryant may have been puzzled by Grace Campbell. He writes in his review: "There is something, also, not altogether prepossessing in the first appearance of Grace Campbell, with whose character the author has evidently taken great pains. Something like pertness and flippancy, not to say rudeness, is detected in her sallies and repartees in the scene, where we are first made acquainted with her; but all this is more than compensated for, by her spirit, frankness, and warmth of heart, as they are brought out in the further progress of the narrative" (p. 266). I suspect that Miss Sedgwick had her eye on Lady Emily in Susan Ferrier's *Marriage* when she developed the character of Grace Campbell.

6. The Shakers were the most successful of communal sects in the United States. Their official name was "The United Society of Believers in Christ's Second Appearing." The sect had its origin among English Quakers, but the American Shakers were disciples of Mother Ann Lee, an Englishwoman who, in obedience to a vision, came to this country in 1774. She believed that the mother element in Christ's spirit was manifest in her. By 1826 there were nineteen Shaker communities in the United States; Shakers numbered at the peak in 1850 about six thousand. The Shakers had some beliefs in common with the Quakers, but they had special millennial doctrines and they enforced a strict rule of celibacy upon their membership, which was made up of both men and women. They were called Shakers in reference to characteristic physical manifestations of religious emotion. Their number was recruited from persons willing to leave the world and its affairs, and sometimes from orphaned children cared for by the community. Any member was free to leave the community at any time. Only a handful of Shakers still remain, in two communities. Nathaniel Hawthorne's "The Canterbury Pilgrims" (1832) and his "The Shaker Bridal" (1837) are the literary results of his visit to the Shaker community at Canterbury, New

Hampshire, in 1831. William Dean Howells's *The Undiscovered Country* (1880) has to do with Shakers at a later time.

7. The Sedgwick family home was at Stockbridge, not far from the Shaker community at Hancock, Massachusetts. In Miss Sedgwick's Introduction she says she is drawing upon "personal observation" of the Shakers, that she hopes not to wound "the feelings even of a single individual of that obscure sect," and that there is little danger of her doing so, since Shakers are unlikely to read fiction (1:x). Apparently her hope was disappointed; we are told that "Shakers protested that her novel treated them with 'irreverence and derision' " (*Literary History of the United States*, ed. Robert E. Spiller and others [New York: Macmillan, 1963], p. 290). Shaker objections may have been to Reuben Harrington, a hypocrite and the villain of the subplot.

8. Mr. Lenox, nevertheless, does represent a Yankee characteristic. See Charles Dickens's account of a question-asker on a canal boat (*American Notes*, pp. 178–80 in *Works*, Riverside ed. [New York, 1874]).

9. The place of the single woman in American life is also Miss Sedgwick's concern in "Old Maids" in *Tales and Sketches*, 1835.

10. Scott in the Introductory Epistle to *The Fortunes of Nigel* makes Captain Clutterbuck say: "In short, sir, you are of opinion with Bayes [in Buckingham's *The Rehearsal*]—'What the devil does the plot signify, except to bring in fine things?' " It is curious that Bryant, with apparent seriousness, should come so close to what Scott writes in wry amusement at his own plots, and so close to paraphrasing Bayes's question.

11. Much of this portion of the review is reprinted as "American Society as a Field for Fiction" in *Prose Writings*, ed. Godwin, 2:351–60.

12. Bryant is here adapting Gardiner, who had said as he began his review of *The Spy* that he was convinced the new country offered a field for fiction. "That nothing of the kind has hitherto been accomplished," he continued, "is a poor argument at best—especially when taken in connexion with the fact, that nothing has as yet been attempted" (*North American Review* 15 [1822]: 250).

13. Gardiner himself became irritated by what some fiction writers were doing with historical materials. For an amusing instance, see his review of James McHenry's *The Wilderness* and *The Spectre of the Forest* (*North American Review* 19 [1824]: 209–23).

14. Bryant writes: "In many parts of our country we see communities of that strange denomination, the Shakers, distinguished from their neighbors by a garb, a dialect, an architecture, a way of worship, of thinking, and of living, as different, as if they were in fact of a different origin, instead of being collected from the families around them" (p. 254).

12

William Leete Stone as Storyteller

William Leete Stone (1792–1844) is remembered by students of Cooper as the defendant in two of Cooper's many libel suits. Stone is more importantly remembered for his exposé of Maria Monk: *Maria Monk and the Nunnery of the Hôtel Dieu* (1836). With the renewed interest in Indian history readers may be turning again to his *The Life of Joseph Brant* (1838) and to his other writings on the Iroquois Confederacy. In the history of journalism he is remembered as the successful editor of the New York *Commercial Advertiser.* But as a writer of short fiction Stone is almost forgotten, even by the literary historians who preserve some memory of fiction writers of his day who were no more successful than he, and of no greater worth.[1] Yet his short fiction has considerable interest, for in it we can see the results in practice of the literary thinking and of some of the fictional purposes of his time, more clearly perhaps than we can in the fiction of writers of greater ability, in whom the same influences may be quite as effective but much less obvious.

We here consider some tales from Stone's first and best collection, *Tales and Sketches* (1834),[2] and one other tale. Now reading the fiction of a minor writer of any period requires some effort of the historical imagination, both in taking into account changes in taste and literary expectation, and in realizing his special problems and intentions, which may belong to his time as well as to him. In reading Stone we need to allow for—or at least to recognize—his jounalistic facility, which may appear as a blemish in his fiction. But there are blemishes beyond that, and if we grimace at a passage that seems stylistically overblown, we need to remember that critics of Stone's time and place were praising a fiction writer capable of such rhetoric by calling him "a true poet"[3]—doubtless intending to dignify fiction, but exerting a baleful influence upon it. We have seen a form of such praise in Bryant's praise of Cooper.

In most of his fiction, Stone seems particularly susceptible to the influences of his time, and in some of his tales there is a disconcertingly literal correspondence between critical sugges-tion and what Stone does. His "The Grave of the Indian King" is such a tale, and it seems to be connected with the beginning of the American materials discussion. The persistence of the influ-ence of that discussion in the work of Stone, Hawthorne, and others is often surprising.

William Tudor, urging the use of Indian materials in an epic vein, emphasizes Indian eloquence. "The speeches given by Homer to the characters in the Iliad and the Odyssey," he says, "form some of the finest passages in those poems. The speeches of these Indians [of the Five Nations] only want similar embel-lishment, to excite admiration." And Tudor particularly rec-ommends to the American writer the epic device of "prophetick narration, a prophecy after the facts have occurred," and suggests that a writer might have the "prescient expounder of fate . . . declare . . . the alliances, contests, triumphs, and utter extinction of his race; that they should disappear with the ani-mals they hunted, and the forests that sheltered both . . . and leave no trace of their existence, but in the records of the white men."[4]

In "The Grave of the Indian King," Stone seems to be writing with his eye on the Tudor passage. The tale has to do with the American phase of King William's War. The scouts of the Onondaga, who are struggling against the French under Count Frontenac, bring news of an overwhelming French force; and the Onondaga, following the counsel of the aged chief Thurens-era, decide to flee in order to fight another day. Thurensera directs that he be left behind; and when Count Frontenac's forces come, they find him seated with his back against a tree. To them he makes his last prophecy:

> Listen to the voice of the Manitto, while he bids Thurensera tell what is to come upon you. Your race is to be as the river dried up—as the dead trees of the forest when the fire has

gone over it. The white man who sent Yonnondio [the French governor] over the great salt lake in the big canoe, will lose his power. A *wolf* is to walk abroad, that will scatter the palefaces at Quebec like a flock of sheep, and drive them out of the red men's land. The white men, with Cayenguerago [the English governor], who is our friend, will come over the land like the leaves. The panther is bounding to the setting sun: the bear moves slowly off the ground: the deer and buffalo leap over the mountains, and are seen no more. The forest bows before the white man. The great and little trees fall before his big hatchet. The white man's wigwams rise like the hill tops, and are as white as the head of the bald eagle. The waters shall remain; and when the red man is no more, the names he gave them shall last. The Great Spirit has said it. [1:219]

There can hardly be a clearer instance of the connection between literary theory and practice in our early national literature; indeed, Stone seems to be making Thurensera expand parts of the Tudor passage into concreteness.[5]

In Stone's tales having to do with Indians, there is another striking correspondence between the literary thinking of the time and Stone's practice, for he shares the impulse to give American scenery a literary record. In "Lake St. Sacrament" his long and impressive description of the northern lights as seen from the headwaters of Lake George (1:122–24) has a motive like that of Cooper's description of the ice storm in *The Pioneers*. Both are examples of the kind of literary record gratifying, and in some sort necessary, to our forebears. But even such descriptions did not fulfill all their needs.

The great need was that American scenery be connected with history or legend or story; beauty without such connection was thought to be but thin literary material. "If we take any glory in our country's being beautiful and sublime and picturesque," John Knapp writes, "we must approve the work which reminds us of its scenery by making it the theatre of splendid feats and heart-moving incidents."[6] Stone and his best contemporaries in fiction were eager to discover or supply associations for American places, either by the action of a narrative or by a calculated description. In this portion of a long description of Lake George (in "Lake St. Sacrament") Stone connects history and place:

> At the point where the lake takes a more eastern direction, a bay sets up amongst the hills to the north-west, beyond which, as far as vision extends, hills rise above hills, surprising for their loftiness, till at length their peaked summits are lost in the clouds. The bosom of the lake itself is adorned with multitudinous little islands, the fresh verdure of which, in summer, being, with the surrounding mountains, reflected back with peculiar vividness from the pure element, adds greatly to the picturesque effect, by thus mingling the beautiful with the rugged and sublime. Wild and desolate as this romantic region then was, and yet continues, its shores have nevertheless been consecrated with more blood than any other spot in America. For a long period it was the Thermopylæ through which alone the French supposed they must pass in their repeated attempts upon the extensive and fertile valley of the Hudson. And fierce and bloody were the conflicts for its possession. [1:134]

The passage is written from the overview—as if the observer were upon some commanding eminence—that we have remarked Cooper using in *The Pioneers*. It may show an influence from the doctrine of the picturesque that stems from William Gilpin. But above all it shows the pervasive influence of Associationism and of the practice of Sir Walter Scott.

In the passages we have been considering, the literary thinking belongs to the critics whose doctrine Stone has absorbed. In Stone's tales in the Gothic vein he is trying to work out the same problems with which some of his contemporaries in American fiction struggled. They quite naturally wished to use a convention of so obvious and pervasive appeal as the Gothic, even though it needed to be adapted if it were to be used in American settings—ruinous castles and ancient abbeys were in short supply. William Howard Gardiner remarks that an American writer can hardly "construct a second castle of Otranto," or amaze his readers "with mysteries, like those of the famed Udolpho," but Gardiner is "by no means sure that a first rate horror, of the most imaginative kind, might not be invented without the aid of

Gothic architecture, or Italian scenery."[7] Stone tries his best to
do so. He usually goes back to around the time of the Revolution
for his Gothic tales, perhaps assuming that a half-century of
elapsed time is enough to avoid the familiarity of present things.
But for one tale he goes back to witchcraft times to find an
American Gothic. In his treatment of witchcraft he is relatively
restrained—restrained at least in comparison with John Neal,
say, or James McHenry.

"Mercy Disborough: A Tale of the Witches" Stone uses to lead
off *Tales and Sketches* (1:1–75). He seems sometimes to have an
eye for subject matter,[8] and as he points out in his introduction
(1:vi), this tale is based upon the trials of Mercy Disborough and
of Elizabeth Clawson in Fairfield, Connecticut. But those trials
took place in 1692; Stone makes the date of his action a time
soon after 1660 in order to accommodate a sort of subplot concerning two of the regicide judges who escaped to New England,
Edward Whalley and William Goffe. They are represented in
the tale as hiding in an empty storehouse belonging to Governor
Leete. (William Leete was an ancestor of Stone, and it is historically true that he aided the regicides.)[9] Their only connection
with the main plot is that mysterious indications of their presence are taken in the course of the story as witchcraft
phenomena. Stone may have included them in his tale in order
to exalt his ancestor, but their inclusion also has an interest as a
matter of literary history. The record of the regicide judges in
New England was considered by literary theorists and writers
alike as literary material par excellence—and in two other instances a regicide judge is made to be present anachronistically
in the time of witchcraft excitement.[10]

The place of the tale in literary history is otherwise interesting.
It may well be the best literary use of witchcraft materials—and
despite liberties with the persons and events of the Fairfield
cases, the most authentic use of them—before the publication of
Hawthorne's "Young Goodman Brown" in 1835. The witchcraft
phenomena are of the sort we know in the records.[11] The chief
evidence against Mercy is "spectral evidence," in this instance
malicious instead of merely deluded, as it may have been also in
some of the actual witchcraft cases. Stone understands that
seventeenth-century witchcraft beliefs had a basis in the misin-

terpretation of Scripture, and he understands the way in which Indian sorcery was associated with witchcraft in the minds of our forefathers. Mercy and Elizabeth suffer the ordeal of "swimming a witch";[12] although that ordeal is not frequent in the New England records, it is indeed a part of the record in the Fairfield cases.[13] It is true that Stone quite unnecessarily departs from the New England records in having Mercy sentenced to be burnt instead of hanged. But in general he does manage to make witchcraft an effective American Gothic; and in his use of a band of Indians as the starting instrument of Mercy's rescue, he manages to make Indians an American Gothic too, as Charles Brockden Brown had recommended long before in the preface to *Edgar Huntley*.

Stone moves his tale along well. Although he remarks of the witchcraft records, truly enough, that "the demons may justly be denounced for the paucity of their ideas, and the poverty of their inventions" (1:39), when he deals with the manifestations that lead to the indictment of Mercy, he resists the temptation to dress up his materials. Instead, he manages an effective narrative point of view, in which phenomena are apprehended as they might have been by the community. This passage is especially interesting because the probability of the deacon's agency is left entirely to the reader's inference:

> The case of a lad, a nephew of the deacon's, is too important to be omitted. He had ventured very near to the old storehouse, to indulge his curiosity by examining the witch-tracks which some people were supposed to have seen; and when there, he declared that he had heard Goody Clawson and Mercy Disborough chattering together in the cellar. He was thereupon sadly dealt with, being often suddenly and violently seized and knocked about at a terrible rate, dashed against the walls, &c. His bed would fly from under him in the night-time; and when one day his uncle attempted to hold him in a chair, the chair itself fell to dancing; and soon afterwards the deacon was also constrained to dance, and afterwards the poor boy likewise—so that all three were obliged to dance around the house, for the amusement of the demons. [1:38]

The narration is most effective when it is closest to the source. As the story progresses, unfortunately, the narrator removes himself from the action and is far too likely to insist overtly upon his own nineteenth-century enlightenment, so that the tale does not fulfill its promise. Even as he is describing the "swimming," Stone says that Mercy's destiny "was in the hands of those whose prejudices would not allow them to pause for an inquiry into the rational or physical causes of the phenomenon they had just witnessed" (1:52). But in the long tradition of fiction about New England witchcraft, few writers have managed the relationship of the storyteller to the story consistently well.

Some of the characters in "Mercy Disborough" are well done: Deacon Goodspeed, whose advances Mercy rebuffs, is a satisfactory hypocrite; his spinster sister, Mehitable, Mercy's chief accuser, is a fine comic figure; the well-meaning minister, Mr. Whitman, is convincingly deluded. Unhappily, Stone is less successful with Mercy herself. In order to exalt her character, he makes her impossibly enlightened; and he endows her with a forbidding fluency, until one wonders if our Puritan forebears would not have been more likely to put a cleft stick on her tongue, as with Mary Oliver, than to execute her. She has a ready eloquence in every exigency. When the ordeal by "swimming" has been determined upon, she seizes the occasion:

> But now that by the devices of the sons of Belial I am about to taste the bitter waters of Meribah, I would testify to these people, which have mouths that speak not, eyes that they see not, and ears that they hear not, that I have ever conducted myself in all my goings out, and all my comings in, like an honest and virtuous maiden, as the Lord inclined and enabled me thereunto. And now peradventure—[1:50]

Here the officers interfere, and the reader is spared the rest of a speech that might have run to a page and more, as does Mercy's admonition to the court when she pleads not guilty (1:42–43).

Stone's way of representing the speech of his Puritans is like Cooper's in *The Wept of Wish-ton-Wish*: he makes them talk in a tissue of biblical idiom and biblical allusion. Even poor old Goody Clawson, given the opportunity, speaks much as Mercy does. Doubtless both Cooper and Stone are trying to emulate

Scott's handling of the speech of his Covenanters, and they fail about equally. Both writers, too, make a pretty ineffectual use of the history of the regicide judges. But Stone's long tale is a good deal more lively than Cooper's novel and would not suffer by comparison with it.

Our two of Stone's Gothic tales with their actions around the time of the Revolution exhibit remarkably different techniques. Although the first of them, "The Skeleton Hand" (2:217–39), is highly derivative, Stone seems to have made a considerable effort in it. He may have wished his readers to recognize the derivative quality and to be glad to think that elements from British romance could be naturalized in an American scene. The reader today will feel that the tale might have been written by Scott in some feverish distemper, although before the end he may think of Charles Robert Maturin's *Melmoth the Wanderer* too. The tale has a long time span—twenty-five years or so—and enough plot materials for an extended romance; the crowded narration has some effect of unintended travesty. But that is characteristic of a good many tales in Stone's time and place. Not many writers knew how to focus a short narrative—Miss Sedgwick often seems unable to. Stone's tale is at any rate a successful adaptation of the Gothic to the American scene.

The action of "The Skeleton Hand" goes on in a village on the Hudson, and begins in the years before the Revolution. It concerns the disappearance of Susan Hazelwood on her bridal eve, the discovery of her skeleton some ten years later, and at last the revelation of the murderer by the "miraculous bleeding of the 'Skeleton Hand' " of Susan—the skeleton hand that an old innkeeper, sure that the murderer would sometime return, had hung over his public table fifteen years before. The most striking character is a mysterious old beldam, Elsie Hallenbake, who is the confederate of Roswell Thornton in the abduction of Susan, but who is horrified by the murder that Thornton commits in desperation when he finds that Susan has gone mad with grief and terror. Thornton is like a less admirable Ravenswood (of *The Bride of Lammermoor*); Stone seems unabashed in making Elsie Hallenbake a close imitation of Nora of the Fitful Head in *The Pirate*:

Had she been mistress of the whirlwind, she could not have

been more delighted with storms. She had been seen, her tall form erect, and with extended arms, standing on the verge of fearsome precipices, in the midst of the most awful tempests, conversing, as it were, with unseen spirits, her long matted hair streaming in the wind, while the thunder was riving the rocks beneath her feet, and the red lightning encircling her as with a winding-sheet of flame. [2:228]

Old Elsie dies at the end of the tale, after Thornton's execution, having "lingered on earth far beyond the period of life allotted to man," as if she could not die until justice was done.

Thornton himself, in the long years between the murder and the revelation of his guilt, had tried to expiate his crime. Some mysterious inhibition had always thwarted his attempts to lose his life, and although he put himself in every peril—as a soldier in the Revolution, at sea, in Paris during the French Revolution, among pirates, in Indian warfare as a member of a band of Indians, in the yellow fever plague at Philadelphia—he is preserved for the preternatural denouement. Within a page Stone outlines an action for a romance such as Maturin might have written.

Stone's "The Skeleton Hand" and "The Spectre Fire-Ship" both appeared in the *Knickerbocker Magazine* in 1834, the latter in May (3:361–71), apparently too late for inclusion in *Tales and Sketches*. The *Knickerbocker* was distinguished for good Gothic tales, among them Hawthorne's "Dr. Heidegger's Experiment." But "The Spectre Fire-Ship" is better than its general run of Gothic tales, and better than the rest of Stone's fiction so far as I know it. The tale will recall the Faust story, but of course what happened to Faust has in its essentials happened to many men in many places. Stone is not naturalizing a legend as Austin does in "Peter Rugg"; we will hardly say that Stone takes the Faust legend to sea as Austin brings the *Flying Dutchman* legend to land. But there is apparently some oblique influence on "The Spectre Fire-Ship" from the Block Island legend of a phantom burning ship that returns to the seas about the island annually.[14] It may be that the legend influenced Stone's source for the tale rather than Stone himself.

The tale begins with a disquisition on sailors' superstitions. It is facile, ill-focused, overlong; nonetheless it succeeds in its narrative function of inviting the readers' initial scepticism of a marvellous action—a scepticism which the tale undertakes to transform into imaginative assent. The introductory passage over, Stone establishes a source for the tale, for it purports to be a redaction of the story of an old Captain Samuel Hoyt, a story of an experience in a time just before the Revolution. In a footnote to the tale, Stone also speaks of a manuscript by Captain Hoyt that he has in his possession. The footnote is probably factitious; and we cannot be sure of the relationship of the tale to its source. But I think we may be sure that the tale does have a source in a sailor's story, and that the economy of the tale, which is not at all characteristic of Stone, is attributable to his good use of a source. It looks as if Stone had really discovered a legend.

As Stone retells the Captain's tale, it is briefly this: As a young man, Hoyt embarks as a seaman on the *Dove*, out of Guilford, Connecticut, bound for St. Bartholomews; a few days out the ship is wrecked, and he and three others are rescued by the *El Dorado*, of Newburyport; the wreck and the rescue are vividly described. The rescued sailors find Captain Warner of the *El Dorado* a man of commanding presence but strangely disturbed; long after their experience on the *El Dorado* they hear stories of him which suggest that he may have been a pirate. Captain Warner is frequently heard at prayer, but his prayers always end: "But oh, if I am to be buffetted, I must be!" At length he discloses to Mr. Seward, his mate, that, in some horrifying exigency, he has made a compact with the devil, and that he must surrender himself the next Friday night—a disclosure that is heard by the crew or some of them. On Thursday evening Captain Warner is sure that he sees a ship, which he calls a fire-ship, approaching from the north; and even the mate thinks there may be a ship with bare poles on the horizon. The next day the Captain informs the mate that the mysterious ship has put over a boat; and he seems to receive a distinguished visitor, the crew obeying his orders, although they see no one. Some time past eleven on Friday night the shadowy ship that has seemed to pursue them suddenly blazes forth "a ship of entire flame." His crew endeavor to secure Captain Warner in his cabin, but in response to a summons from the fire-ship, he crashes through the window and leaps into the sea. The fire-ship disappears. The mate brings the *El Dorado* safely to her destination, Antigua; he and his crew abandon her there; and no seaman ever sails in her again.

The tale is managed well. Although we are to suppose we have Stone's account of Captain Hoyt's recollection of the action, none of Hoyt's own emotions are recorded, and Stone's narrative is often skillfully restrained. In Stone's redaction of Hoyt's story, Hoyt disappears after the account of his rescue, and, by the time of the account of the Thursday, Stone himself no longer intrudes into the narrative. There seems no term for the narrative point of view; it is not objective narration, for sometimes conduct is interpreted and emotions assigned to the crew collectively or to individuals. But the narrative is curiously impersonal; no emotion in it seems to belong to Hoyt or to Stone; and the frequent constructions in the passive voice seem to fit. Stone succeeds in letting the reader feel with the crew that Captain Warner is under some strange delusion, and to let him keep feeling so for a time even after the crew has accepted Captain Warner's confession of his compact with the devil.

> Sailors are, as we have seen, always superstitious, and under the circumstances of the present case—the wildness of the night, the angry looks of the billows rolling beneath them, and the agitation of the captain, upon whose face large drops of sweat stood trembling, induced them to yield a ready belief to the dreadful tale, without once dreaming that it might be nothing more than the dark and wayward fancy of "a mind diseased." [P. 366]

The sailors, like Mr. Seward, come almost to think they see a shadowy ship, although they do not see the messenger Captain Hoyt believes comes to him from her. In this account of the curious pantomime of the messenger's reception, the point of view may be that of the crew collectively:

> The captain informed Mr. Seward that the fire-ship had put off a boat, which was now just alongside. This communication—for the boat did not become visible, even to the imaginations of the sailors—was followed by the order—"On deck there! Boys man the sides!" With equal

terror and alacrity, the preparations were made for receiving a distinguished visitor on board. The sailors descended to the side of the ship with their hats beneath their arms, and Captain Warner, stepping to his post, made the usual compliment of receiving a gentleman on board, though with emotions of indescribable perturbation.

"Sir," said he to his invisible visitor, "will you please to walk below?"

He then descended into the cabin, as though in company with a guest, whom he was conducting thither with marks of consideration. He returned in about twenty minutes—gave orders again to have the sides of the ship manned, which were punctually obeyed,—and dismissed his still invisible guest. [P. 368]

Stone carefully avoids fixing a precise time at which the crew begin to be sure they see a phantom ship, but the reader shares their increasing conviction; and when, just before midnight on the fatal Friday, "the shadowy vessel that had been chasing them" appears in flames, no vestige of the attitude of critical appraisal that Stone had allowed the reader as the action began remains with him.

Indeed, Stone manages skillfully to enforce the feeling of inevitability that arises from the fixing of the time at which the catastrophe must come. "The contract," the Captain says when he makes his confession, "will expire precisely at 12 o'clock on Friday night next. I shall then be sent for, and must go, though floated away in a river of flame." The Captain sees the fire-ship coming for him; the men are increasingly sure that a shadowy ship does approach; when she does appear as a ship of flame and the Captain gets his last summons, an expectation that Stone has contrived in the reader himself is strikingly fulfilled. Of course one is reminded of Marlowe's Dr. Faustus, but Stone's tale does not suffer thereby. Captain Warner, who carries out his compact without anything like Dr. Faustus's eloquence in despair, has a dignity of his own.

The full title of Stone's collection is *Tales and Sketches,—Such as They Are.* In his introduction Stone says: "As to the title of these volumes—the production of occasional hours of relaxation, snatched from the demands of a laborious profession—the author has chosen it exactly for its fitness." It may be difficult to decide whether the statement is an indication of Stone's humility about his fiction or of a certain arrogance that seems to have been part of his nature. At any rate, Stone was an active journalist, he was soon to turn to his historical writing, and he may well have thought of his fiction as a minor activity, although he cherished it enough to collect it. He uses as a title-page motto the tag "scribimus indocti doctique,"[15] and indeed his fiction is an evidence of the surprising strength of the impulse among Americans of his time to write and publish fiction, even though very few writers could reasonably hope for any appreciable reward in money or reputation. But Stone and scores of other contributors to the magazines and annuals were working out a fiction for the still-new nation. As we look at their work from our perspective, it seems a concerted effort in a way unparalleled elsewhere. Hawthorne's best work surpasses that of his forgotten fellow-workers, yet it is from their work that his work emerges.

NOTES

1. After connections with various newspapers (and with three short-lived literary periodicals), Stone in 1821 became editor and part owner of the New York *Commercial Advertiser*, a Federalist and later a Whig newspaper. He devoted himself and his paper to a number of causes, and was active in educational matters, becoming superintendent of the common schools in New York City (1843–44). He had a wide acquaintance with literary and political figures; among his friends were James Gates Percival and Robert Charles Sands (Sands was associated with Stone on his newspaper). For Stone's legal troubles with Cooper, see James Grossman, *James Fenimore Cooper*, pp. 140–41, 160–61, 217–18. Stone's important historical works on the Iroquois Confederacy were written during the later part of his life in addition to his heavy duties as editor. He wrote other books, and he was a contributor to magazines and annuals. His collections of fiction are *Tales and Sketches* (1834), *The Atlantic Book Club* (1834), and *The Mysterious Bridal and Other Tales* (1835). A memoir, "The Life and Writings of William Leete Stone," by his son William Leete Stone (1835–1908) is printed in the elder Stone's *The Life and Times of Sa-go-ye-wat-ha, or, Red Jacket* (Albany, 1866), pp. 9–101.

2. *Tales and Sketches*, 2 vols. (New York: Harper & Brothers, 1834). Except for references to "The Spectre Fire-Ship," all the parenthetical page references in this chapter are to this book.

3. For example, Stone (like Hawthorne) seems to become overstimulated in the act of describing any moonlit scene: "The bosom of the lake was partially illumined by the beams of the declining moon, as they played through the foliage of the trees, which but for those silvery rays would have left darkness, as of old, brooding upon the face of the deep" (1:1). "But ere twilight had darkened into night, just as our travellers had reached the brow of the hill . . . the queen of night arose in all her brightness and beauty; and, by the aid of her mild and mellow light, they descended and arrived in safety" (1:89). The "true poet" expression may indicate a failure in early American criticism to distinguish clearly between the purposes of the poet and the purposes of the fiction writer. See John Stafford, *The Literary Criticism of "Young America"* (New York: Russell & Russell, 1967), pp. 55, 71.

4. *North American Review* 2 (1815): 26, 30–31.

5. There is another curious Tudor parallel. Autumnal scenes were thought to be especially an American resource, and Tudor recommends to writers "the singular appearance of the woods; where all the hues of the most lively flowers, the vivid colours of tulips, are given to the trees of the forest," and the groves are attired "in the gaudiest and most fantastick livery" (*North American Review* 2 [1815]: 16–17). Tudor's comparison seems even less happy in Stone's use of it. In "A Romance of the Forest," describing "the rich and variegated autumnal livery of the American forests," Stone writes of "a landscape of apparent flowers, rivalling in variety and beauty the spectacle which, to a poet's eye, would be presented by a magnificent undulating bed of tulips, of illimitable extent" (1:88).

6. *North American Review* 8 (1818): 173–74.

7. *North American Review* 15 (1822): 253–54. Gardiner has no great interest in the Gothic tale in itself, but he values the Gothic as a way of attaining aesthetic distance. He praises Cooper for his skill in *Lionel Lincoln* in removing scenes in the Province House and other Boston places from the familiarity of everyday associations by the "sort of magical authority" he shares with Scott, Mrs. Radcliffe, Walpole, and Brockden Brown (*North American Review* 23 [1826]: 152–53).

8. For Stone, unhappily, promising material does not always result in a good tale. His son in his memoir of Stone (pp. 45–61) reprints from Eliza Leslie's annual, the *Gift* for 1836, a tale called "The Language of Flowers." It is based upon an episode in the lives of Aaron Burr and the striking Margaret Moncrieffe during the Revolution. It is a very poor tale yet, according to his son, Stone had the story from Aaron Burr

himself. There is an entertaining account of Margaret Moncrieffe in Morris Bishop's *The Exotics* (New York: American Heritage Publishing Co., 1969), pp. 63–71.

9. William Leete (ca. 1613–83) was governor of the New Haven Colony at the time of the action of the tale. He was governor of the Connecticut Colony 1676–82. In his introduction Stone mentions Ezra Stiles, *A History of Three of the Judges of King Charles I* (1794), but he seems to have made little use of it.

10. James McHenry, *The Spectre of the Forest* (1823), and James Nelson Barker's play *Superstition* (1824).

11. Sometimes Stone draws directly from the record of the Fairfield trials. An instance is Deacon Goodspeed's troubles with a bewitched skiff (1:26), which follows closely the testimony of one Edward Jesop at the trial of Mercy Disborough. See John M. Taylor, *The Witchcraft Delusion in Colonial Connecticut, 1647–1697* (New York: The Grafton Press, 1908), p. 64.

12. King James I in his *Dæmonologie* states the principle for "swimming" a suspected witch this way: "It appears that God hath appointed (for a supernatural signe of the monstrous impiete of Witches) that the water shall refuse to receive them in her bosome, that have shaken off them the sacred water of Baptisme, and willfully refused the benefite thereof" (quoted in G. L. Kittredge, *Witchcraft in Old and New England* [1929; reissue New York: Russell & Russell, 1958], pp. 290–91).

13. Taylor prints generous portions of the evidence at the trials of Mercy Disborough and of Elizabeth Clawson. Both women were accused of malicious evil done their neighbors; some of the evidence against both was spectral evidence. A committee of women searchers alleged that they found "witch marks" on both. Two men deposed that at the ordeal by "swimming" both women, who had been bound hand and foot, "swam upon the water like a cork" and could not be pressed down into it. Despite the evidence of the "swimming," Elizabeth Clawson was acquitted. Mercy Disborough was convicted, but later reprieved and then pardoned. This result seems to have been brought about by the formal protests of a group of ministers and another group of citizens somehow functioning as friends of the court. The ministers denied the validity of spectral evidence, of the evidence of the unexplained deaths of cattle, of witch marks, and of the "swimming." The other group warned against the same evidence, pointing out what a "miserable toyl they are in in the [Massachusetts] Bay for adhereing to these last mentioned litigious things," and also citing an irregularity in the jury. See Taylor, *The Witchcraft Delusion*, pp. 73, 75–78.

14. According to the legend, in 1738 the *Palatine*, carrying a number of Dutch families bound for Philadelphia, was wrecked on Block Island,

off Rhode Island, after its crew had abandoned the ship and its passengers in fear of an epidemic. It was believed that wreckers on Block Island had decoyed with a false light the amateur sailors from among the passengers who were trying to navigate the ship. Apparently a belief in the annual return of a phantom burning ship still persists. Whittier's poem "The Palatine" (1867) has helped to extend the life of the legend.

15. Horace, *Epistles*, 2.1.117.

13

Hawthorne's Showman and His Audience

Nathaniel Hawthorne's "Main Street" was first printed in *Aesthetic Papers* (1849), a collection of miscellaneous pieces (among them Thoreau's "Civil Disobedience") edited by Hawthorne's sister-in-law, Elizabeth Peabody; Hawthorne included the sketch in *The Snow-Image, and Other Twice-Told Tales* (1851). "Main Street" is one of the few pieces he wrote during his years at the Salem Custom House; and it is quite different from any one of the others. It is not clear that, before he lost his place in the Custom House, he really intended to continue his career as a professional writer, to make his writing anything more than an avocation. "Main Street" is at any rate retrospective and, despite its comedy, a kind of estimate of the genre of historical fiction Hawthorne began writing in college or soon thereafter, continued to the time of his marriage and residence at the Old Manse, and later returned to in *The Scarlet Letter*.

Hawthorne's work is connected in important ways with the literary discussion that went on for about fifteen years before his first tales appeared. The tales in which he works with the materials of New England history are clearly of a different order from his other pieces of short fiction and his essay-like sketches. They are so because in them the influences of literary theory, of Scott, of his ancestral inheritance, and of his reading in New England history combine into something like a tradition. In some of the early historical tales—"The Gray Champion," for example—Hawthorne follows critical prescription closely. In some of them—"Young Goodman Brown," for example—he discovers possibilities in the use of historical materials hardly suspected by the literary theorists.

But in all of his historical tales, Hawthorne searches out such materials as William Tudor and his colleagues had insisted were to be found in our early history: "perilous and romantick adventures, figurative and eloquent harangues, strong contrasts and important interests." And in all of them the literary discussion that went on during his formative years pointed him toward his accomplishment. In "Main Street" he looks back on his own work, wryly but doubtless with some satisfaction. The sketch is a too much neglected indication of Hawthorne's idea of himself as storyteller.

Some of Hawthorne's tales have been carefully examined for their implications about his literary thinking—notably "The Prophetic Pictures," "Drowne's Wooden Image," "The Birthmark," "The Artist of the Beautiful," and "The Snow-Image." The interest is certainly a legitimate one, but the inquiry has been disappointing. For one thing, whatever literary theory may be inferred from these tales seems to have but little reference to Hawthorne's best work. For another, nothing we can infer from them touches questions important to any writer: For whom am I writing? What is my relationship to them?

From his beginnings as a writer, these questions were difficult for Hawthorne.[1] In "The Old Manse" he speaks of "my limited number of readers, whom I venture to regard rather as a circle of friends"; and in two subsequent prefaces he uses much the same image.[2] He may be conforming to the lingering notion that an overt professionalism was not quite admirable in a writer, the fading survival of the notion that led Washington Irving into the "Geoffrey Crayon" persona for his *Sketch Book* and *Bracebridge Hall*. Yet I think that the attitude and even the manner of its expression have a clear relationship to the concept of Hawthorne as a writer which some of his first friendly critics, faced with the problem of giving high praise to a writer virtually unknown, thought it tactful to suggest. Hawthorne was, Park Benjamin, Henry Wadsworth Longfellow, and Evert A. Duyckinck told their readers, a writer for a special and limited sort of audience, with a temperamental preference for personal obscurity.[3]

Hawthorne's talk about his readers as a limited circle of friends may seem merely a pose, even an irritating one, although perhaps useful to him in envisioning an audience. But in the retrospective "Main Street" Hawthorne envisions his audience quite differently, and suggests an attitude toward his readers and toward himself as a writer at once more complex and more professional than that of the prefatory pieces. Even in "Main Street," however, our insight is limited, for what is said in it applies clearly only to work that uses historical materials.

In scheme, structure, and general intention "Main Street" is without parallel in Hawthorne's writing, but the element of self-ridicule is not quite without parallel therein. "Here is thy husband in his old chamber," Hawthorne once wrote to his fiancée, "where he produced those stupendous works of fiction, which have since impressed the Universe with wonderment and awe!"; and he went on to detail the furnishings of that chamber as they were connected with his work, down to "the worn-out shoe-brush with which this polished writer polished his boots."[4] Even in writing intended for publication we find pleasant countertendencies to a romantic notion of the artist that emerges in some letters and some tales. There are the graceful depreciations of his work in the prefatory pieces for his collections, the occasional self-parody, and the whimsical little preface to "Rappaccini's Daughter." In the preface the pretense that Hawthorne is the French writer M. de l'Aubépine[5] being introduced to the American public not only makes Hawthorne's characteristic self-depreciation amusing, but provides an opportunity for a list of French titles—bits of self-satire—for some of the pieces now in *Mosses from an Old Manse*: "Roderic; ou le Serpent à l'estomac," "L'Artiste du Beau; ou le Papillon Mécanique," "Beatrice; ou la Belle Empoisonneuse."

In "Main Street," however, the self-ridicule is but one element in a piece in which many things go on, and go on so nearly at once that the effect is not single and not easily described; an analysis of "Main Street," moreover, runs the risk of reducing it to something less than it is. The self-ridicule inheres in the figure of the showman, in the machinery of his show, and in the comment of members of his audience. But the self-ridicule includes—or is included in—consideration of the nature and the problems of historical fiction, especially Hawthorne's own. One does not hesitate to identify the showman with Hawthorne, for the showman's entertainment represents the history of Salem,[6] enacted on the principal thoroughfare. A good many of the events and persons are those Hawthorne had used in his tales.

"Main Street" begins, "A respectable-looking individual makes his bow and addresses the public." The showman speaks of himself as a "public man"; when criticism has momentarily disturbed him, he resumes his composure "with the inevitable acquiescence of all public servants." This showman has no romantic notion that an artist should be independent and contemptuous of his audience. He intends to interest a public and asks for approval.

We are to imagine the showman as a puppet-master, whose puppets perform by elaborate mechanical contrivance and, apparently, before a panorama—one of those continuous paintings on a strip of canvas many yards long moving between two rollers. In the nineteenth century, when panoramas were very popular, they were accompanied by lectures; and the showman accompanies his entertainment with one. He operates his equipment with a crank; the "little wheels and springs" of the machinery are well oiled but, the showman remarks, the mechanism is complicated and hence liable to casualties. He controls the lighting too: the lights can brighten into noonday sunshine, or fade into moonlight, or be obscured in November cloud—they seem to represent Hawthorne's own facility with chiaroscuro—and the showman speaks of his "pictorial exhibition," his "pictorial mechanism," his "pictorial puppet-show." But, whatever the implications of passages in Hawthorne's work elsewhere, there is here no magic mirror, there are no esoteric artistic means beyond understanding. The means of representation have been constructed; they are manipulated through devices that may go wrong; the show does indeed break down at the end. Yet if nothing goes wrong, and if the audience is receptive, the illusion may be almost complete; the audience may have "the action represented in this life-like, this almost magic, picture!" But the rapport between the showman and his audience is by no means complete.

The audience at the entertainment is represented by but three of its members. There is a courteous gentleman who points out two historical anomalies. The showman has no defense: apparently such things are nearly inevitable in historical fiction. The

two anomalies, however, seem to be of somewhat different
kinds. One is the bringing together of a number of figures on
the main street of Salem who in actuality could never have been
there all at one time. We may suppose that the showman, by his
silence, admits a calculated anachronism for his own purposes,
as Hawthorne sometimes allows himself an anachronism[7] or
other historical discrepancy for his. The other anomaly seems to
represent an uncalculated mistake. The showman speaks of the
descendants of the first wife of Governor Endicott, who, the
courteous gentleman points out, had no children. Despite this
gentleman's awareness of historical inaccuracies, he maintains
both his courtesy and his interest.

But there is, too, an "acidulous-looking" critic whom nothing
pleases. Now the showman is quite ready to admit that he is
presenting puppets worked by wires; that his panoramic
background seen too closely and in an improper light is but
daubed canvas; that he is representing, not the verity of history,
but an illusion. His machinery stands for the procedures and
privileges of the writer of historical fiction. He protests to his
critic that verisimilitude must depend partly upon the spectator's
willingness to find it: "Human art has its limits, and we must now
and then ask a little aid from the spectator's imagination." We
remember Theseus's words in *A Midsummer-Night's Dream*: "The
best in this kind are but shadows; and the worst are no worse, if
imagination amend them"; and Hawthorne doubtless was remembering them too.

As well as he can, the showman has provided an aesthetic
distance; his critic has simply refused to accept it. The showman
remonstrates with him: "But, sir, you have not the proper point
of view. You sit altogether too near to get the best effect of my
pictorial exhibition." But the critic is not to be moved; he
examines the puppets too narrowly, and they appear to him but
crudely cut and colored pieces of cardboard jerking on all too
apparent wires; the figures of Captain Gardner and his mettled
horse, on which the showman had particularly prided himself,
seem to the critic like figures of a tame and diminutive devil
astride a pig.

There is in the audience, however, as the showman points out
to his critic, a "young lady, in whose face I have watched the

reflection of every changing scene." It is a subtlety of the piece that we know so little of this member of the showman's audience—and of the segment of Hawthorne's public that she represents. Hawthorne is recognizing that the public for his fiction, as for fiction in general, is largely a feminine public, and accepting it. But this young lady, who shows such appreciation of the showman's art, does not speak; she has a capacity for enjoyment and she accepts the conditions of the puppet show. We know no more of her than that. Yet she furnishes the showman with his most effective explicit defense of his artistry: it can be delighted in.

The showman's entertainment is presented not only to his audience within the hall but, through the record of his discourse, to us as readers. And his narrative techniques are so much those especially characteristic of Hawthorne that his discourse seems a kind of restrained parody. Like Hawthorne, the showman slips from one narrative point of view to another, and within very rapid narration. The action may come to us with immediacy, and almost as if we were viewing it through the eyes of a Salem Puritan—almost, but not quite, for, as often in Hawthorne's tales, there is slight, ironic intrusion of another attitude. Here, for example, is part of the showman's account of the arrival of the first Quakers in Salem. "See!" the showman says,

> they trample upon our wise and well-established laws in the person of our chief magistrate; for Governor Endicott is passing, now an aged man, and dignified with long habits of authority,—and not one of the irreverent vagabonds has moved his hat. . . . Here comes old Mr. Norris, our venerable minister. Will they doff their hats, and pay reverence to him? No: their hats stick fast to their ungracious heads, as if they grew there; and—impious varlets that they are, and worse than the heathen Indians!—they eye our reverend pastor with a peculiar scorn, distrust, unbelief and utter denial of his sanctified pretentions, of which he himself immediately becomes conscious; the more bitterly conscious, as he never knew nor dreamed of the like before.

The account of the witchcraft distress also comes to us from the point of view of Salem Puritans. They are disturbed and hardly able to believe their neighbors guilty, but they are reassured when Cotton Mather tells them that all has been religiously and justly done, and they know well enough that there are desires and temptations which might lead even such as Martha Carrier or the Reverend Mr. Burroughs into the devil's power. The substantial passage in "Main Street" on the troubles of 1692 seems to me one of Hawthorne's great pieces of historical reconstruction, firmly based in the record, but written with a kind of insight that the historian as historian, even if he be capable of it, must not allow himself.

In his discourse the showman also uses other narrative points of view. He may, for instance, use a historical perspective within an immediate account of an event, and so interpret it, as Hawthorne often did in his tales.[8] Here is part of an account of a muster-day:

> There they come, fifty of them or more. . . . Do they not manœuvre like soldiers who have seen stricken fields? And well they may; for this band is composed of precisely such materials as those with which Cromwell is preparing to beat down the strength of a kingdom; and his famous regiment of Ironsides might be recruited from just such men. In everything at this period, New England was the essential spirit and flower of that which was about to become uppermost in the mother-country.

And there are too, even within the showman's rapid narration, such passages of reflective interpretation as we know in *The Scarlet Letter*. Two passages of reflection on the quality of Puritan life are of particular interest.

Hawthorne, directed in his quest for fictional material by the literary theorists, had been able to find striking incidents and personages in Puritan life, so that the experience he represents looms in our imaginations. But his comments in "Main Street" show that he thought he had been dealing in his fiction, not at all with the norm of Puritan life, but with its vivid exceptions. In a passage which restates what Hawthorne had written in "Doctor Bullivant" about twenty years before,[9] the showman is made to say that, when the first emigrants came, "the zeal of a recovered faith burned like a lamp within their hearts," but that even within their lifetimes, and certainly within those of their children, the lamp began to burn dimly, "and then it might be seen how hard, cold, and confined was their system,—how like an iron cage was that which they called Liberty." And in a later passage the showman remarks that the daily life of Salem "must have trudged onward with hardly anything to diversify and enliven it, while also its rigidity could not fail to cause miserable distortions of the moral nature. Such a life was sinister to the intellect, and sinister to the heart." Hawthorne apparently never had any full sympathy with Puritanism either as a faith or an ideal. No fiction of his is concerned with the zeal of a recovered faith that in "Main Street" he seems to recognize but does not represent. Even in *The Scarlet Letter*, where the time span is 1642 to 1649, there is no representation of that initial spirit of New England Puritanism.

The reflection on the quality of Puritan life, however, may be aside from the showman's primary function. His unfriendly critic complains: "What is all this? A sermon? If so, it is not in the bill." And the showman admits the stricture: "Very true, and I ask pardon of the audience." Perhaps he is saying that reflection may be allowed him as an indulgence, but that his function is representation, not reflection; reflection, he admits, "is not in the bill." Yet Hawthorne often asks of us the indulgence, not only in the romances, but in so early a tale as "The Maypole of Merry Mount," and in the later "The Birthmark" and "Ethan Brand," two tales in which the persistent authorial instruction may be a blemish.

The daily life of Salem, the showman says, ordinarily trudged along unenlivened; indeed, he insists that "a funeral feast" was the only occasion in the social customs of New England "where jollity was sanctioned by universal practice"—a spirituous and grisly jollity. Yet the account of Salem life in the showman's discourse often seems lively enough—partly because we are so often reminded of Hawthorne's tales. There are Endicott, Peter Palfrey, and Thomas Morton—and we remember "The Maypole of Merry Mount." When the showman speaks of Endicott and Roger Williams within successive sentences, we recall "Endicott

and the Red Cross," and we recall the tale again when we come
to a passage that describes some Puritan punishments. Perhaps
unconsciously, Hawthorne repeats in "Main Street" the image
from "Endicott and the Red Cross" of the wolf's head affixed to
the church door, with the plash of blood beneath. The accounts
of the coming of the Quakers and of the witchcraft time of
course connect in our minds, as they do in Hawthorne's, with
"The Gentle Boy" and with "Young Goodman Brown." These
remarkable penetrations of the past should be considered with
the tales more often than they are.

Yet some questions about our ability to penetrate the past
emerge for us as a result of the showman's discourse—emerge so
clearly that I think Hawthorne surely intended them to. One
becomes keenly aware of that curious irony he experiences in
some small degree on any return to a span of history with which
he is familiar and from which his mind can go on to subsequent
events. When, for instance, the showman remarks, "How sweet
must it be for those who have an Eden in their hearts, like Roger
Conant and his wife, to find a new world to project it into, as
they have," we remember too well how soon it was impossible to
think of the Bay Colony as an Eden. Such ironic realization may
reinforce another feeling. The showman remarks how soon the
heavy tread of white men beats down "the wild woods, the wild
wolf, and the wild Indian" all alike. "Even so it shall be. The
pavements of the Main Street must be laid over the red man's
grave." And later, when the showman has represented some
schoolboys making game of the drunken grandson of the great
Squaw Sachem, he asks, "Does it not go far towards telling the
whole story of the vast growth and prosperity of one race, and
the fated decay of another?"

We hardly know how to answer; the image, moreover, is a
disquieting one. History is the record of what was, so far as can
be ascertained; and we are prone to feel that what did happen
had to happen, that it was fated. We hardly know whether the
sense of inevitability we have so strongly has its basis in history
itself or in something else—perhaps in a desire to absolve our
ancestors from moral responsibility and to escape it ourselves. At
any rate, Hawthorne himself avoided dealing with Indian material, although he recognized that it was one of the great re-

sources of the American writer.[10] Even "Roger Malvin's Burial," which develops from an incident in Indian warfare, is focussed so that the moral implications of the struggle between white men and Indians do not arise in the tale, although they seem to be recognized in its first paragraph.

When the showman has represented the great snow of 1717, a wire breaks and his entertainment comes to a sudden end—an acknowledgment of the historical period in which Hawthorne had worked best. But the showman laments; how the interest of his audience would have deepened, he exclaims, could he have led them at last "into the sunshine of the present" and given them "a reflex of the very life that is flitting past us!" "Not a gentleman that walks the street," the showman continues, "but should have beheld his own face and figure, his gait, the peculiar swing of his arm, and the coat he put on yesterday." That lament, I believe, is also Hawthorne's.

The subtlety of intention and the balance of interest in "Main Street" are perhaps too delicate—so delicate that either a slight misapprehension on the reader's part or a slight failure in keeping on Hawthorne's part can too much affect the sketch. Hawthorne uses the curious and the dangerous scheme of letting his showman's discourse become a sort of sampling of both his characteristic subject matter and his characteristic techniques—an attempt that will succeed fully only when the reader knows the Hawthorne tales that have subject matter in common with the showman's entertainment. And the piece as a wry representation of critical doctrine seems not to have succeeded well with most readers. It does not consider the function of the writer as much early- and middle-nineteenth-century literary theory leads us to expect. Indeed the showman has trouble with his audience and with his devices—which he readily confesses are devices. All told, the sketch makes surprisingly modest claims. As the showman's defense is finally that his representation can be delighted in, so the defense of historical fiction must be that, when it is written with insight, the reader can accept it with enjoyment. Given their assumptions, there is no answer either to the courteous gentleman or to the unfriendly critic, for fiction is neither literal history nor reality.

Here and there in his discourse, the showman remarks his

power over time. The dwellings of the first settlers, he says, "such is the ingenious contrivance of this piece of pictorial mechanism,—seem to have arisen, at various points of the scene, even while we have been looking at it." He can select from time: "under cover of a mist that has settled over the scene, a few years flit by, and escape our notice." He can condense or terminate the representation of some span of time in a regard for his audience's measure of interest: a typical Puritan day can be made to pass before their eyes in the space of a few minutes; the representation of a long winter can be cut off lest its monotony try the audience's fortitude as an actual New England winter does. The showman's power over time seems virtually complete; even when his representation has been interrupted by his unfriendly critic, he can at once resume his control: "The showman bows, and waves his hand; and, at the signal, as if time and vicissitude had been awaiting his permission to move onward, the mimic street becomes alive again."

Perhaps after all that apparent mastery of time is the great achievement of a writer like Scott or Thackeray who can make his readers feel that the personages he represents escape out of time and live in the present of his art. Hawthorne too means to achieve that feeling for period that Scott brought into fiction in English. And often he does. The past as it is present in his tales and in some sort summarized in "Main Street" is thronged with personages vivid to us, and more alive, more in their habits as we think they must have lived, than history shows them or our unaided imaginations can conceive them. But Hawthorne knows that the writer's power over illusion may fail; that readers are capricious; that critics, sometimes for ends of their own, may not wish to understand or approve. He chooses to make his claim in "Main Street" with ironic reservation, and only through the comic but attractive figure of the showman.

NOTES

1. Elizabeth Peabody remembered Hawthorne saying of his early career as a writer: "It was like a man talking to himself in a dark place." See Moncure D. Conway, *Life of Nathaniel Hawthorne* (London, 1895), p. 32.

2. In the 1851 preface to *Twice-Told Tales* Hawthorne says that at the

time of their composition and long thereafter the author "was merely writing to his known or unknown friends." In the same year, in the preface to *The Snow-Image and Other Twice-Told Tales*, he uses the same image, although modified by an addition: "Ever since my youth," he says, "I have been addressing a very limited circle of friendly readers, without much danger of being overheard by the public at large; and . . . the habits thus acquired might pardonably continue, although strangers may have begun to mingle with my audience."

3. Park Benjamin, in a review of *The Token* for 1837, wrote of Hawthorne as "this voluntarily undistinguished man of genius." "His modesty," Benjamin said, "is the best proof of his true excellence. How different does such a man appear to us from one who anxiously writes his name on every public post!" (*American Monthly Magazine*, n.s. 2 [1836]: 406). Longfellow, in his review of the 1837 *Twice-Told Tales*, wrote: "These flowers and green leaves of poetry . . . have been gathered fresh from the secret places of a peaceful and gentle heart. . . . And a very delightful volume do they make; one of those that excite in you a feeling of personal interest for the author. A calm, thoughtful face seems to be looking at you from every page" (*North American Review* 45 [1837]: 59–60, 62). Evert A. Duyckinck, preparing the way for the 1842 *Twice-Told Tales*, wrote: "It need be no cause of regret to the friends of Hawthorne that he is not popular in the common acceptation of the word, for popularity is not essential to his success. . . . His merit does not need the verdict of multitudes to be allowed. . . . The writings of Hawthorne can bear the delay of favor, they cannot perish, for they spring from the depths of a true heart" (*Arcturus* 1 [1841]: 331). It is to such statements that Hawthorne refers in the 1851 preface to *Twice-Told Tales* when he remarks that "he is by no means certain that some of his subsequent productions have not been influenced and modified by a natural desire to fill up so amiable an outline."

4. See *Love Letters of Nathaniel Hawthorne* (Chicago: The Society of Dofobs, 1907), 2: 73–76.

5. A young Frenchman, Monsieur Schaeffer, whom Hawthorne met on a visit to Horatio Bridge in 1837, used to address Hawthorne playfully by the French word for "hawthorn"; apparently the fancy took root. See *The American Notebooks by Nathaniel Hawthorne*, ed. Randall Stewart (New Haven: Yale University Press, 1932), p. 11.

6. Hawthorne borrowed Joseph B. Felt's *Annals of Salem* (1827) from the Salem Athenaeum on 2 January 1849. He had known it at least since 1833 when he first borrowed it from the Athenaeum, and he had used it extensively in "Endicott and the Red Cross." See Marion L. Kesselring, "Hawthorne's Reading, 1828–1850," *Bulletin of the New York Public Library* 53 (1949): 180.

7. The showman remarks the possibility of "the misplacing of a picture, whereby the people and events of one century might be thrust into the middle of another." Hawthorne in his fiction does not quite do that, but there are glaring anachronisms. In "Endicott and the Red Cross," for instance, Roger Williams is described as "elderly," with a "gray beard," of "apostolic dignity." The historical Williams was about thirty years old at the time of the action of the tale (1634). Or, to take another instance, in chapter 6 of *The Scarlet Letter*, the Puritan children play "at scourging Quakers"; the first Quakers to arrive in Boston came in 1656.

8. Hawthorne uses historical perspective in various manners. The reader may remember the long passage of historical interpretation interpolated in "The Maypole of Merry Mount," and how Hawthorne resumes his narrative by saying, "After these authentic passages from history, we return to the nuptials of the Lord and Lady of the May." Even in "My Kinsman, Major Molineux," which keeps almost entirely to one point of view, we do find, within the most immediate account of Robin's adventures, this sentence: "Nearly all, in short, evinced a predilection for the Good Creature in some of its various shapes, for this is a vice to which, as Fast Day sermons of a hundred years ago will testify, we have a long hereditary claim." And in "The Gray Champion," when Hawthorne is describing, as an eyewitness might have seen it, the progress of Andros and his party down King Street, he stops to say: "The whole scene was a picture of the condition of New England, and its moral, the deformity of any government that does not grow out of the nature of things and the character of the people."

9. See *Tales, Sketches, and Other Papers*, Riverside ed., p. 81.

10. In "Our Evening Party among the Mountains" Hawthorne says that "the biographer of the Indian chiefs" has "a right to be placed on a classic shelf, apart from the merits which will sustain him there." But he goes on to reject Indian subject matter for himself with what seems a gratuitous emphasis; see *Mosses from an Old Manse*, Riverside ed., p. 483. The discussion of John Eliot in *Grandfather's Chair* suggests that Hawthorne was fully aware of the bitter irony in the history of the Bay Colony and the Indians; see *Grandfather's Chair*, Riverside ed., pp. 467–77.

14

Hawthorne
and the Immunities of Romance

Nathaniel Hawthorne's romances are justified in their prefatory pieces by the literary theory of the years 1815 to 1830. Although they do not by their publication dates belong to the period on which we have concentrated, they do belong to it by Hawthorne's use of the literary thinking of that period in the exigencies of his later career. It has been contended, and denied, that the romance is inherently the American genre in long fiction,[1] and of course Hawthorne's romances and their prefatory pieces are important exhibits in the discussion. But the discussion has gone on without enough attention either to Hawthorne's peculiar problems in the writing of his romances, or to the implications of his carefully calculated prefatory pieces to them. Neither his concepts of romance nor the prefaces to his three later romances can be comprehended without the recognition of the effect of literary thinking that clearly belongs to the period of his youth and young manhood. We need to understand just what Hawthorne meant when he said in the preface to *The House of the Seven Gables* that he proposed "to keep undeviatingly within his immunities"—the immunities of the romance writer—and just why he required them. And we need to see how his response to the conditions under which the romances were written makes each one of them not only distinct in design from the others but a new thing in fiction.

Hawthorne may never have heard of realism, but if he did not know the literary term, he had yet an unfulfilled inclination toward what we call realism. In the frame sketches of his projected collection "The Story Teller" he was working on the outskirts of realism and toward a genre quite different from that of his tales.[2] Many passages in the *American Notebooks* are records of close observation of ordinary life and look like the practice work of a realist. In "Main Street" the lament of Hawthorne's showman that his entertainment did not get to the ordinary life of his present has a significant implication.

But an inclination toward realism is most significantly indicated in that passage in "The Custom House" in which Hawthorne wistfully reflects upon what he might have done had he used the materials of his immediate experience, had he sought "resolutely, the true and indestructible value that lay hidden in the petty and wearisome incidents, and ordinary characters" of his daily experience and observation. "The fault was mine," he goes on; ". . . a better book than I shall ever write was there." But he suggests that "at some future day" he may yet do something with the commonplaces of custom-house life, and find "the letters turn to gold upon my page." He never did; he had cast himself in the role of romancer and he continued to claim its privileges and immunities. One may have some speculative regret that he did not become the transitional figure in American literature he might have been.

But Hawthorne could not have changed the direction of his work at the time of the composition of *The Scarlet Letter*. When he lost his place in the Salem Custom House, he set about preparing a collection of short pieces in the hope of quickly gaining some income by it. A projected title for it was "Old-Time Legends: Together with Sketches, Experimental and Ideal"—clearly a catch-all title that would allow the inclusion of the few pieces he had written in the Salem custom house years, any of the older pieces he had passed over in making his previous collections, and the newly-conceived old-time legend, the piece James T. Fields calls "the germ of 'The Scarlet Letter.'" Fields's account of his urging Hawthorne to extend that piece into a romance is familiar and, although the account is ambiguous and Fields's memory after more than twenty years may not be entirely trustworthy, there seems no reasonable ground to doubt that without Fields the germ would have remained a tale, although possibly, as Fields seems to say, a longer tale than it had been Hawthorne's habit to write.[3]

The expansion of the tale into a book without extending the action largely accounts for the quality Hawthorne metaphorically describes in a letter to Fields as the "turning different sides of the same dark idea to the reader's eye." That quality—that persistent reflective and analytical concern with moral and spiritual predicament—distinguishes *The Scarlet Letter* from romances before it and makes it a markedly new development in a romance tradition that began with *Waverley*.

The Scarlet Letter draws extensively upon some of Hawthorne's early tales,[4] and it is much more like the work done in the early Salem years than that done at the Old Manse or in the Salem custom-house years. It has a scene in the past and historical connections, the ordinary sanction for romance; and it has therefore an inherent aesthetic distance. Yet, although Hawthorne was working in a way, and with materials, in which he had had artistic success, he was careful to define in a well-known passage in "The Custom House" the quality of "strangeness and remoteness" that belongs to romance—the "neutral territory, somewhere between the real world and fairy-land, where the Actual and the Imaginary may meet"—and to claim its immunities. In the three following romances, which deal in some sort with his present, he had to find—for each romance—ways to keep those immunities secure.

The success of *The Scarlet Letter* made a new work expedient, and it put Hawthorne's writing under the publishing control of Fields, who shrewdly directed the spacing of the publication of Hawthorne's books so that the popularity of a work still selling helped in the promotion of the next.[5] *The Scarlet Letter* was published 16 March 1850. Hawthorne began *The House of the Seven Gables* in late August 1850 and completed *The Blithedale Romance* on 30 April 1852.[6] In a bit more than twenty months he wrote those two romances, *A Wonder-Book*, and "Feathertop," and he made his last collection of short pieces, *The Snow-Image, and Other Twice-Told Tales*. For a writer who had long been of indolent habit, Hawthorne was working very rapidly. Indeed, when one remembers how little he wrote in the three years and more of his residence at the Old Manse, his production in this period is amazing. The fact is not extraneous to his art; it is a condition of it.[7]

When *The Scarlet Letter* was out and succeeding, Hawthorne cast about for a subject for a romance that he could write quickly, and that would not too much resemble his first successful romance. He found one that required no new reading, but that might embody his feeling for the New England past and re-use devices that he had succeeded with in his "Legends of the Province House."[8] Yet he was happy to find himself writing in a new vein; the *House*, he wrote to Horatio Bridge, was a work more characteristic of his mind, and more proper and natural for him to write than was *The Scarlet Letter*. But he did not turn to his present without reservation and elaborate safeguards, nor did he at all abandon his role as a romancer; had he wished to, he could hardly have developed a new technique when his public in the person of Fields was calling for a new work that should be written quickly.

The distinction between the romance and the novel with which Hawthorne begins the preface to *The House of the Seven Gables* (1851) is a standard one and much like Sir Walter Scott's distinction.[9] But Hawthorne devises a more important safeguard. *The House of the Seven Gables* has two imaginative centers, the time of Hawthorne's own present, and the time of the late seventeenth-century Pyncheons and Maules. The latter gives the sanction of a historical past to the romance, and it allows the mingling of "the Marvellous . . . as a slight, delicate, and evanescent flavor," as he describes the procedure in the preface—although in a letter to Fields, he speaks of himself "careering on the utmost verge of a precipitous absurdity," as, he says, a romance writer ought always to be doing.

The passage in the preface to the *House* that shows us most about the persistence in Hawthorne of the literary thinking of the time of his youth and young manhood comes as he disclaims any important relationship between his romance and the actualities of the Salem of his day:

> The reader may perhaps choose to assign an actual locality to the imaginary events of this narrative. If permitted by the historical connection,—which, though slight, was essential to his plan,—the author would very willingly have avoided anything of this nature. Not to speak of other objections, it exposes the romance to an inflexible and exceedingly

dangerous species of criticism, by bringing his fancy-pictures almost into positive contact with the realities of the moment.

The passage has an extensive background in early American literary thinking. Down to the time of Bryant's review of *Redwood*, we remember the *North American Review* critics insisted that fiction in the new nation could not deal interestingly or effectively with its readers' own time.

Edward T. Channing, for instance, in an 1819 review of William Dunlop's life of Charles Brockden Brown, feels sure that Brown's use of American scenes in or near his present cannot be altogether fortunate, since there must come into the story "mention of some place or circumstance which is too stubbornly familiar and unpoetical for any thing but common incidents and feelings."[10] Even William Howard Gardiner, exulting in the emergence of the first successful American romance, *The Spy*, takes it for granted that the fiction writer cannot work in his present, but is happy to find that he requires no very long retrospect, and says, to quote the passage once more: "Neither need we revert to any very remote period of antiquity to rid us of this familiarity, which forever plays about present things with a mischievous tendency to convert the romantic into the ludicrous."[11] Now that Hawthorne was not working altogether in the Puritan past, which he could make seem antiquity, he feared this mischievous tendency.

Hawthorne's preface would teach his readers how to read his romance. And in the romance itself he takes care that his scene will not be stubbornly familiar and unpoetical. The figures in the romance are types—excellent types though they may be—and the scene they move in virtually out of time. Although we are told of Judge Pyncheon's nefarious political activities (in general and even trite terms), we do not see him function in his world. Holgrave, as a disciple of the "newness," makes some of his ideas clear to us, but we do not see him among his fellows. Even Phoebe we do not see in her ordinary walk. We see all the characters in the Pyncheon house or grounds, as they are caught into "a legend prolonging itself": when they break out of the house, the legend, and the past—when the scene is really in the present—the romance ends.[12] Yet it is just Hawthorne's success with this strategy, just his awareness of an old literary assumption and his new way of conforming to it, that gives to *The House of the Seven Gables* its peculiar interest and appeal.

So, too, *The Blithedale Romance* (1852) is partly directed by the literary assumptions of the period of Hawthorne's early development. But this time Hawthorne, needing a book to follow the *House* so soon, turned to his own experience as ready-to-hand material. His extensive use in *Blithedale* of the memories of his life at Brook Farm, and of his letters to his fiancée and his notebooks of the time of his residence there (and for the death of Zenobia, of a passage from his notebooks at the Old Manse) required a strategy different from that of the *House*, where the notebooks are used only for some details.[13] The extensive use in fiction (other than in sketches and prefatory pieces) of his own recorded observation he had not practiced except in that "Chapter from an Abortive Romance," "Ethan Brand," where he uses his North Adams journal.

Hawthorne's materials in themselves might have been put to uses quite different from the use he makes of them in *Blithedale*. Emerson and Hawthorne had discussed the desirability of a history of Brook Farm,[14] and Hawthorne ends his preface to *Blithedale* with an elaborate expression of a hope that someone will write one; although he toyed with the notion of writing history, it was never likely that he would write any. Of course the materials of his Brook Farm experience would never have made a novel as he had defined the novel in his preface to the *House*: a piece of fiction "presumed to aim at a very minute fidelity, not merely to the possible, but to the probable and ordinary course of man's experience." The Brook Farmers were not ordinary, perhaps not even probable. Yet those materials might have been used in a satire or in a comedy of highly special manners, and *Blithedale* does have elements of both comedy and satire. But Hawthorne had to write a book to follow up the success of the *House* and to get it out soon enough to have that success help carry it; he could scarcely slip far out of the genre of the *House*. He recognized in his Brook Farm materials ways of solving problems in the writing of a romance, problems that literary theorists had insisted were especially problems for American writers.

It is difficult or impossible, Jared Sparks had said, to interest readers who "are near the time and place of the supposed action," for a man's "own house, his own city, or his own time, can scarcely be made to appear picturesque or romantic to himself."[15] Now a scene at Brook Farm—with which virtually no reader had any familiarity—took care of that difficulty. But there was held to be another, one that stemmed from the wide acceptance of the doctrine of Associationism. Edward T. Channing, for instance, had pointed out that the American writer could hardly surmount "the want in his readers of romantic associations with the scene and persons he must set before us."[16] That difficulty Hawthorne undertook to obviate by a skillful treatment of an unusual scene and group. Brook Farm had some notoriety and readers therefore some initial interest in it, but it could be made the scene of a romance without danger of the intrusion of the reader's knowledge or his ordinary expectations. If the reader had curiosity rather than romantic associations to bring to a Brook Farm scene, Hawthorne was at least free to make it seem as picturesque or romantic as he pleased, to make sure that the reader carried romantic associations away from the romance. Hawthorne explains what he is about in the somewhat labored second paragraph of his preface to *Blithedale*, a paragraph with echoes of the literary thinking of the 1820s.

Hawthorne's intention, he says, is "to establish a theatre" in which the figures in his romance may be made to carry out an action "without exposing them to too close a comparison with the actual events of real lives." He would not have them "compelled to show themselves in the same category as actual living mortals," and "with the idea of partially obviating this difficulty (the sense of which has always pressed very heavily upon him)," he has used Brook Farm as the scene of his romance. The parenthetical clause is striking. Certainly more than twenty-five years earlier Edward T. Channing, William Howard Gardiner, Jared Sparks, and other critics had told American writers that the difficulty pressed heavily upon them. But here it looks as if Hawthorne, when he turned to materials of his immediate observation, welcomed a justification in critical theory—even if somewhat worn and frayed—for the use of those materials in a romance, for adapting them to a genre he felt sure of, and sure that he could work in rapidly enough to carry out Fields's strategy of publication.

The preface to *Blithedale*, indeed, makes clear a design for the romance that, along with the complex narrative point of view, accounts for its special effect. The action, Hawthorne lets us know, is a quasi-allegorical one, in which representative figures—"the self-concentrated Philanthropist; the high-spirited Woman . . .; the weakly Maiden . . .; the Minor Poet"—work out their fictional destiny against a background of real and observed detail, but one which may seem a "Faery Land . . . with an atmosphere of strange enchantment, beheld through which the inhabitants have a propriety of their own." The allegorical action goes on against a background—"essentially a day-dream, and yet a fact"—that has at once the convincingness that belongs to reality observed and recorded, and a strangeness that belongs to Brook Farm's removal from anything the reader is likely to know in his own experience.

Apparently satisfied with the use of notebook material in *Blithedale*, Hawthorne, during his stay in England and in Italy, quite consciously designed his notebooks to be sourcebooks for romances—romances that even as he recorded his observations were taking some vague shape in his mind. The materials of the English notebooks he never succeeded in using for a romance: in Italy he wrote in 1858 the draft manuscript now called *The Ancestral Footstep* and put it aside, writing *The Marble Faun* before again trying, and failing, to make a romance out of the materials recorded in England. In the preface to *Our Old Home* he tells his readers that the sketches he offers them, as well as other materials that remain in his notebooks, "were intended for the sidescenes and backgrounds and exterior adornment of a work of fiction of which the plan had imperfectly developed itself in my mind." The statement is significant in that it indicates—more clearly, perhaps than does the preface to *Blithedale*—how far the fable and the background were initially two things in Hawthorne's mind, two things which it belonged to his art to combine into one.

Since *The Marble Faun* (1860) comes after Hawthorne's consulship at Liverpool and his stay in Italy—so long after the other three romances—it might have been written, one would suppose, without the pressure to publish that is a condition of the other three. But it did not escape such pressure. Hawthorne completed a draft of the book on 30 January 1859 in Italy, intending to write the final copy after his return to the United States. But in England he found that Fields had secured an offer of English publication ahead of an American edition, with its attendant advantage of an English copyright, an offer the more attractive since Hawthorne was in need of income. He stayed in England long enough to write the final copy, which he completed in about three and a half months.[17] It may well be that, had he completed *The Marble Faun* at the Wayside and at his leisure, the characteristics of the romance that so bothered his first readers and have since extended his critics would not have appeared in the final version. The pressure of time probably does account for a quality of the romance that disturbs readers today.

For the reader of *The Marble Faun* is conscious, even as he reads, not only of a distinction, but of a separation between the fable on the one hand and side-scenes, background, and exterior adornment on the other; Hawthorne's art has not made them into one. "There are, to put it bluntly," Sir Leslie Stephen wrote, "passages which strike us like masses of undigested Guide-book."[18] And even a recent critic, John Caldwell Stubbs, who sees the setting as "almost always symbolic as well as descriptive of the Italian scene," and descriptions of art objects significantly associated with the major characters, also sees Hawthorne as like "the American tourist with his slide collection [who] has brought back too many recollections of Italy."[19] Hawthorne may have been conscious of this guide-book quality; in his preface to the romance he professes himself surprised to find how much of it is notebook material. But at any rate, he felt that the notebook material gathered in Italy assured him immunity from any familiarity his readers were likely to have with his scene—from the difficulty that the literary assumptions of our early criticism had taught him to fear, and that his literary habit had been to avoid.

An atmosphere of "suitable remoteness," Hawthorne had said in the preface to *Blithedale*, "is what the American romancer needs." In *The Marble Faun* he uses his Italian experience to furnish remoteness of another sort, but not of an entirely differ-

ent order. His Brook Farm experience had furnished him with
what he thought the best equivalent for the "Faery Land"
American experience ordinarily denied the romancer; Italy, he
says in the preface to *The Marble Faun*, afforded him "A sort of
poetic or fairy precinct, where actualities would not be so terribly
insisted upon as they are, and must needs be, in America."

There follows at once a sentence that Henry James in his
Hawthorne (1879) has made famous by using it as a point of
departure for his discussion of the blankness of American life
and the consequent difficulties for the fiction writer. "No author, without a trial," Hawthorne writes, "can conceive of the
difficulty of writing a romance about a country where there is no
shadow, no antiquity, no mystery, no picturesque and gloomy
wrong, nor anything but a commonplace prosperity, in broad
and simple daylight, as is happily the case with my dear native
land." Now perhaps Hawthorne wrote this sentence, and
perhaps James quoted it about twenty years later, without per-
ceiving that it is—on the face of it—nearly nonsense. Hawthorne
had most successfully used the American seventeenth century as
antiquity, and found within it shadow and mystery; the peculiar
institution of slavery and the whole history of the Indians and
white men were gloomy but picturesque enough wrongs; what
Hawthorne designates as commonplace prosperity was both
complex and ruthless. But one cannot understand the sentence
on its face, even though he may see that it is saying what had so
often been said thirty or forty years earlier, as American writers
and critics were finding their way into an American literature; it
is, indeed, strikingly like the passage in Letter 23 of Cooper's
Notions of the Americans that we have noted.

In *The Marble Faun* Hawthorne found himself offering his
readers a piece of fiction with a scene not American; he had not
done so before in any piece in which the scene matters except in
"Rappaccini's Daughter"—and there the scene is an Italy of
literary convention, not of observation. He knew why he was
doing so; he seems to have felt he owed his readers some explanation. But it may seem curious that for an explanation he reverts to a theory which held that American experience did not
supply the materials from which a literature could be made, and
which predicted that such a writer as Nathaniel Hawthorne

could scarcely emerge.

Yet the recurrence in Hawthorne's prefaces to an obsolescent sort of literary thinking is understandable. He had developed in a period in which literary theory had turned the mind of American writers to the American past, and in which romance attached itself to history and was justified thereby. He had cast himself in the role of romancer in *The Scarlet Letter*; he could hardly have broken out of that role under the exigencies of the composition of *The House of the Seven Gables* and *The Blithedale Romance*. Yet he found himself in *Blithedale* and still more in *The Marble Faun* depending upon notebook materials that in themselves made for realism. He was insisting that he was a romancer, even when he worked with the materials of his experience or observation with his scene in the present. The prefaces to the *House, Blithedale*, and *The Marble Faun* are all intended to define for himself as well as for his readers what he is doing, and how it is that pieces of fiction not set in the past are romances.

Hawthorne is saying in all three prefaces that he has not stepped out of his role as a romancer, although he is now trying for an aesthetic distance different from that inherent in the historical tales and the seventeenth-century scene of *The Scarlet Letter*. He is saying in the prefaces to *Blithedale* and to *The Marble Faun* that even personal observation may be used within the limits of romance if the provenance of that observation is unfamiliar to the reader. He seeks, he says, a "fairy-land" (the term or a variant appears in three of the four prefatory pieces). It has seemed to me that Hawthorne failed to find the term he needed, but whatever else he may mean by "fairy-land," he means a scene unfamiliar to his reader. In saying all this with frequent allusion to obsolescent literary theory, Hawthorne is returning to that theory at his need, as he is impelled to explain mutations that have taken place in the genre of romance as he has been dealing with it.

The prefaces to *The House of the Seven Gables, The Blithedale Romance*, and *The Marble Faun* read in the context of Hawthorne's experience as a writer of fiction reveal more about the problems of the romances than he ever intended them to reveal. Yet, as those prefaces show the interplay between the exigencies of Hawthorne's publication and the habit of mind that led him back to old strains of literary thinking, they help to account for the special quality of the romances: the delimiting in each of its own precinct for its own imaginative life.

NOTES

1. See Nicolaus Mills, *American and English Fiction in the Nineteenth Century* (Bloomington: Indiana University Press, 1973), pp. 11–28.

2. The "Sketches from Memory" in *Mosses from an Old Manse* are examples of sketches originally intended as frame-sketches in the projected "The Story Teller." They appeared as separate sketches in the *New-England Magazine* in 1835 and were added to the second edition of *Mosses*, 1854. Hawthorne intended, he says, that the frames should be "perhaps more valuable" than the tales, "since they will be embossed with groups of characteristic figures, amid the lake and mountain scenery, the villages and fertile fields, of our native land" (*Mosses*, Riverside ed., p. 461). That fine sketch "The Canal Boat" represents the intention as it was most nearly fulfilled. In another frame-sketch, "Our Evening Party among the Mountains," Hawthorne outlines a plan for careful observation of teamsters passing through Crawford Notch in sleighing time—a plan, apparently, for a realistic work. A curious passage in "The Old Manse" may also be significant: Hawthorne laments the thinness of his work during the Old Manse period, from which came "no novel even, that could stand unsupported on its edges." Since he is not likely to have said "novel" when he meant "romance," it looks as if he is indicating an unfulfilled aim.

3. See James T. Fields, *Yesterdays with Authors*, pp. 49–52. A plan to print some tales along with *The Scarlet Letter* persisted almost to its publication; in "The Custom House" Hawthorne speaks of a collection of tales, but attaches a footnote to say that the projected collection has been deferred. "A new volume of tales" was advertised in January 1850. See William Charvat's introduction to the Centenary edition of *The Scarlet Letter*, pp. xx–xxv.

4. See N. F. Doubleday, *Hawthorne's Early Tales, a Critical Study* (Durham, N. C.; Duke University Press, 1972), pp. 107–8, 177–78, 210–12.

5. In the period 1850–54 Ticknor, Reed & Fields published ten Hawthorne books, only three of which were new editions of earlier books. What Hawthorne called in the preface to *The Snow-Image* "the magic arts of my friendly publishers" required his cooperation.

6. Randall Stewart, *Nathaniel Hawthorne*, pp. 112, 122.

7. Fields seems to have hurried Hawthorne as much as he could.

Some of *The Scarlet Letter* was in type before Hawthorne had finished writing the book; Fields could not persuade him to allow the same procedure with the *House*, but did advertise the book as in press before Hawthorne had finished writing it. See Charvat's introduction to the Centenary edition of the *House*, p. xvii. Another condition of Hawthorne's art is his discovery that long fiction was more profitable than short fiction. In refusing to furnish other tales after "Feathertop" (1852) for Rufus W. Griswold's *International Magazine* he wrote: "The thought and trouble expended on that kind of production is vastly greater, in proportion, than what is required for a long story" (quoted in Stewart, *Nathaniel Hawthorne*, p. 115).

8. See Doubleday, pp. 134–37.

9. Hawthorne writes: "When a writer calls his work a Romance, it need hardly be observed that he wishes to claim a certain latitude, both as to its fashion and material, which he would not have felt himself entitled to assume had he professed to be writing a Novel. The later form of composition is presumed to aim at a very minute fidelity, not merely to the possible, but to the probable and ordinary course of man's experience." Scott had written in his "Essay on Romance": "We would be rather inclined to describe a Romance as 'a fictitious narrative in prose or verse; the interest of which turns upon marvellous and uncommon incidents;' being thus opposed to the kindred term Novel . . . which we would rather define as 'a fictitious narrative, differing from the Romance because the events are accommodated to the ordinary train of human events and the modern state of society' " (quoted in Mills, *American and English Fiction*, p. 12).

10. *North American Review* 9 (1819): 65.

11. *North American Review* 15 (1822): 255.

12. Despite this strategy, Hawthorne seems to have been a little uncomfortable with his scene even nominally in the present. He wrote to Fields on 27 January 1851: "It has undoubtedly one disadvantage in being so close to the present time; whereby its romantic improbabilities become more glaring" (Fields, *Yesterdays with Authors*, p. 56).

13. See Randall Stewart's introduction to *American Notebooks*, pp. xxviii–xxxiii. William Dean Howells apparently recognized the authenticity of the background material in *Blithedale* and liked it the best of Hawthorne's romances; it is, he says, "more nearly a novel, and more realistic than the others" (*My Literary Passions* [New York, 1895], p. 186).

14. *American Notebooks*, ed. Stewart, p. 176.

15. *North American Reveiw* 21 (1825): 82.

16. *North American Review* 9 (1819): 65.

17. See Stewart, *Nathaniel Hawthorne*, pp. 207–10.

18. In the *Cornhill Magazine*, 1872, reprinted in *Hawthorne: The Critical*

Heritage, ed. J. Donald Crowley (New York: Barnes & Noble, 1970), p. 492. When Stephen reprinted the essay in *Hours in a Library*, he softened the expression.

19. See Stubbs's interesting discussion of *The Marble Faun* in *The Pursuit of Form: A Study of Hawthorne and the Romance* (Urbana: University of Illinois Press, 1970), pp. 138–57.

15

Roads Out of the
Land of Fiction

Our writers, as their work and sometimes their comments on it
show, thought hard about what they could do with the means of
fiction. But they have no very elaborate theories of fiction. We
hear nothing from them that needs to be called "romanticism";
they are not prone to exalt their vocation. Indeed, they are conscious that fiction had been and still was held in ill repute: it is a
virtue in Mary Douglas in *Marriage* that she "scarcely ever read a
novel in her life," and Jane Austen is impelled to her defense of
novel-reading in the fifth chapter of *Northanger Abbey*. The prejudice embraced the very term "novel"; Richard Whately tells us
of a woman of his acqaintance who forbade her daughters to
read any novel but allowed them to read any play that fell into
their hands.[1] And Scott remarks in his review of *Emma* that
apparently novel-reading belongs to that class of frailities widespread and concealed, like drinking, "since among the crowds
who read little else, it is not common to find an individual of
hardihood sufficient to avow his taste for these frivolous
studies."

As Edward Everett saw it in 1823, the moral objection to the
novel had begun to lessen with the popularity of Fanny Burney
and then of Maria Edgeworth: "Miss Burney introduced a new
era and a new style in works of fiction, and was thought safe
reading, as far as a novel could be so; and next to her succeeded
Miss Edgeworth."[2] No one of the writers of our examples would
have willingly added any reason for the moral objection to fiction. Scott says in the Introductory Epistles to *The Fortunes of
Nigel*, "I care not who knows it—I write for the general amusement," but then adds at once, "I will never aim at popularity by

what I think unworthy means." The world agreed that his means were worthy; it was particularly the Waverley novels that made the novel respectable.[3]

An overconscious concern about the reputation of the novel may have put restraints on writers that limited the fiction of the period. The reader today is likely to find the representation of sexual relationships pretty intangible. But that may seem less important to him than it did to readers earlier in our century, bored as he probably is with the persistent exploitation of sex in the novel of his own time. And restraints that foster variety are no bad restraints. It does seem certain that the reactions against the coarseness and the limited preoccupations of the eighteenth-century novel widened the interests of fiction in the nineteenth century, and brought experience into fiction that had scarcely been used before.

Scott is reluctant to claim for his own work much value beyond that of relieving the tedium or the ills of the lives of his readers;[4] and that is the first value he ascribes to good fiction in general. "In truth," he writes in his review of *Emma*, "when we consider how many hours of langour and anxiety, of deserted age and solitary celibacy, or pain even and poverty, are beguiled by the perusal of these light volumes, we cannot austerely condemn the source from which is drawn the alleviation of such a portion of human misery, or consider the regulation of this department as beneath the sober consideration of the critic." But Scott is quick to claim value beyond relief or entertainment for "works which, like this before us, proclaim a knowledge of the human heart, with the power and resolution to bring that knowledge to the service of honour and virtue."

No one of our writers would have quarreled with Scott's statement of the values of fiction, which is close enough to the Horatian formula of the blending of delight with instruction.[5] Some of them had a more overtly didactic purpose than that Scott implies; some of them had worthy intentions not specifically ethical. But all of them were aware of a social responsibility incumbent upon fiction writers. Irving's statement of it is at once unpretentious and profound. "I have always had an opinion," he says in "The Author" (*Bracebridge Hall*), "that much good might be done by keeping mankind in good-humor with one another."

Particularly our American writers, in their desire to make the new nation a storied land, realized the importance of fiction as shared imaginative experience.

Certainly the social value of fiction was recognized by readers. We remember Miss Mitford saying that the Waverley novels were what civilized people talked about. They talked of them no less in the United States. Edward Everett says that "the rising generation must be at a loss to know what their elder brothers and sisters talked about, before such things existed," but assures the rising generation that "we were not a wholly forlorn race before the Scotch novels appeared," for "though inferior to Scott, Miss Edgeworth is inferior to him alone." Susan Cooper, daughter of the novelist, has left us a vivid account of the way in which new books from London became the subjects "for social talk and clever discussion about the firesides of the whole neighborhood."[6] There was apparently an excitement in the realization that fiction had found its way out of an imaginatively sterile period.

In our examples of early nineteenth-century fiction, we have seen each of the British writers take his own road out of what Scott calls "the land of fiction": that land of amazing and persistent suffering and perils, of extravagant sensibility, and of final happy outcome—a land readers scarcely tried to assimilate to any actuality they knew. And although some of our writers influence others, no one of the British writers is subservient to any influence, nor, I believe, much conscious of himself as part of a literary movement. There are, to be sure, fiction writers who make a more decided break with the conventions of fiction than any we have considered.[7] The specimens of variety of attempt here discussed, although they surely alter the tradition of fiction, fit into it and develop it.

Our American writers, with the new national feeling, and with a vigorous company of critics affirming, often repetitively, the possibilities of an American literature, were more consciously a part of a literary movement than were our British writers. Although as readers they had known the land of fiction, they had not themselves much occupied it as writers, nor was it likely much to attract them. Something they could and did do in adapting the Gothic to the American scene—sometimes effectively and ingeniously. But the only British fiction that could influence them importantly as writers was that which they could adapt to their scene, experience, and peculiar needs.

There were Americans to read and enjoy Jane Austen,[8] but her novels scarcely suggested anything that might be done with an American scene. Maria Edgeworth, we have realized, influenced Miss Sedgwick; she apparently influenced women writers for the annuals and, I suspect, Cooper. But American fiction was not really under way before 1820, and Miss Edgeworth's career as a writer of fiction was then virtually at an end, and her influence already overborne by that of Scott. Scott's enormous popularity, with the easy adaptability of his ways of working with the recent past in Scotland, dominated all other influences.[9] Americans, almost on a sudden, needed to realize imaginatively their own pasts, and Scott's work showed them the way. Its influence persisted; chapter 2 of *The Scarlet Letter* is a striking example of that feeling for period that Scott brought into fiction.

In our examples of both British and American fiction, we have been aware of the interplay between convention and the new attempt. Perhaps we should remind ourselves that a thoroughly conventional work may be highly regarded; in "The Fall of the House of Usher," for instance, Edgar Allan Poe polishes the Gothic convention until it seems, as we say, like new. And the most successful fiction retains much that is conventional, although readers are more aware of it in historical perspective than in the work of their contemporaries. Conventional elements appear even in work interesting for extensions of the uses or the means of fiction.

In coming out of the land of fiction, some of our writers bring with them its assumptions about plot. It is perhaps surprising to realize that among our examples Cooper's *The Pioneers* best achieves what Scott calls a "combined plot," the sort he was aiming for in *The Antiquary*, the plot in which all the important characters are somehow involved in the denouement.[10] But we can see that figures in *The Pioneers* we took at first to be only representative of "character and manners" do, most of them, have a part in the latter action and denouement. Miss Sedgwick's *Redwood* hardly has a combined plot, for in it two actions intersect. Nevertheless Cooper in *The Pioneers* and Miss Sedgwick in

Redwood (and Scott in *The Antiquary*) have much the same problem. Bryant in reviewing *Redwood* says that Miss Sedgwick presents us "not merely with the picture of what she has imagined, but with the copy of what she has observed." He might have made the same sort of comment about either of the other two novels. And readers since Bryant's time generally have been interested in what was observed, increasingly less interested in the plots designed to meet the expectations of the novelists' first readers.[11]

Jane Austen has a good deal of fun with the combined plot in the concluding chapters of *Northanger Abbey*; in her novels written later she has such plots as will hold together her dealings with small groups of people in restricted localities; even then, as we have noticed, she may show some amused embarrassment as she gathers things up in the last pages. It seems likely that Miss Ferrier in *Marriage* intended a tighter plot than she achieves, and the variety of her interests somewhat disrupts it. The reviewers of her own time complain about the lack of plot interest, and praise passages in the book that have the least to do with the plot.

But in some of our examples the writers leave behind them the exigencies of plot. In *Castle Rackrent* Miss Edgeworth escapes plot conventions that seem to us so sadly to hamper her in her other novels, and that she handles in such fashion as to dismay or amuse us. Galt in his *Literary Life* says of *Annals of the Parish*: "It is so void of any thing like a plot, that it lacks in the most material feature of the novel" (and that, therefore, he does not consider it his best work), but he clearly sees that a plotted novel could not have accommodated his intention or his materials for the *Annals*. Miss Mitford in *Our Village* escapes the problems of plot entirely, and is enabled to people her fiction with the multitude of lively figures that interest her.

Miss Mitford's sketches would hardly have been feasible without initial periodical publication, and the development of periodicals fostered the development of short fiction; even Scott contributed three tales to an annual. Magazines and annuals were particularly important to the development of American fiction, for publishers in the United States, who did not pay royalties for the British novels they reprinted, were not anxious to publish American novels at their own risk. American fiction writers therefore often turned to short pieces for the magazines and annuals; Miss Sedgwick surely had a larger public in the annuals than she did for *Redwood*. Hawthorne wrote tales and sketches for most of his career and (save for the early and almost abortive *Fanshawe*) did not face the problems of the combined plot until the time of the romances. William Austin and William Leete Stone, for whom fiction was an avocation, would have been unlikely to have written it at all without periodical outlets for it.

The tale in the period of our concern becomes in its best specimens something other than just a short narrative, and gains techniques of its own. Irving in committing himself to short pieces says that he has chosen a line of writing peculiar to himself, and in his best tales he does succeed in designing for his material structures that are quite unlike anything in the short fiction before him. In "Main Street" Hawthorne is thinking back over his early tales, tales in which he discovered his ways of using historical materials for purposes beyond themselves. Even William Leete Stone, drawing a tale from witchcraft records, manages passages of considerable technical interest, and for a tale of the sea-going preternatural finds a technique to fit his striking materials. William Austin in "Peter Rugg" achieves what seems a self-existent legend.

Fiction short and long in all periods tends to feed upon itself, but in the land of fiction the material of one novelist had been particularly the work of his immediate forerunners. As Scott remarks, "the man of genius as well as his wretched imitator" must work with materials; it is in his adventure into new materials that Scott's example benefited his fellow workers most. Among our writers, Irving in his mysterious portrait stories and Miss Austen in *Northanger Abbey* amuse themselves and us with a wry consideration of fiction before them, but the extensions of uses of fiction are for the most part departures into new materials.

Maria Edgeworth found her materials for *Castle Rackrent* in recent Irish history; and on Scott's own testimony it was her example that brought him to the realization of the fictional possibilities of the recent history of his own country. After the achievements of Miss Edgeworth and Scott, Galt's achievement in the *Annals of the Parish* and Cooper's in *The Pioneers* are nearly as striking, for those novels represent whole communities in ways not paralleled in fiction before them. Miss Mitford's *Our Village* has an important antecedent only in Irving's *Bracebridge Hall*, which is so curiously also an influence on *The Pioneers*. In the United States, critics identified the problem of fiction in the new nation as one of materials, and fiction began with the search for what were called American materials, and developed as the search extended.

New materials may need new forms and sometimes new subsidiary techniques. The materials of New England life in *Redwood*—materials so new to fiction that they impel Bryant to forecast a new kind of novel—Miss Sedgwick manages to work with, but they seem at odds with her conventional plotting. The somewhat disconcerting shifts of technique in *Marriage* are the result of Miss Ferrier's effort to include her diverse materials without finding an adequate form for them. If in *The Pioneers* Cooper conforms to the conventions of the combined plot, he yet imposes on it a new structure marked off by the progress of the seasons, a structure that accommodates the materials he delights to use. Galt, for his wealth of knowledge and feeling about the recent past in lowland Scotland, borrows a structure sometimes used for historical writing and imagines a narrator to use it as it had never been used before.

The development of the narrator who tells, not primarily his own story, but of the experience of others, is surely the most striking development within our examples. Irving's narrators in their complex frames are an important interest in his work, carefully designed for the stories they have to tell, and the product of a great literary skill—as we are a little too much aware even as we read. But among our examples we have four narrators of another order—Thady Quirk, Wandering Willie Steenson, the Reverend Mr. Balwhidder, and Jonathan Dunwell. Each of them has a character quite his own, a character that emerges from his narrative. Each of them has a narrative style that seems quite his own, a style that is part of his character as we apprehend it. All four seem to us completely distinct from their authors, and they have no real antecedents in fiction in English.

Our writers come out of the old land of fiction that Scott so amusingly describes, and they leave many of its preoccupations behind. But they are of course still in a land of fiction; perhaps they have only in a variety of ways extended the borders of the old land and peopled it anew. Yet the territory they occupy seems a much more varied land, with better air, and wider vistas—often a pleasant and an interesting place for readers who return to it.

NOTES

1. See *Jane Austen: The Critical Heritage*, p. 92.

2. See Everett's review of a collected edition of Miss Edgeworth's works, *North American Review* 17 (1823): 383–89. Everett remarks an amusing aspect of the attitude toward the novel. Many libraries that did not admit Fielding and Smollett, he says, tolerated Richardson, "protected as he was supposed to be, by number of tomes and stiffness of manner, from the danger of being generally read."

3. A relief that the novel had with Scott become clearly respectable may partly account for the often exultant praise of Scott's work. In 1827 William H. Prescott wrote that Scott's example had brought about a revolution in fiction, and that "we of the present generation can hardly estimate our own good fortune, in having lighted upon this prolific and entertaining epoch" (*North American Review* 25: 184).

4. Scott's intention is, he says in the Introductory Epistle to *The Fortunes of Nigel*, "to amuse in one corner the pain of body; in another, to relieve anxiety of mind; in a third place, to unwrinkle a brow bent with the furrows of daily toil; in another, to fill the place of bad thoughts, or to suggest better; in yet another, to induce an idler to study the history of his country; in all, save where the perusal interrupted the discharge of serious duties, to furnish harmless amusement." See also the dedication to George IV of the collected Waverley novels.

5. The Horatian formula was enough in people's minds so that Irving uses it in the prefatory piece for *Tales of a Traveller* to make fun of himself, and perhaps of overt didacticism; he writes of his tales: "They may not possess the power of amusement, which the tales told by many of my contemporaries possess; but then I value myself on the sound moral which each of them contains. This may not be apparent at first but the reader will be sure to find it out in the end." He has often hidden his moral from sight, he goes on, so that the reader "may have a bolus of sound morality popped down his throat, and be never the wiser for the fraud."

6. *Pages and Pictures from the Writings of James Fenimore Cooper* (New York, 1861), pp. 16–17.

7. James Hogg, for instance, in his *The Private Memoirs and Confessions of a Justified Sinner* (1824), or John Gibson Lockhart in his *Some Passages in the Life of Mr. Adam Blair* (1822).

8. The American edition of Jane Austen's collected novels published by Carey & Lea of Philadelphia in 1832–33 is a trifle earlier than the first English collected edition published by Bentley in 1833.

9. Scott's influence not only cut off other influences, but apparently the reading of the novels of his predecessors. A writer in the *American Quarterly Review*, probably Robert Walsh, complains that "the Mysteries of Udolpho could no longer keep people awake at night; Tom Jones was ignominiously turned out of doors . . . ; Sir Charles Grandison gave place to a race of heroes who never made a bow in their lives; Miss Edgeworth was eclipsed, though we hope only for a time, to emerge more brightly" (2 [1827]: 33). Interestingly, it is Washington Irving who seems most aware of a danger of an overinfluence from Scott. "Scott's manner," he admonishes himself, "must . . . be widely avoided" (quoted in *Washington Irving: Representative Selections*, p. lxi).

10. In the Advertisement to *The Antiquary* Scott writes: "I have been more solicitous to describe manners minutely, than to arrange in any case an artificial and combined narrative." He adds at once and ruefully, "and have but to regret that I felt myself unable to unite these two requisites of a good Novel." By "artificial" Scott means, of course, contrived by art; he conveniently defines "combined plot" for us in his review of *Emma*: "that combined plot, (the object of every skilful novelist,) in which all the more interesting individuals of the dramatis personæ have their appropriate share in the action and in bringing about the catastrophe." For Scott the great exemplar of the combined plot is Henry Fielding in *Tom Jones*. But he thinks that he himself works best in the tradition of Smollett and Le Sage. See the introduction to *The Monastery* and the Introductory Epistle to *The Fortunes of Nigel*.

11. Along with the conventional plot comes one of its frequent figures, the hero or heroine of mysterious birth. To limit the examples to work by our writers, there is a hero of mysterious birth in Scott's *The Antiquary*, and heroines of mysterious birth in Miss Edgeworth's *The Absentee* and in Miss Sedgwick's *Redwood*. Even Miss Ferrier (perhaps remembering the critical objections to the lack of plot interest in *Marriage*) has a mystery about the parentage of her heroine in *The Inheritance*. The parentage of the hero of *The Pioneers* we learn only in its next-to-last chapter. So late as Hawthorne's *The Blithedale Romance*, we are expected to be curious about the parentage of Priscilla. Mystery of identity has been, of course, an element in narrative and drama since

ancient times, and there may be some psychological reason for its persistence. But the early nineteenth-century fiction writers could not escape the examples of the successes with it in Fielding's *Tom Jones* and Fanny Burney's *Evelina*. And even in Smollett's *Humphry Clinker* the title character carries the evidence of his parentage about with him in a snuff box.

Index

Crabbe, George, 109
Crosby, Richard, 19

Dante Alighieri, *Inferno*, 56
Defoe, Daniel, 11, 50; "True Relation of the Apparition of one Mrs. Veal," 118
Dickens, Charles, 69; *American Notes*, 159 n. 8; *Pickwick Papers*, 48 n. 8; *Pickwick Papers* (Preface), 93 n. 12
Disborough, Mercy, 164
Durand, Asher B., 133
Duyckinck, Evert A., "Nathaniel Hawthorne," 177

Edgeworth, Maria, 61, 143, 148, 203; *The Absentee*, 7, 8, 15, 16, 134,149; *Belinda*, 7, 8; *Castle Rackrent*, 5–6, 7–17, 19, 78, 207, 208, 209; *Ennui*, 18 n. 14, 154; letter to Mrs. Stark, 11–12; *Ormond*, 8
Edgeworth, Richard Lovell, 7, 8
Edinburgh Review, 74
Emerson, Ralph Waldo, 194; Address for Bryant's seventieth birthday, 133; "The American Scholar," 96, 157; "The Poet," 157
Everett, Edward, "The Works of Maria Edgeworth," 203, 205

Faust legend, 168
Ferrier, Susan, 3, 5; *Destiny*, 75 n. 1; *The Inheritance*, 75 n. 1, 211 n. 11; *Marriage*, 61–77, 148, 158 n. 5, 203, 207, 209
Fielding, Henry, *Amelia*, 75 n 2; *The History of . . . Joseph Andrews*, 26; *Jonathan Wild the Great*, 11; *Tom Jones, a Foundling*, 212 n. 11; *A Voyage to Lisbon*, 4
Fields, James T., 191, 197, 200 n. 7; *Yesterdays with Authors*, 110 n. 3, 190
Flying Dutchman legend, 114, 118, 119

Galt, John, 5; *Annals of the Parish*, 16, 78–94, 95, 207, 209; *The Ayrshire*

Legatees, 92 n. 2; *The Entail*, 92 n. 2; *Literary Life*, 78, 91, 93 n. 8, 207; *The Provost*, 92 n. 2
Gardiner, William Howard, 118, 195; review of Cooper's *The Pioneers*, 144 n. 1; review of Cooper's *The Spy*, 125, 128, 148, 154, 156, 159 n. 12, 163, 193
Gilpin, William, 24, 163
Godwin, William, 39
Goffe, William, 164
Goldsmith, Oliver, *The Vicar of Wakefield*, 78, 143
Gothic convention, the, 5, 9, 20, 36, 38–40, 163, 168, 205–6
Grierson, Sir Robert, 51
Grossman, James, *James Fenimore Cooper*, 146 n. 15
Guiney, Louise Imogen, "Peter Rugg, the Bostonian," 122, 126 n. 12

Hall, Bishop Joseph, 68
Hawthorne, Nathaniel, 3, 46–47, 125, 172, 208; *The American Notebooks*, 190, 194; *The Ancestral Footstep*, 196; "The Artist of the Beautiful," 177; "The Birthmark," 177, 183; *The Blithedale Romance*, 191, 194–96, 199–200; "The Canal Boat," 126 n. 4, 200 n. 2; "The Custom House," 190, 191; "Dr. Bullivant," 182–83; "Dr. Heidegger's Experiment," 168; "Drowne's Wooden Image," 123, 177; "Endicott and the Red Cross," 183, 188 n. 7; *The English Notebooks*, 196; "Ethan Brand," 183, 194; "Feathertop," 191; "The Gentle Boy," 184; *Grandfather's Chair*, 188 n. 10; "The Gray Champion," 176, 188 n. 8; *The House of the Seven Gables*, 39, 189, 191, 192–94, 199–200; "Legends of the Province House," 192; "Main Street," 176–88, 190, 208; *The Marble Faun*, 196–200; "The Maypole of Merry Mount," 183, 188 n. 8; "My Kinsman, Major